Margaret Cavendish

For Richard Edward Wilson:
Carpe diem, baby!

Margaret Cavendish

Gender, genre, exile

Emma L. E. Rees

MANCHESTER UNIVERSITY PRESS
Manchester and New York

distributed exclusively in the USA by Palgrave

The right of Emma L. E. Rees to be identified as the author of this work has been asserted by her in accordance with the Copyright, Designs and Patents Act 1988

Published by Manchester University Press
Oxford Road, Manchester M13 9NR, UK
and Room 400, 175 Fifth Avenue, New York, NY 10010, USA
www.manchesteruniversitypress.co.uk

Distributed exclusively in the USA by
Palgrave, 175 Fifth Avenue, New York,
NY 10010, USA

Distributed exclusively in Canada by
UBC Press, University of British Columbia, 2029 West Mall,
Vancouver, BC, Canada V6T 1Z2

British Library Cataloguing-in-Publication Data
A catalogue record for this book is available from the British Library

Library of Congress Cataloging-in-Publication Data applied for

ISBN 0 7190 6072 9   *hardback*

First published 2003

11 10 09 08 07 06 05 04 03   10 9 8 7 6 5 4 3 2 1

Typeset in Photina
by Carnegie Publishing, Lancaster
Printed in Great Britain
by Biddles Ltd, Guildford and King's Lynn

Contents

Acknowledgements

I should like to thank my colleagues in the English Department at Chester College, especially Chris Walsh and Melissa Fegan, who have done a huge amount to help this book to completion. Margaret Cavendish Society members have also helped, in particular Jim Fitzmaurice, Nancy Weitz and Deborah Taylor-Pearce. Lizzie Rees, Sue Foster, Alexis Waitman, Graham Rees, Maria Wakely, Sue Lawson, Judy Hayden, Helen East and Sapphire each, in very different ways, helped me to see this project through. I thank them all. Without the support and patience of people associated with Manchester University Press, this book would not have seen the light of day.

A version of Chapter 2 first appeared in *In-between: Essays and Studies in Literary Criticism* 9.1 & 2 (2001), and appears here in an extended and altered form with the kind permission of the editor, Gulshan Taneja, University of Delhi, New Delhi. A version of Chapter 3 first appeared in *Women's Writing: The Elizabethan to Victorian Period* 4.3 (1997), edited by the author, and appears here in extended and altered form with the kind permission of Roger Osborn-King of Triangle Journals, Oxford. A version of Chapter 4 first appeared in *A Princely Brave Woman*, edited by Stephen Clucas (Hampshire: Ashgate, 2003), and appears here in extended and altered form with the kind permission of the editor.

My greatest thanks go to my husband, Richard. Without his patience and love, this book could not have come about. He is a man of extraordinary patience and spiritual strength, with whom it has been my privilege to spend many years. In expressing my love for his person and his integrity, I would recall the self-effacing and unstinting support which William Cavendish gave to Margaret, *per tot discrimina rerum*. To Richard my emotional debt is immeasurable.

Introduction:
a glorious resurrection

*Who knows but after my honourable burial, I may have a glorious resurrection
in following ages, since time brings strange and unusual things to passe.*
(Margaret Cavendish, 'To the Two Universities', *Philosophical and Physical Opinions* (1655)).

Here lyes the Loyall Duke of Newcastle and his Dutches his second wife
by whome he had noe issue[. H]er name was Margarett Lucas yongest
sister to the Lord Lucas of Colchester a noble familie for all the brothers
were Valiant and all the Sisters virtuous[.] This Dutches was a wise
wittie & learned Lady, which her many Bookes do well testifie[;] she
was a most Virtuous & a Louieng & carefull wife & was with her Lord
all the time of his banishment & miseries & when he came home never
parted from him in his solitary retirements.

It may seem a little perverse to start the story of episodes in someone's
life with an account of their death. However, this inscription, which
William Cavendish, Duke of Newcastle, wrote for the tomb in West-
minster Abbey in which his beloved wife was interred on 7 January
1674, and in which he was to join her two years later, is poignant
in its apparent self-effacement and depth of affection. The epitaph's
author allocates to himself just a few words, choosing instead to focus
on his wife. Clearly it is an exceptional relationship which this epitaph
records. The no less exceptional woman at its centre was 'wise wittie
and learned', produced 'many Bookes', and provided support for her
husband in his 'banishment'. This woman was Margaret Cavendish,
the subject of this book and one of the most vibrant and creative
Englishwomen of the seventeenth century. That vibrancy was not
celebrated by all of her contemporaries, however, and the sentiment

1

of William's memorial was, shortly afterwards, maliciously subverted by the clerk John Stansby, correspondent of the royalist antiquarian Elias Ashmole:

> Here lies wise, chaste, hospitable, humble ...
> I had gone on but Nick began to grumble:
> 'Write, write,' says he, 'upon her tomb of marble
> These words, which out I and my friends will warble.
> Shame of her sex, Welbeck's illustrious whore,
> The true man's hate and grief, plague of the poor,
> The great atheistical philosophraster,
> That owns no God, no devil, lord nor master;
> Vice's epitome and virtue's foe,
> Here lies her body but her soul's below'.[1]

It's a verse shot through with vitriol and disapprobation, calculated to effect maximum harm. Calling Cavendish a 'great atheistical philosophraster' not only impugns her intellectual validity (the derogatory suffix *aster* being suggestive of the triumph of pretension over merit) but also denigrates her reputation by tainting it with a suspicion of godlessness. Further, the emphasis on 'true man's hate' serves to condemn William too. It is Cavendish's philosophising, her brazen attempt to participate in contemporary intellectual debate, that has so provoked Stansby. The accusation of atheism is charged with meanings immediately familiar to Cavendish's contemporaries, and 'atheistical' functions as a convenient catch-all way of dismissing both the woman and her ideas.

The story of Margaret Lucas, born in Essex in 1623, the youngest of eight children, later Margaret Cavendish, Duchess of Newcastle, is astonishing. It is a life which she herself documented, both in the pages of her autobiographical *True Relation*, and in numerous other places in her copious publications. Of course there have ever been – long before Barthes articulated them – problems inherent in constructing too close a connection between an author and her work, and intentionality rightly remains a thorny issue. In the extraordinary case of Margaret Cavendish, however, attempts to separate writer and work are doomed because of the author's dogged textual insistence and presence. Her determination to be so present in her texts has much to do with her anomalousness; far from being an impediment to her, the singularity in which she delighted proved, during the hazardous years of the middle of the seventeenth century, to be the very means by which she could make her voice and contentious opinions heard. Widely dismissed as eccentric, or indulged as bizarre, Cavendish could publish ideas and opinions under the mantle of obscurity or frivolity. The ways in which she went about this form the basis of this book.

At the age of twenty, in 1643, Cavendish left the increasingly fraught atmosphere of Essex and went to Oxford. There she attached herself to Henrietta Maria's court, moving with her to the Continent shortly afterwards. It was in Paris that she met and married one of the most charismatic figures of the age, and one of Henrietta Maria's favourites, William Cavendish, Marquis of Newcastle, some thirty years her senior. The courtship, the exchange of more than seventy love poems, the wedding and the subsequent marriage were all remarkable. Not wanting to displease their queen through the inequality of the match (an inequality of social station, as well as of age), the couple wed secretly in Sir Richard Browne's chapel in Paris in 1645.

The passionate courtship; the Cavalier husband old enough to be her father; the absence of any children in an age when women were expected to be mothers; the travails in Europe, living a nomadic existence in constant anticipation of an unpredictable end to exile – all are elements which shaped Cavendish's writing. Vast in both scope and length, this writing bears testimony to its creator's eclectic and varied interests. Its diversity is matched by its originality – no other woman produced anything like the volume or content of Cavendish's work. That said, the originality is combined with a desire to be part of the literary-philosophical tradition which is the focus of this book.

William Cavendish, the archetype of the rakish and attractive Cavalier, disgraced following the Royalist defeat at Marston Moor, turned out to be no less unusual than his young wife. In an age of patriarchy when family structure replicated state, William seems to have acted as *éminence grise* to Margaret, actively encouraging and promoting her writing. Such support may too easily be read as a kindly indulgence, but, when Cavendish's texts are read in the way I propose in this book, the relationship becomes more equitable – William's wife's anomalous role as a writing woman allowed her a licence to propagate at times uncompromisingly contentious ideas which a *man* – in the context of the age, the only proper pretender to the title of 'writer' – would not have dared to have published.

This inextricable relationship of life and writing, then, was one she cultivated, and there are key events in this woman's life, as in any life, which define her and her work. One of these (and one to which I return in my first chapter) took place in December 1651 when Cavendish appeared before the Committee for Compounding at Goldsmith's Hall, in an attempt to raise revenue. This parliamentarian committee allowed royalists whose assets had been sequestered to apply to buy them back. The enormity of the impact of this event cannot be overstated – the previously tongue-tied Margaret, self-confessedly bashful, and painfully self-conscious, was fairly summarily dismissed by the Commissioners. Other central events in determining the character of this incomparable woman included the execution of a brother; the ransacking of her relatives' tomb by parliamentarian forces; living for a period in the grand setting of the artist Rubens's house in Antwerp; dining with intellectual luminaries; visiting the Royal Society in near-regal pomp after the Restoration; eventually dying in mysterious circumstances, contrary to all possible predictions more than two years before her elderly husband in Welbeck, and the pomp of her funeral at the beginning of 1674. The writing to which such episodes (some of which I shall return to in later chapters) gave rise surely deserves consideration.

In this book I examine critical assessments of the woman and her work (again, that almost unavoidable conflation) from the seventeenth century to the twenty-first. The woman who emerges from my study is not the one *hampered* by anomaly, depicted as spectacularly eccentric, even mentally (or, as some critics would have it, physically) ill. Instead she is a sane and wily contributor to mid-century intellectual debates, aware of others' opinions and expectations of her, and exploiting these same with the aim of propagating a unique and intrepid voice under a set of circumstances where others – like her husband – could not (or dared not) make themselves heard. As a woman, cultural expectations of her were more to do with her propriety than with any suspicion that she might actually have an important contribution to make to contemporary philosophical or political debate. The woman who drew crowds in Hyde Park, causing people – Pepys included – to strain to get a glimpse of her fantastical outfits, by attracting such attention to her person simultaneously deflected it from where it would really have mattered – her writing. By focusing attention on the image, the appearance, Cavendish kept censorial attention away from the content – her publications.

4

In the pages which follow I do turn my attention to this content in an attempt to answer the question: How did a mid-seventeenth-century woman, not just a royalist, but married to one of the most prominent royalist military leaders of the day, manage to publish material which not only engaged with the latest thinking on philosophical matters, but actually, once 'unlocked', can be read as being highly politically controversial? The best answer I can find is that it is through a careful choice of genre that Cavendish succeeds in formulating controversial arguments. Repeatedly she lulls the reader into believing that he or she is reading a generically familiar text. When that genre's antecedents are examined, however, Cavendish's unique take on it emerges in all its tantalising and subversive force.[2]

This book is on one level an attempt to rebuff John Stansby and others like him, but its aims are, of course, more far-reaching than that. I want to convey some of the creative energy of Cavendish and her work in the middle years of the seventeenth century. More importantly, though, I want to show how her work was politically charged, not in any immediately evident way, but in a highly complex and imaginative way. These are the aims of this book.

In this introduction, then, the constituent parts of this study – genre, politics and exile – will be defined, and in the chapters that follow I will illustrate and expand upon the book's central hypothesis: that Cavendish used *genre* in her writings of the 1650s as a means of articulating her powerlessness in the face of what I shall come to define as a 'triple exile'. That is, it will become apparent that she is exiled not only in a legislative sense (by being married to a man who was politically designated a delinquent and banished) but in two other interrelated senses, too. She is analogously exiled firstly, as a woman trying to write in a hostile culture (thanks not least to Stansby and his peers) when this was seen as promiscuously transgressive, and secondly as a royalist maintaining and promoting the prohibited aesthetic of theatricality in various forms in her writing. It is not only the content of Cavendish's publications of the 1650s that registers the key concerns – genre, politics and exile – but, in the relationship between peritext (the mass of prefatory material Cavendish produced, for example) and main text, the material organisation of Cavendish's very publications registers her exile too. Despite, indeed, precisely on account of, this triple exile, Cavendish produced in the 1650s a series of publications which I read as

intensely and articulately polemical. In the production of these publications, genre is the key to unlocking the mystery of how Cavendish
makes her political commentary. This idea of 'exile', so crucial to this
book, needs some contextualisation. As twenty-first-century readers
with 20/20 hindsight, we conceptualise the seventeenth century as
being punctuated by the Restoration of 1660. From the frantic and
myopic reality of the 1650s, though, the vista must have looked
entirely different. What we see as a temporary state of affairs must,
at the time, have felt like an awful permanency, with all of the feelings
of dejection and fear that accompany such a situation.

No one book could do justice to the vast corpus of Cavendish's
material: between 1653 and 1671 she published some twelve original volumes of writing, and oversaw the sometimes extensively
revised second or third editions of seven of these.[3] In the chapters
which follow, then, two of Cavendish's exilic texts, *Poems, and Fancies*
and *Natures Pictures*, are explored in depth. I concentrate particularly
on the atomist poems and *The Animall Parliament* in the former, and
on *Heavens Library* and *Assaulted and Pursued Chastity* in the latter.
An identification of the relation of these texts, in a generic sense, to
earlier texts or literary or philosophical paradigms not only brings
into focus the whole volumes of which they are a part but also
illuminates much of Cavendish's oeuvre and the literary techniques
she employed. What I have done then is to identify for each of the
texts under discussion a select few of the dominant generic paradigms
which, in being adopted and subverted by Cavendish, seem most
closely to reflect her attitudes to exile, politics, and genre.

In some important respects my use of the term 'genre' is akin to
that of Sharon Cadman Seelig in *Generating Texts*.[4] However, if Seelig's
concern, as articulated in her subtitle, is to identify the *Progeny of
Seventeenth-century Prose*, mine is rather to find the progenitors – and
not only of prose. A text is not *sui generis*, nor is it inevitably straightforwardly influenced by another text, but it may, in either a formative
or a substantive sense, have certain characteristics as the result of a
stylistic or ideological adoption of 'a similar method, a similar set of
assumptions'.[5] It is an authorial mindset which generates a literary
mode or choice of genre. This notion of idea generating form is especially applicable to Cavendish's exilic writings. The concept of genre
I am utilising, therefore, incorporates not just the purely structural
or external but the thematic, too. Similarities in apparent impetus or

approach can overcome generic differences, and may be, to quote Seelig again, 'rhetorical as well as conceptual'.[6]

In this book I have, further, identified affinities in intention and circumstances surrounding the writing of texts earlier than those of Cavendish. Her take on earlier authors' rhetorical stances facilitates her own, acutely contemporary, comment and creativity. 'Bigger' ideas or beliefs can create productive and very real similarities between texts and ages which otherwise might appear superficially so disparate as to be unconnected.

In my exploration of Cavendish's work of the 1650s I consider earlier works to which she, either through a kind of cultural osmosis perhaps inevitable in the intellectual milieu she inhabited in the 1650s or through her own reading (which, given her frequent professions not to understand any language other than her native tongue, would have had to have been in English), had some form of access. Further, there are earlier texts which, for one reason or another, appealed to her in such a way that she could adopt and adapt them to make her own voice heard – a voice which, because of the triple exile, was subversive almost as soon as it was articulated. Her engagement with *genera mista* is consistent with, as Seelig expresses it, a 'desire to adapt the formal structures of the past to new occasions and purposes, to combine previously distinct approaches for particular rhetorical occasions'.[7] In Cavendish's case, as her biography demonstrates, such occasions included her economic dispossession, her gendered disempowerment and her exclusion from dominant modes of political and literary discourse and production.

The identification of similarities in politics or mindsets between Cavendish's and previous works should not eradicate differences between the texts, but rather serve to emphasise these. Historical specificity and generic interconnectedness need not be mutually exclusive categories. Differences between texts may serve to highlight even more clearly connections between them, the 'intersections of literary forms that let us examine the relationship between the conception and the articulation'.[8] These 'intersections' run more deeply than a simplistic notion of influence, which suggests that a text may offer quite precise indications of which texts or authors a writer has encountered and consciously brought to their own text; intersections with the 'progenitors' of *attitude, circumstance* or *literary execution* in Cavendish's texts may be less conscious or deliberate.

7

What does remain precisely so conscious and deliberate throughout Cavendish's work is a subversive political sentiment. To promulgate such a sentiment, to distribute works which, once the generic lock has been picked, are controversial, one first must avoid censorship. A useful model for reading early modern texts which is productive in the context of Cavendish's work is found in Annabel Patterson's *Censorship and Interpretation*.[9] The act of censorship (to follow Patterson's terminology) produces its very own discourse which is characterised by deliberate ambiguities and obliquity. What these writerly strategies result in is an avoidance of confrontation with dominant authorities, who may tacitly turn a blind eye to avoid implementing the force of state censorship. Ancient literary paradigms could facilitate oblique political commentary and so the events of the mid-seventeenth century gave rise to new models of generic synthesis. Genres which acquired more gravity mid-century, spawning many subgenres and growing increasingly politicised, included the romance and the lyric.

Cavendish's vast peritextual self-displays (the multiple prefaces and elaborate frontispieces which characterise her volumes) and her anxieties over how her readers would receive her works are directly symptomatic of – to return to Patterson for a moment – 'functional ambiguity', and its repercussions for authorial intentionality.[10] Cavendish's own 'oblique communication' takes the form of a presentation of generic conventionality undercut by covert political content.[11] Cavendish also engages in the potential of 'private' genre (the lyric, but especially in her case the letter) for subversive purposes, and is a committed player in the mid-century re-engagements with romance.

The concept of 'genre' found in my book is, as should by now be clear, an interpretative, and not merely a classificatory, notion. It is a dynamic interpretation which contradicts some influential theoreticians who perceive a far greater degree of stasis and rigidity in 'genre'. The theories of genre with which Cavendish and her contemporaries would have been familiar were born of social as much as aesthetic imperatives. Genre and hierarchy were inextricably linked. Sidney, for example, and other Renaissance genre theorists such as Scaliger, had constructed a hierarchy which maintained an Aristotelian identification of a mimetic social dimension to literary modes, with, put simply, epic at the top and pastoral at the bottom.[12]

Cavendish, in her 1656 text *Heavens Library*, generates a similar sort of hierarchy, central to which is Plato's own hierarchic production of ideals. In a later chapter I will examine the potency for the exiled poet Cavendish, of the image of Plato banishing poets from his Republic, and the additional irony that he was widely viewed, as Sidney expressed it, as having produced a body of work of which it might be said that 'though the inside and strength were Philosophy, the skin as it were and beauty depended most of Poetry'.[13]

In his characterisation of the poet Sidney has recourse to a Lucretian image which, as I'll go on to show, had resonance for Cavendish in her first published work, *Poems, and Fancies*. The didactic poet operates on the reader 'even as the child is often brought to take most wholesome things by hiding them in such other as have a pleasant taste'.[14] The importance attributed by Sidney to a poetic didacticism conducive to virtuous conduct – 'no learning is so good as that which teacheth and moveth to virtue' – is echoed by Cavendish in a preface to the reader of *Natures Pictures* thus: 'I hope this work of mine will ... beget chaste Thoughts, [and] nourish love of Vertue'.[15] Further, when Cavendish declares in her preface to *Poems, and Fancies* that she chose to explicate her atomist theory in verse, 'because I thought Errours might better pass there, then in Prose', she is recalling an older set of generic theories and assumptions, echoing not only Lucretian modes but also Sidney's description of the poet who 'nothing affirms, and therefore never lieth'.[16]

For Cavendish's generic dissimulations to work effectively she needs some of her readers to come to her texts expecting a degree of rigidity, and others to read through that, to see the text as flexible, and to decipher some of what it conceals. In other words, in *Natures Pictures*, or more specifically in the short story in it, *Assaulted and Pursued Chastity*, the reader expects to encounter one genre but actually they may discover that, for very specific political reasons, Cavendish has reinvented or rediscovered the romance genre's plastic potential.[17] If, as Bakhtin argues, 'studying other genres is analogous to studying dead languages', then what Cavendish does in her use of genre is to find an idiolect informed by the peculiar personal and political circumstances of her life in the 1650s.[18]

Cavendish's treatment of genre undergoes a transformation during and because of the civil wars which, to royalist minds, spelled the end of an epic past. In royalist literary sensibilities the civil wars were a cusp marking a move from epic to novelistic discourse. Read in this way, passages of Cavendish's work such as the first book of *Natures Pictures* are to be understood as a novelistic adaptation of Socratic discourses, and so are able to focus and comment on contemporary reality without the bounded, closed-off distance associated with the epic. Thus, elements of the first book serve to emphasise the 'low' nature of the serio-comical genre, just as the archetypally low characters found in William's *Beggars Marriage* do.[19]

'Genre', then, is an inherently unstable and mutable category, particularly so in the unsettled years of the mid-seventeenth century. Generic parameters are constantly changing and, over time, an inverse relationship often emerges between a text's utility, and its literariness.[20] Put another way, early modern scientific theories may since have been entirely discredited on *scientific* grounds, but retain a poetic or literary quality. Cavendish's play with genre is interpretative: highly imaginative and creative. In her hands genre is less a prescriptive force than a modulation which alters the generic code from which it is a departure, or of which it is a version. Critics such as Alastair Fowler have gone so far as to suggest that the changeable form of genres means that satisfactory definitions are impossible, since once a genre operates within literature it is subtly changed.

A culture which views genre as fixed or prescriptive actually and paradoxically encourages precisely the kind of innovative generic play which, it will be argued in the course of this book, is manifested repeatedly in Cavendish's writings. That is, in order to write beyond the parameters of the genres which interest her, and in order to reinvent them to accommodate her own political agenda, she had first to be of a literary culture sufficiently well acquainted with the genres in their widely or popularly perceived form, in order to know how to effect such adaptations.[21] In terms of literary communication, generic assumptions colour the reader's interpretation of, presumptions about or responses to, a work of literature. Consistently throughout Cavendish's work, genre bears meaning (or, despite the death of the author, intention).

In an Aristotelian sense, generic grouping has both internal and external operations, being both substantive and formal. In the following chapters this broader conception of 'genre' is the one being applied. When approaching a work of literature, the reader engages in a complex hermeneutic task, which is made possible by the generic indicators which permeate a work.[22] These, in turn, direct the reader to think about and approach the text in a specific way, with a specific set of assumptions operating upon it. What Cavendish does in her work is to exploit these assumptions, frustrate and reverse them, precisely by appearing to make them work in and for her text. In *Natures Pictures*, for example, the comprehensive title – discussed in detail in Chapter 1, below – influences the reader's mindset. Modal transformation produces precisely those hybrid genres Cavendish advertises – '*Comical, Tragical, and Tragi-Comical, Poetical, Romancical*'.[23] *Genera mista* result from a mode, for example the heroic, operating on a kind, for example a romance, thus producing an heroic romance. Kate Lilley argued in 1992 that Cavendish's 'imagination is not primarily focused on normative or pure kinds. It is most engaged by that which troubles or resists categorization.'[24] I would qualify this statement by arguing that it is through her engagement with precisely such 'normative' kinds that Cavendish's own, largely politically motivated, departures from them have their full, subversive impact.

This book differs in its emphasis from earlier examinations of Cavendish's writings. Criticisms such as Stansby's, with which this introduction opened, account for the appalling image of Cavendish and her works which has endured, with the result that it is only very recently that she has begun to be taken seriously. The impression which lasted for many years was of an eccentric, disturbed and arrogant woman. Condemnation from her contemporaries – diarists, scientists and poets – was aimed at both her literary- and self-publication. Recent critical studies, however, have witnessed a movement away from attempts simply to portray Cavendish as a manifestation of all that is somehow nefarious about a woman's literary self-promotion. The general recuperation of her image has developed into more focused and insightful studies, and there now exists a considerable body of scholarship on Cavendish's work.

What of criticism from her contemporaries? In 1653 Dorothy Osborne, self-confessedly rather the worse for 'ale', wrote to William Temple asking whether he had read *Poems, and Fancies*, Cavendish's first published work.[25] 'Sure', Osborne wrote of Cavendish, 'the poor woman is a little distracted, she could never be so ridiculous else as to venture at writing books, and in verse too'.[26] For Osborne, by

4 February 1654, Cavendish's reputation was modified, and the 'distracted' poet was mentioned because of 'all her philosophy'.[27] Osborne's contemporary, the diarist John Evelyn, epitomised the priorities early critics had in discussing Cavendish. On 18 April 1667 he visited the Cavendishes in London and 'was much pleased with the extraordinary fanciful habit, garb, and discourse of the Duchess'.[28] Evelyn was evidently so 'pleased' that he visited twice more in late April and early May, accompanied by his wife on these occasions.[29] Mary Evelyn wrote to Dr Bohun that she was 'surprised to find so much extravagancy and vanity in any person not confined within four walls', continuing of Cavendish that:

> Her face discovers the facility of the sex, in being yet persuaded it deserves the esteem years forbid ... Her mien surpasses the imagination of poets, or the descriptions of a romance heroine's greatness; her gracious bows ... and various gestures of approbation, show what may be expected from her discourse, which is as airy, empty, whimsical and rambling as her books, aiming at science, difficulties, high notions, terminating commonly in nonsense, oaths, and obscenity.[30]

As her husband had done, so Mary Evelyn prioritises the 'romance heroine's' demeanour and appearance over her 'discourse'.

Samuel Pepys also questioned Cavendish's sanity, declaring her to be 'a mad, conceited, ridiculous woman, and [her husband] ... an ass to suffer her to write what she writes to him, and of him'.[31] A letter written in 1667 emphasises brutally a connection between public display and open sexuality – Cavendish is described as 'all ye pageant now discoursed on: Her breasts all laid out to view at a playhouse and her scarlet painted nipples'.[32] Even in the twentieth century, Virginia Woolf's concern was with the woman who 'frittered her time away scribbling nonsense and plunging ever deeper into obscurity and folly', becoming a 'crazy' spectacle, 'a bogey to frighten clever girls with'.[33] Conversely, Charles Lamb's positive assessment was ahead of its time, as he wrote of 'that princely woman, the thrice noble and virtuous but somewhat fantastical and original-minded Margaret Newcastle. No binding could be too fine for such a good and rare book, no casket rich enough to honour and keep safe such a jewel.'[34]

Even recent commentators such as Douglas Grant, Cavendish's first full biographer, writing in the 1950s, concentrate primarily on her eccentricities. His biography opens with a chapter, 'A Visit to

London', which focuses on her visit to the exclusively male Royal Society on 30 May 1667. The rest of the biography is chronological, a treatment that serves to accentuate this extraordinary event (a further three centuries were to pass before another woman could enter the Royal Society) as the apotheosis of her career. He relates how six women in waiting were needed to carry Cavendish's train, and prints extracts from John Evelyn's ballad composed especially for the occasion, which describes his alleged fright upon catching sight of her: 'God bless us! when I first did see her: / She looked so like a Cavalier, / But that she had no beard.'[35] In 1955 another critic declared that 'perhaps the best description that can be given of the Duchess of Newcastle is that she was mildly mad and immoderately devoted to Cartesian rationalism'.[36] In the same era B. G. MacCarthy was prompted to praise the woman and her writing in terms so extraordinarily exuberant and yet equivocal that they warrant quoting at length:

> Who could depict with a mere pen's point this dear, delightful, opinionated, child-like, fantastic genius? One may draw a rhombus to represent a diamond, and sketch in some radiating lines to suggest the effulgence of light, the depth, the colours, the fluctuating radiance. But such a sketch would only be a crude diagram, unless the mind which knows the quality of the precious stone evokes from memory its dazzling light. The Duchess of Newcastle was a diamond of the first water, partly obscured by its original covering of clay, uncut save for a facet or two which sent out a fitful and ill-balanced brilliance. Her genius was so productive and so various, her ideas so original and so ill-regulated, her vision so exalted, her ignorance so profound, her style alternately so preposterous and so perfect, that one despairs of ever reducing to the cold canons of criticism the inspired confusion of her works.[37]

Modern critics have examined the image Cavendish projected which provoked such a panoply of contemporary and subsequent denunciation, and in many cases have provided their own rehabilitative assessments. Helen Cocking's early attempt to locate Cavendish in an intellectual matrix of precedence and influence was a useful contribution to studies of the writer.[38] Several works examine Cavendish's spectacular public self-presentation, eliding autobiographical information, historical anecdotes and evidence from Cavendish's own works, in particular from her prefatory material.[39]

As Dorothy Osborne recognised in her contemporary's work the different threads of poetry and philosophy, so recent studies of Cavendish's scientific writings have begun to give credence to the notion that, far from being the strange, incoherent eccentric which her earlier critics represented her to be, she produced in her scientific writings a cogent analysis of, and contribution to, contemporary theory.[40] Carolyn Merchant's work on Cavendish's philosophical works has been continued by Sophia B. Blaydes, who contextualises Cavendish's early materialism in terms of the thinking of her contemporaries, Hobbes, Gassendi and Descartes.[41]

In this book I propose an extension of some of these critical opinions, and the revision, or in some cases the rejection, of others. For example my focus on 'exile' is shared by Anna Battigelli, who discusses Cavendish's 'self-created role as an isolated exile', but Battigelli looks at Cavendish's entire corpus rather than focusing, as I do, on the exilic texts.[42] I do consider such 'self-creation' to be paramount, however, and in my exploration of Cavendish's portrayal of female heroism in Chapter 4, I find it to be more complex than critics such as, for example, Dolores Paloma suggest.[43] I identify in these texts of the 1650s an ultimate frustration for the author, but not for her characters, of the fantasy of autonomy and order. Further, I characterise Cavendish's adaptability and eclecticism as stemming from a pragmatic responsiveness to political events, and the expediency or otherwise of appearing to be on one side or the other of contemporary intellectual and political debates.

I show how such debates had as their locus 'theatre'. Sophie Tomlinson's 'My Brain the Stage' takes an image from Cavendish's 1664 work, CCXI Sociable Letters, in which the exiled writer records her enjoyment of a public mountebank show, and uses it to explore her plays' 'use of performance as a metaphor of possibility for women'.[44] I concur with Tomlinson's depiction of the interrelationship between gender and theatre, especially as an alliance which operates similarly between royalism and the exiled genre of drama. Allied with issues of performance is the public agency of the female characters in Cavendish's works, an issue which Tomlinson discusses in relation to Cavendish's plays, and the implications of which I apply to her Interregnum texts. Tomlinson's broad definition of the idea of 'acting' as operating 'simply as a metonym for female public utterance' is one which I also adopt.[45] Tomlinson also usefully identifies the disparity between Cavendish's tongue-tied appearance before the

Committee for Compounding at Goldsmith's Hall in 1651 and her fictional characters' far superior eloquence.[46]

In the chapters that follow, different versions of Cavendish's generic play will be examined. For example Cavendish reinvents genres such as the romance in specific, political ways. It is a reinvention which is crucial to an understanding of, for example, *Assaulted and Pursued Chastity*. This text, Cavendish's blueprint for her post-Restoration *Blazing World*, also draws some of its impetus from Shakespeare's *Tempest*, a text which had great resonance for the royalists of the mid-seventeenth century. The ideas and themes of the Dryden–Davenant *Tempest* of 1667, and Cavendish's *Assaulted and Pursued Chastity* and *Blazing World*, relate directly to the experiences and affiliations of their authors during the Interregnum. Their concerns include usurpation, involuntary exile, construction of a social utopia which in fact has dystopic elements and, in keeping with the speculations of the new science, the possibility of the existence of non-corporeal entities. These are themes which would have directly affected royalist sympathisers in the 1650s (perhaps true artistic freedom of expression and publication of these themes could be found only in the next decade, an issue I touch on in Chapter 6). The enchanted imagined isle, be it that of Davenant's imagination or Cavendish's, is a space wherein the disenfranchised have the power to experiment with different versions of rule and absolutism. For the fictional or dramatic characters, it is the brave new world they inhabit of which they may declare 'this isle's our own, that's our comfort'; their creators derive like comfort from being analogous absolute rulers of the texts they indite.[47]

The first chapter of this book, then, opens with an examination of how the triple exile is negotiated by Cavendish in her peritextual material. I argue that Puritan objections to, and legislation against, drama obliquely suggested to Cavendish that subversive political commentary might be made possible by a careful engagement with genre. A specific example of such an engagement is the focus of Chapter 2, a consideration of Cavendish's first published work. Generically, this work, *Poems, and Fancies*, owes much to Lucretius's *De rerum natura*, the influence of which pervades Cavendish's text, not being confined to the explicitly atomist poems. In the 1640s Cavendish's personal universe had been metaphorically atomised, and her decision to versify scientific theories became an implicitly political act. She shared with Lucretius the status of a pioneer engaged in a controversial project: in his case the dissemination of a radical Epicurean philosophy; in hers the publication of a woman's writing which, further, is characterised by explicitly anti-Puritan sentiment.[48] Cavendish was not unique among seventeenth-century women in her fascination with Lucretius. In the Appendix I return to *De rerum natura* and I briefly examine its translation by Cavendish's contemporary, Lucy Hutchinson.

The selection or banishment of exemplary figures which forms the basis for Cavendish's prose piece *Heavens Library* is an imaginative subversion of Socratic genre theory, which has repercussions for the rest of the text, *Natures Pictures*, of which it is a part. This is the focus of Chapter 3. Once the essence of Cavendish's treatment of Plato in *Heavens Library* has been identified, apparently Platonic texts such as the dialogic opening book of the volume emerge as rather more polemical than their prima facie structures indicate. Chapter 4, 'Travellia's travails: Homeric motifs in *Assaulted and Pursued Chastity*', focuses on Cavendish's creation of a figure of an heroic woman – a creation which exceeded the bounds of her text and which she wished to be applied to her self, too. The protagonist Travellia's triumphant emergence as a nation's leader arguably sees her cast in a Ulyssean role, and is enhanced by a literally spectacular performance. This staging, however, is not confined to the specular, but is characterised by the female character's oratory. This creation of a woman orator is closely linked with Cavendish's depiction of a woman able to move into full citizenship, and her reworking of the figure of the Homeric Penelope.

The last of the texts to be analysed at length involves a return to *Poems, and Fancies. The Animall Parliament* appears to be a straightforwardly allegorical political tale written in the genre of Livy's fable of the Belly. However, and this is the argument of Chapter 5, when it is read in the context of how Cavendish's contemporaries William Harvey and Thomas Hobbes constructed a relationship between monarchical systems of rule and human physiology, *The Animall Parliament* moves from a quasi-scientific genre to a generically complex critique of the Puritan administration. It is a critique which is prodigious in its utopian optimism and political audacity.

Chapter 6 is a brief consideration of whether the Restoration changed Cavendish's use of genre, and the way in which many of her later texts function as the culmination of earlier generic experiments. An analysis of Cavendish's 1662 *Orations of Divers Sorts* identifies how, as a concerted generic experiment, it privileges the author's own, singular voice whilst curtailing any suggestion of a wider female engagement either with the genre or, concomitantly, in public life. A brief discussion of certain of Cavendish's plays, some of which were written in the 1650s, but which were published in two volumes in 1662 and 1668, is appropriate here. Thus I have avoided in part my own banishment of the genre of drama, which Cavendish published only after the chronological scope of the main part of my project.

In my conclusion I return to the 'rehabilitative' nature of recent work on Cavendish and her writings, demonstrating how my own study has participated in this process of rehabilitation. Literary canonicity was, analogously, another 'place' from which Cavendish was for centuries exiled. This book represents a redemption of the writer from, at the very least, that particular iniquitous cultural corollary to the triple exile.

Notes

1 John Stansby, quoted in Douglas Grant, *Margaret the First: A Biography of Margaret Cavendish, Duchess of Newcastle, 1623–1673* (London: Rupert Hart-Davis, 1957), p. 199. Stansby (1629–80) was described by Elias Ashmole as 'an ingenious enquirer after things worthy memoriall'. See C. H. Josten, ed., *Elias Ashmole (1617–1692): His Autobiographical and Historical Notes, His Correspondence, and Other Contemporary Sources Relating to his Life and Work*, 5 vols (Oxford: Clarendon Press, 1966), III, 1287. Katie Whitaker argues that Stansby (she calls him 'Stainsby') may not have written the verse himself, but instead collected it on his travels. Katie Whitaker, *Mad Madge* (New York: Basic Books, 2002), p. 348.

2 On the rigorous, if haphazard, application of literary censorship during the Puritan Commonwealth see Dorothy Auchter, *Dictionary of Literary and Dramatic Censorship in Tudor and Stuart England* (Westport, Connecticut: Greenwood Press, 2001).

3 I use the term 'oversaw' because, in the case of the 1668 Latin reissue of the 1667 *Life* of William Cavendish, the translation had been done not by Cavendish but by Walter Charleton. The Wing catalogue, however, does class this under Cavendish's works, as Item N848. The 1655 *Philosophical and Physical Opinions* was reissued in 1663, and in a substantially altered form in 1668. The full title of this latter edition is: *Grounds of Natural Philosophy: Divided into thirteen Parts: with an Appendix containing five Parts*.

The Second Edition, much altered from the First, which went under the name of Philosophical and Physical Opinions, Wing Item N851. See Bibliography, below.

4 Sharon Cadman Seelig, *Generating Texts: The Progeny of Seventeenth-century Prose* (Charlottesville: University Press of Virginia, 1996).

5 *Ibid.*, p. 1.

6 *Ibid.*, p. 3.

7 *Ibid.*, p. 10.

8 *Ibid.*, p. 12. Importantly, Seelig chooses to use the word 'intersections' rather than 'similarities', because this latter does not convey the full complexity of what she is trying to do, and nor does it of my own project.

9 Annabel Patterson, *Censorship and Interpretation: The Conditions of Writing and Reading in Early Modern England* (Madison: University of Wisconsin Press, 1984).

10 *Ibid.*, p. 18. Despite William calling prefatory epistles '*the common and Dunstable rode*', Cavendish's works contain many of them. Her 1662 volume of plays, for example, has twelve. See William Cavendish, 'An Epistle to justifie the Lady Newcastle and Truth against falshood', in Margaret Cavendish, *The Philosophical and Physical Opinions* (London, 1655), sig. A2v. See also Margaret Cavendish, *Playes* (London, 1662), sigs A2–6.

11 Patterson, *Censorship and Interpretation*, p. 45.

12 This hierarchy was implicitly recalled by Northrop Frye in his proposition of five mimetic modes ranging from myth, down through romance, to irony. It is a proposition which has been criticised for its 'fixed, synchronic system'. See Alastair Fowler, *Kinds of Literature: An Introduction to the Theory of Genres and Modes* (Oxford: Clarendon Press, 1982), p. 243. Fowler's critique of Frye is faulted by Seelig, pp. 9–10.

13 Sir Philip Sidney, *An Apology for Poetry or The Defence of Poesy*, ed. Geoffrey Shepherd (Manchester: Manchester University Press, 1984), p. 97.

14 *Ibid.*, p. 113.

15 *Ibid.*, p. 123; Margaret Cavendish, *Natures Pictures Drawn by Fancies Pencil to the Life* (London, 1656), sig. c3v. All further quotations from *Natures Pictures* will be from this edition.

16 Cavendish, 'To Naturall Philosophers', *Poems, and Fancies* (London, 1653), n.p. All further quotations from *Poems, and Fancies* will be drawn from this edition.

17 On such discoveries by the reader see White, who argues that the recognition and contextualisation of generic elements is a crucial part of the reading process: 'The original strangeness, mystery, or exoticism of the events is dispelled, and they take on a familiar aspect ... in their functions as elements of a familiar kind of configuration'. Hayden White, *Tropics of Discourse* (Baltimore: Johns Hopkins University Press, 1978; repr. 1992), p. 86. It is this process that Cavendish manipulates.

18 Mikhail Bakhtin, 'Epic and Novel: Toward a Methodology for the Study of the Novel', in *The Dialogic Imagination: Four Essays by M. M. Bakhtin*, ed. Michael Holquist (Austin: University of Texas Press, 1981), pp. 3–40 (p. 3).

19 Cavendish, *Natures Pictures*, pp. 94–6.
20 On this see, for example, Fowler, pp. 12–13.
21 As Alastair Fowler expresses it: 'Only by knowing the beaten track, after all, can [one ...] be sure of leaving it'. Fowler, p. 32. In other words, even if an author writes against a genre, it is still, within that very act of resistance, somehow a determining force on what is being written.
22 Alastair Fowler identifies the various features which constitute different 'kinds' of literature, that is, the factors critics have used to determine genres. Among them are: structure (both external and metrical); size; subject; mood and style. See Fowler, pp. 60–72.
23 Cavendish, *Natures Pictures*, title-page.
24 Cavendish, *'The Description of a New World Called The Blazing World' and Other Writings*, ed. Kate Lilley (London: Pickering, 1992), p. xi. This account of Cavendish's relationship to categorisation recalls, in its suggestion of the anxiety of classification, Foucault's description of the frenetic aphasiacs in *The Order of Things*. They are characterised as 'creating groups then dispersing them again, heaping up diverse similarities, destroying those that seem clearest, splitting up things that are identical, superimposing different criteria, frenziedly beginning all over again, becoming more and more disturbed, and teetering finally on the brink of anxiety'. See Michel Foucault, *The Order of Things* (London: Tavistock, 1970; London: Routledge, 1991), p. xviii.
25 Kingsley Hart, ed., *The Letters of Dorothy Osborne to Sir William Temple, 1652–54* (London: The Folio Society, 1968), p. 53.
26 *Ibid.*, p. 53.
27 *Ibid.*, p. 157.
28 Austin Dobson, ed., *The Diary of John Evelyn*, 3 vols (London: Macmillan, 1906; repr. London: Routledge/Thoemmes, 1996), II, 269.
29 In May Evelyn was 'discoursing with her Grace' in her bedchamber, later in the month seeing her at the Royal Society. *Ibid.*, p. 272.
30 *Ibid.*, p. 271, n. 3.
31 John Warrington, ed., *The Diary of Samuel Pepys*, 3 vols (London: Everyman, 1964), III, 195. The entry is dated 18 March 1668.
32 Quoted in Susan Wiseman, 'Gender and Status in Dramatic Discourse: Margaret Cavendish, Duchess of Newcastle', in Isobel Grundy and Susan Wiseman, eds, *Women, Writing, History, 1640–1740* (London: Batsford, 1992), pp. 159–77 (p. 160).
33 Virginia Woolf, *A Room of One's Own* (London: Hogarth Press, 1929; repr. London: Grafton Books, 1990), p. 60.
34 Lamb, *Last Essays of Elia*, quoted in Kenneth Baxter, 'Mad, Vain and Thrice Noble', *Independent*, 12 September 1992, p. 27. Lamb was enthusing specifically about Cavendish's biography of her husband, the anomalous generic status of which is discussed in Gloria Italiano, 'Two Parallel Biographers of the Seventeenth Century: Margaret Newcastle and Lucy Hutchinson', in Mario Curreli and Alberto Martino, eds, *Critical Dimensions: English, German and Comparative Literature Essays in Honour of Aurelio Zanco* (Cuneo: Saste, 1978), pp. 241–51.

35 Quoted in Grant, *Margaret the First*, p. 24. Evelyn does not mention this ballad in his diary account of the visit to the Royal Society, recounting instead the pomp of the occasion, and how he 'conducted her Grace to her coach'. See *Diary of John Evelyn*, p. 272.

36 Gerald Dennis Meyer, *The Scientific Lady in England, 1650–1760: An Account of Her Rise, With Emphasis on the Major Roles of the Telescope and Microscope* (Berkeley: University of California Press, 1955), p. 2. Meyer is unusual amongst critics in making an, albeit cursory, mention of *Heavens Library* on pages 7–8. He also touches on the notion of the placatory power of genre. In her *Blazing World*, he argues, '[Cavendish] sugar-coated the bitter bolus of natural philosophy in the hope that women readers, once they had acquired a taste for it when diluted with Romancy, would repair to the forepart of [*Observations Upon Experimental Philosophy*]'. Meyer, p. 9.

37 B. G. MacCarthy, *The Female Pen: Women Writers and Novelists, 1621–1744* (Oxford: Blackwell, 1945), pp. 81–2. The equivocation is especially evident in MacCarthy's assessment of Cavendish's 'scientific poppycock'. MacCarthy, p. 123.

38 See Helen Muriel Cocking, 'Originality and Influence in the Work of Margaret Cavendish, First Duchess of Newcastle' (unpublished MPhil dissertation, University of Reading, 1972). Other critics who focus on Cavendish's engagement with contemporary ideas include Sylvia Bowerbank and Maria de Santis. See Sylvia Bowerbank, 'The Spider's Delight: Margaret Cavendish and the "Female" Imagination', *English Literary Renaissance*, 14 (1984), 392–408. Bowerbank is taken to task by Maria de Santis for misinterpreting 'Cavendish's arguments as [she ...] overstate[s] the efficacy and the unity of the experimental method'. See Maria de Santis, 'Projecting a New Science: Restoration and Eighteenth-century Scientific Method' (unpublished doctoral dissertation, Columbia University, 1992; abstract in *Dissertation Abstracts*, 54 (1993), p. 186), p. 106.

39 See, for example, Dolores Paloma, 'Margaret Cavendish: Defining the Female Self', *Women's Studies*, 7 (1980), 55–66; James Fitzmaurice, 'Fancy and the Family: Self-characterizations of Margaret Cavendish', *Huntington Library Quarterly*, 53 (1990), 198–209. On Cavendish's autobiography see Elspeth Graham, *et al.*, eds, *Her Own Life: Autobiographical Writings by Seventeenth-century Englishwomen* (London: Routledge, 1989); Sandra Findley and Elaine Hobby, 'Seventeenth-Century Women's Autobiography', in Francis Barker, *et al.*, eds, *1642: Literature and Power in the Seventeenth Century* (Proceedings of the Essex Conference on the Sociology of Literature) (Colchester: University of Essex, 1981), pp. 11–36; Bella Brodzki and Celeste Schenck, eds, *Life/Lines: Theorizing Women's Autobiography* (Ithaca: Cornell University Press, 1988), pp. 1–15; *A True Relation* is also discussed in Estelle C. Jelinek, *The Tradition of Women's Autobiography: From Antiquity to the Present* (Boston: Twayne, 1986), pp. 28–32. Jelinek discusses the text in relation to that of Anne Halkett who wrote 'the other exceptional autobiography of the period'. Jelinek, p. 29. See also Mary G. Mason, 'The Other Voice: Autobiographies of Women Writers', in Brodzki and Schenck, pp. 19–44. In a more recent

article, Judith Kegan Gardiner uses psychologist Heinz Cohut's theories about narcissistic personality types to analyse Cavendish's autobiography, which she characterises as being quite different from the 'paradigmatically masculine individualism' of Hobbes's autobiography. See Judith Kegan Gardiner '"Singularity of Self": Cavendish's *True Relation*, Narcissism, and the Gendering of Individualism', *Restoration: Studies in English Literary Culture, 1660–1700*, 21 (1997), 52–65 (p. 62).

40 On Cavendish's science see Jay Stevenson, 'The Mechanist-vitalist Soul of Margaret Cavendish', *Studies in English Literature*, 36 (1996), 527–43; Stephen Clucas, 'The Atomism of the Cavendish Circle: a Reappraisal', *The Seventeenth Century*, 9 (1994), 247–73; John Rogers, 'Margaret Cavendish and the Gendering of the Vitalist Utopia', in *The Matter of Revolution: Science, Poetry and Politics in the Age of Milton* (Ithaca: Cornell University Press, 1996), pp. 177–211. See also Lisa T. Sarasohn, 'A Science Turned Upside Down: Feminism and the Natural Philosophy of Margaret Cavendish', *Huntington Library Quarterly*, 47 (1984), 289–307; Deborah T. Bazeley, 'An Early Challenge to the Precepts and Practice of Modern Science: The Fusion of Fact, Fiction and Feminism in the Works of Margaret Cavendish, Duchess of Newcastle' (unpublished doctoral dissertation, University of California at San Diego, 1990; abstract in *Dissertation Abstracts International*, 51 (October 1990), 1235-A). Sarasohn usefully contextualises Cavendish's atomist doctrine, and identifies both 'radical feminism' and 'condemnation of women' in her work. Sarasohn, p. 298. Further, her identification of an intellectual subversion in Cavendish's work is informative in terms of my own project, and its identification of generic subversion.

41 Carolyn Merchant, *The Death of Nature: Women, Ecology and the Scientific Revolution* (New York: Harper and Row, 1980; repr. London: Wildwood House, 1982); Sophia B. Blaydes, 'Nature Is a Woman: the Duchess of Newcastle and Seventeenth-century Philosophy', in Donald Mell, Jr, Theodore E. D. Braun and Lucia M. Palmer, eds, *Man, God, and Nature in the Enlightenment* (Studies in Literature, 1500–1800) (East Lansing: Colleagues Press, 1988), pp. 51–64.

42 Anna Battigelli, *Margaret Cavendish and the Exiles of the Mind* (Lexington: The University Press of Kentucky, 1998), p. 9.

43 Paloma, pp. 55–66. As Elaine Hobby expresses it, in *Assaulted and Pursued Chastity* 'Cavendish recombined the elements of romance in such a way as to undercut an ideology that would define women as passively virtuous and preoccupied solely with their lovers' prowess, leaving all the fun, and all the power, to men'. Elaine Hobby, *Virtue of Necessity: English Women's Writing, 1649–88* (Ann Arbor: University of Michigan Press, 1989), p. 92.

44 Sophie Tomlinson, '"My Brain the Stage": Margaret Cavendish and the Fantasy of Female Performance', in Clare Brant and Diane Purkiss, eds, *Women, Texts and Histories, 1575–1760* (London: Routledge, 1992), pp. 134–63 (p. 137).

45 *Ibid.*, pp. 144–5.

46 On 'performance itself [as] a fantasy space for aristocratic women' like
   Cavendish, see Ros Ballaster, 'The First Female Dramatists' in Helen Wilcox,
   ed., *Women and Literature in Britain, 1500–1700* (Cambridge: Cambridge
   University Press, 1996), pp. 267–90 (pp. 273, 276). In my own project I do
   not concentrate on Cavendish's plays, because of their post-Restoration
   publication. It is, then, on the analogous 'theatre' of *res publica* that the
   argument of this book is played out. However, the daringly autonomous
   strategies of, for example, the female protagonist of *Assaulted and Pursued
   Chastity* must, because of the dictates of circumstance, ultimately remain a
   fictional substitute for Cavendish's own circumscribed life. Linda Payne, like
   Jacqueline Pearson, whom she cites, examines women's access to power
   through language, an important cultural phenomenon and literary strategy.
   Repeatedly, public speech (of Cavendish's characters or of herself) is figured
   as the process by means of which power and status may be accessed. This
   is the theatre of public affairs where, as Cavendish reiterates in a variety of
   ways, performance is constituted by public utterance. See Lynda Payne,
   'Dramatic Dreamscapes: Women's Dreams and Utopian Vision in the Works
   of Margaret Cavendish, Duchess of Newcastle', in Mary Anne Schofield and
   Cecilia Macheski, eds, *Curtain Calls: British and American Women and the
   Theater, 1660–1820* (Athens: Ohio University Press, 1991), pp. 18–33;
   Jacqueline Pearson, "Women may discourse … as well as men': Speaking
   and Silent Women in the Plays of Margaret Cavendish, Duchess of Newcastle', *Tulsa Studies in Women's Literature*, 4 (1985), 33–45. Pearson notes
   that 'In the 1662 Folio, fifteen plays out of twenty-one begin and seven end
   with women speaking. This is strikingly unusual in the dramatic practice
   of the time'. Pearson, p. 33.
47 Quotation from Ventoso, mariner, in Dryden and Davenant's *Tempest*, II.i.
   See James Maidment and W. H. Logan, eds, *The Dramatic Works of Sir William
   D'Avenant*, 5 vols (New York: Russell & Russell, 1872–74; repr. 1964), V,
   437. This optimistic sentiment is especially true of Davenant, who expressed
   in his *Proposition* of 1654 a belief in the social amelioration Restoration
   drama might bring about. See James R. Jacob and Timothy Raylor, 'Opera
   and Obedience: Thomas Hobbes and *A Proposition for Advancement of Moralitie* by Sir William Davenant', *The Seventeenth Century*, 6 (1991), 205–50.
   The article includes a reproduction of the full text of the *Proposition* (pp. 242–
   8). See also Eckhard Auberlen, 'The *Tempest* and the Concerns of the
   Restoration Court: a Study of *The Enchanted Island* and the Operatic *Tempest*', *Restoration*, 15 (1991), 71–88. Auberlen argues that 'the play was
   made to support the conservative political myth that monarchy was the
   natural form of government'. Auberlen, p. 72. See also George R. Guffey,
   'Politics, Weather, and the Contemporary Reception of the Dryden–
   Davenant *Tempest*', *Restoration*, 8 (1984), 1–9. Guffey offers a highly specific
   contextualisation of the play, examining weather reports contemporaneous
   with its first performances.
48 By 'anti-Puritan' I mean here and elsewhere in my study to suggest 'Puritanism' as the Cavendishes imagined it to be, and am really referring to

perceptions rather than truths, and the cultural need to articulate and dramatise political difference. For more on the slipperiness of such terms see Ivan Roots, ed., *'Into another mould': Aspects of the Interregnum* (Exeter: University of Exeter Press, 1998), especially his chapter on 'Union and Disunion In the British Isles, 1637–1660', pp. 1–29.

1

The 1650s:
genre and exile

As for an History, said she, it cannot be exactly true, because there are so many severall intentions interwoven with several accidents, and severall actions divided into so many severall parties and severall places, and so many severall Reporters of severall opinions. (Margaret Cavendish, *The She Anchoret, Natures Pictures* (1656), p. 354)

I beleeve (Sir) you have seene a curious kind of perspective, where, he that lookes through a short hollow pipe, upon a picture conteyning diverse figures, sees none of those that are there paynted, but some one person made up of their partes, conveighed to the eye by the artificiall cutting of a glasse.[1]

So Thomas Hobbes praises William Davenant's dramatic heroic romance, *Gondibert*, published in 1651. Hobbes's style here suggestively intimates how an author's vision might compose disparate elements into a harmonious literary whole. Writing with close connections with the exiled court in Paris in the 1650s, Hobbes similarly elides the various moral qualities of Davenant's fictional characters with the poet's own, composite 'vertue'.[2] The compliment comes at the conclusion of Hobbes's attempt concisely to delineate a theory of genre which, in turn, due to the circumstances surrounding its composition, is intensely political in nature.[3] Hobbes identifies 'three sorts of Poesy[:] *Heroique, Scommatique*, and *Pastorall*', an hierarchic tripartite structure which echoes the philosophers' division of the Universe 'into three Regions, *Caelestiall, Aëriall*, and *Terrestriall*', and is, crucially, likened to 'the three Regions of mankind, *Court, Citty,* and *Country*'.[4] The critique itself functions like a perspective glass, generating a unified literary image from the diverse components of exile, genre, and politics – the three elements, indeed, which are placed under the lens of this book.

My perception of Cavendish's literary history is strongly dia-chronic; her texts are inseparable from the very particular times in which they were written. Some critics have claimed that she swept away convention, both literary and social, in her eclecticism. Con-trary to that, as I suggested in my introduction, it is my belief that through her careful manipulation of genre she forged many links and continuities with an intellectual past. In this chapter I am going to foreground the literary implications of Cavendish's experience of the triple exile, probing still more its interconnectedness with both genre and politics. The central importance placed upon exile is evi-dent not only in Cavendish's generic play but in the material and spatial configuration of the publications themselves.

During her sixteen years in exile Cavendish sent five volumes into London to be published.[5] Despite the fact of her being politically speaking *persona non grata*, Cavendish appears to have encountered little resistance to having her large, opulent volumes published. Her publications bore the imprint of John Martyn and James Allestry, a very successful commercial press. As Leona Rostenberg writes:

> During their association of eighteen years Martyn and Allestry together, or in partnership with Dicas, published an approximate total of 102 books, many of which were of unique importance in the progress of science and intellectual development. The largest proportions of their output represent the fields of science, belles-lettres and theology. Among the best-sellers in literature were the plays of Madame Scudéry, Butler's *Hudibras*, Cowley's *Poems* and, for the bluestocking, the various compositions of Margaret Cavendish, Duchess of Newcastle.[6]

The only exception to publication by Martyn and Allestry throughout the 1650s is the unique bound version of Cavendish's opus (minus *Philosophicall Fancies*) that she had specially assembled, then presented to Leiden University, using Constantijn Huygens as inter-mediary, in 1658. The original binding for this volume was English, with a newly added Latin index. As this is the only known printed copy of the Latin index, it would appear that this particular presen-tation copy could have been a joint effort of private and commercial presses. Whatever the circumstances of the production of her texts, though, whether Cavendish's publications were simply considered harmless, even faintly ridiculous, whereas in fact, when carefully read, they demonstrate an incisive political awareness, remains in part the object of this book. The self which Cavendish articulates in her direct addresses to her readers is repeatedly constructed so as to appear unthreateningly conventional in its multiple professions of humility. As she writes in *Natures Pictures*, 'I *Desire my Readers to judge this Book of mine according to the harmless Recreations of my idle time, and not as a laborious, learned, studious, or a methodical work*'.[7] What this construction creates is the opportunity for the writer to seize the potential of the liminal status of this material for seducing a readership – a readership she needs, in order for the polemical goals of her generic manipulations to succeed, to be alert to the possibility that appearances can be deceptive.

The critic Gérard Genette provides in *Seuils* some informative ways of theorising such prefatory or 'paratextual' material.[8] As the French title of his work suggests, *Seuils* is a study of the 'thresholds' of a publication, that is, its prefatory, dedicatory and titular components, and in his formulation the paratextual threshold comprises two parts: the epitext and the peritext.[9] It is with the latter of these two that this section of this chapter is more closely concerned. An examination of the paratextual, or more precisely peritextual, material of Cavendish's exilic publications *Poems, and Fancies, Philosophicall Fancies, The Worlds Olio, The Philosophical and Physical Opinions* and *Natures Pictures*, suggests that their very form is informed by and may be read as a response to her experience of exile. In other words the physical organisation of Cavendish's texts is politicised in ways directly related to the triple exile already identified.

Cavendish is as manipulative of her readership or, perhaps more precisely, her public, in her peritextual material as she is in her intratextual use of genre.[10] In this liminal zone of contact Cavendish endeavours to generate in her readers a mindset conducive to receiving the main body of the text in a quite intentional way, and to be in some degree alert to the possibility that all may not be as it seems, that is, that the author is capable of ingenious literary or generic operations. Further, in her peritexts Cavendish's presence and voice are explicitly present. What is more, in her intratextual generic interventions Cavendish does not altogether exile this peritextual voice. There is a slippage over the threshold, the effect of which is analogous to the inroads Cavendish attempts to make in her act of publishing out of exile. Her voice does not remain in the liminal, confined space of the peritext, but seeps into the main body of each publication. Cavendish will not succumb to the triple exile, and in the very structuring of her texts this refusal is reiterated. This peritextual, literary contestation of the condition of exile is another attempt by the exiled to seize an element of discursive power. The multiplicity and intimacy of Cavendish's peritexts, and her explicit self-presentation within them, register the anxiety behind her appeal to be heard – 'if not favour'd, then my Book must dye, / And in the Grave of Dark Oblivion lye'.[11] She goes to great lengths to reach the public poised on the thresholds of her texts.

How exactly does Cavendish's exilic peritextual material suggest that it is not only the content but also the very physical presence of her works which registers her triple exile? Before any part of a publication is read, its size and shape make an impression. Most of Cavendish's volumes are quarto or folio, thereby immediately making a visual impact. Even this has a political element to it – in their very ostentation, their impudent presence, her texts declare that her writing will not be exiled. This presentation also has a generic implication, since, in Genette's words, such large sizes 'were reserved for serious works (that is, works that were religious or philosophical rather than literary)'.[12] The very format, then, is suggestive of an audacious and somewhat ostentatious response to those authorities which would have Cavendish triply exiled. Similarly assertive is Cavendish's delight in what Genette would term 'onymity', in other words, rejecting both anonymity and pseudonymity in favour of having her own name appear as author of her texts. Such self-promotion constitutes Cavendish's legalistic assumption of responsibility for her work.[13] Further, her emphasis of her nobiliary status could be read as a deliberate refusal to acknowledge as anything other than temporary and illegitimate her social and political exclusion. *Poems, and Fancies* is advertised as being 'WRITTEN *By the Right* HONOURABLE, *the Lady* MARGARET Countesse of NEWCASTLE'.[14] In *The Philosophical and Physical Opinions*, she is described as a marchioness, and her delight in her status and degree reaches a peak in her last exilic publication, *Natures Pictures*, which is 'Written by the thrice Noble, Illustrious, and Excellent Princess, the Lady Marchioness of NEWCASTLE'.[15]

The titles of Cavendish's publications of the 1650s differ one from

27

another in length and complexity. Before departing for England in 1651, she had started to compose *The Worlds Olio*, which was published in 1655, when *Philosophicall Fancies* was revised and reissued as *The Philosophical and Physical Opinions*. This new nomenclature arguably marks a growing sense of confidence in Cavendish's publishing activities. The titles of her works began to shift from suggesting the purely imaginative to asserting the rational or scientific. Gone, then, were the 'Fancies', the more emphatic 'Opinions' replacing them; generic expectations were being indicated or suggested by the works' titles.[16]

Alongside Cavendish's first publication, *Poems, and Fancies*, the volume which receives most attention in this book is the 1656 publication:

NATURES PICTURES DRAWN BY FANCIES PENCIL TO THE LIFE. *In this Volume there are several feigned Stories of Natural Descriptions, as Comical, Tragical, and Tragi-Comical, Poetical, Romancical, Philosophical, and Historical, both in Prose and Verse, some all Verse, some all Prose, some mixt, partly Prose, and partly Verse. Also, there are some Morals, and some Dialogues; but they are as the Advantage Loaves of Bread to a Bakers dozen; and a true Story at the latter end, wherein there is no Feignings.*[17]

As Douglas Grant writes, 'A more specific and inclusive title could hardly have been devised'.[18] This synopsis title may be understood as a way – to borrow Genette's terminology – of delimiting the possible interpretations a reader might 'transport' over the peritextual threshold into the text. A title is always arbitrary, a short one more so, and its openness to multiple interpretations, and its ultimately extrinsic relationship to the text it designates, are problems which Cavendish here tries wittily to confront. Indeed, *Natures Pictures* marks a change in Cavendish's choice from the non-synoptic titles of her earlier works to the inclusivity of the title of the 1656 work, in which she plays with conventions and classifications in the title's juxtaposition of 'Nature', 'Fancy' and 'Life'. A connection thus begins to emerge between peritext and genre. Cavendish experiments with both in full awareness of the quasi-official status they grant to a text, a status which 'no reader can justifiably be unaware of or disregard this attribution, even if he does not feel bound to agree with it'.[19]

More of the peritextual material comes in the form of dedications.

Cavendish's first dedication, her epistle to Charles Cavendish at the beginning of *Poems, and Fancies*, may be read as topical in terms of the subject matter of the ensuing text.[20] The sewing imagery she employs in the epistle re-emerges in the main body of the text, and in subsequent exilic publications, especially *Natures Pictures*. It is highly pertinent to the author's self-identification, as I will demonstrate in Chapter 4. This personal relevance marks Cavendish's move away from the primarily remunerative purpose of early modern dedicatory material to a less private prefatory format which demonstrates a greater awareness of an active readership spoken to 'over [the] … addressee's shoulder'.[21] The performative act of dedication may also be understood as another way in which the exiled Cavendish attempted to appropriate a degree of power.[22] This is further emphasised by her careful choice of addressees. Not only does she address dedications to her readers, or to her husband or brother-in-law, but also, in *The Philosophical and Physical Opinions*, to 'The Two Universities' of Oxford and Cambridge.[23] This direct appeal to and concomitant implication of two such eminent and long-standing institutions is a shrewd move on Cavendish's behalf.[24] It is just such a move as she makes intratextually through her generic manoeuvres. In this same text Cavendish's lavish use of prefaces is apparent. It begins with William's allographic prefatory dedication to his wife, and is followed by his 'Epistle To justifie the Lady Newcastle'. These in turn are followed by Cavendish's dedications 'To the Reader' and 'To The Two Universities', her altogether inappropriately titled 'Epilog[u]e to my Philosophical Opinions' and no fewer than four epistles to her readers.[25]

The text is also punctuated by occasional intertitular epistles: 'To Condemning Readers', 'To the Unbeleeving Readers in Natural Philosophy', 'To all Learned Physitians', 'To My Readers', and 'To My Just Readers'.[26] On occasion the apparent anxiety of the writer's peritextual voice is carried over into the text without the use of such intertitles. Her interventions do not remain exiled on the far side of the textual threshold. In an exposition in *The Philosophical and Physical Opinions* entitled '*The sympathies and antipathies of sound to the minde and actions*', for example, Cavendish's voice is intrusive as she again attempts to define her project and defy her (textual and political) marginality. 'If I have not matched my strains and notes, with words and thoughts properly', she begins:

let those that understand musick, and Rhetorick mend it, for I understand neither, having neither fed at the full table, nor drank at the full
head of learning, but lived always upon scattered crums, which I pick
up here and there, and like a poor lasie begger, that had rather feed on
scraps then work, or be industrious to get wealth, so I had rather write
by guesse, then take the pains to learn every nice distinction.

And if my book will not please the learned, yet it may please the
vulgar, whose capacity can onely dig in the earth, being not able to
reach the celestial Orbs by speculation.[27]

This characteristic move to flatter the reader and simultaneously to
promote her own natural wit is unusual in its utter incorporation
into a wholly unrelated text, unannounced by any form of intertitle.
Such authorial interventions emphasise the degree of intimacy and
rapport Cavendish attempts repeatedly to assume with her reader.
Unlike a work's main title or designated peritextual material, such
interventions are only stumbled upon in the course of the text being
thoroughly read. Genette allows that a preface may be situated other
than at the opening of a work. What a preface essentially is, he
stresses, is 'a discourse produced on the subject of the text that follows
or precedes it'.[28] This formulation provocatively suggests another
way of reading those authorial interventions such as the one quoted
above from *The Philosophical and Physical Opinions*. If Genette's argument is logically pursued, then Cavendish may be seen as
transforming herself into her text. That is, much of her prefatory
material – preludial or otherwise – is about herself, her humility,
natural wit, professions of ignorance and so on.

Such deliberate conflation of self and text, such explicitly trans-
liminal interventions, suggests once more that, as I have been
arguing, the material and spatial arrangement of Cavendish's texts
is psychologically motivated and specifically a response to her condition of triple exile. However, it is important that the 'sender' of a
preface is not automatically assumed to be its 'actual writer ... whose
identity is sometimes less well known to us than we suppose'.[29] That
is, the reader must be alert to the possibility that the peritextual
material of Cavendish's publications may constitute her deliberate
presentation of a persona which may or may not correspond exactly
to 'Margaret Cavendish' but rather to a political or literary point
which she is attempting to convey.

In the case of Cavendish's exilic works, the peritexts function to point the reader towards a specific way of reading the texts that follow them, or into which they are embedded. My examination later in this book of the connection between *Natures Pictures* and the peritextual material of *Poems, and Fancies* illustrates this point, and I shall not pre-empt that argument here other than to suggest that Cavendish was acutely aware of the potency of the topos of humility or modesty in such peritextual material. As I argue later, such claims of inadequacy are immediately and quite deliberately undermined by Cavendish by their very context, that is, by their presentation in extremely competent and wittily polemical works. Further, the hyperbole of William's allographic prefaces is the antithesis in tone to such humility. In *Poems, and Fancies*, for example, he situates his wife quite firmly in a poetic tradition whereby 'Spencers Ghost *will haunt you in the* Night, / *And* Johnson *rise, full fraught with* Venom's Spight', such poets having been '*rob[b]'d . . .* of their Glorious Fame' by her.[30] In *The Worlds Olio* he pursues the culinary metaphor suggested by the title and calls his wife 'the Mistris of the Feast', declaring 'here's a Sumptuous Banquet for your Brain', and, in a concluding rhyming couplet which suggests an awareness of the text as commodity, pleads: 'this Imaginary Feast pray try, / Censure your worst, so you the Book will buy'.[31] This market-oriented attitude to the material book is also a theme in his 'Epistle To justifie the Lady Newcastle' in *The Philosophical and Physical Opinions*, where the '*Corrector, and the Printer*' are held responsible for any errors which may be present in the text. Such awareness of the physicality of the texts Cavendish was producing accentuates the material reality of their intervention from a condition of exile into a country from which their originator was banished. This is a manifestation of a variety of what Genette terms the 'generic hyperconsciousness' of allographic preface-writing, that is, the predominating feeling 'that what's most obvious about the whole business is that he is engaged in writing a preface'.[32] William is not adding to an understanding of the content of the text for which he is writing a preface, but is manipulating that paratextual material's political potential. He is banished, but his voice and, equally defiantly and at greater length, that of his wife, is still forcibly articulated and put into public circulation.

The elaborate frontispieces of Cavendish's exilic publications are similarly contumacious. The function of such illustrations clearly exceeds the purely decorative, and they participate in the paratextual project of reiterating Cavendish's purpose. Her frontispieces are engravings taken from paintings by the Dutch artist Abraham van Diepenbeke. One shows Cavendish in a classical pose, draped with a toga-like gown and looking, as one critic expresses it, 'very much like a statue of a Greek goddess'.[33] Another shows the author in a library or study whose shelves are empty, two putti with a crown of laurels hovering over her head, and a third frontispiece shows a group of people gathered around a fire, Cavendish and William seated next to each other. The frontispieces appeared attached to different volumes, bound next to their title-pages, and each served to portray its author in a confident pose.[34] This confidence is at once astonishing and yet curiously characteristic when viewed in the context of the triple exile of their author. Her paratexts at once register and are a response to this exile, an exile which she refuses to impose structurally, by refraining from banishing her voice to the peritextual margins of her own texts. It is to a further examination of this exile that my argument now turns.

In her introduction to *Women's Writing in Exile*, Angela Ingram explicates what she perceives to be the specifically gendered varieties of exile as experienced by women. It is worth quoting at length because, although she is writing about the experience of twentieth-century women writers, her words are equally applicable to Cavendish:

> Others are exiled less by geography than according to received literary criteria, which, in obscuring the complex interactions of race, class, and sexuality, in delineating hierarchies in matters of genre, arbitrarily determine canons and canonicity. And then, in a century and in a world disrupted by clashing armies and ideologies, destabilized by monumental stupidity and violence, women frequently excluded from what is considered significant action by immobilizing notions of 'protection' have produced exilic texts which, in reflecting the master discourses, subvert them.[35]

Cavendish, to return to the triple exile, was a woman writer at a time when print culture was almost exclusively male; a royalist when the dominant political ideologies were Puritan; married to an aristocrat but dependent on the good will of creditors, and an Englishwoman unable to live in England. Despite all this – or more precisely *because* of all this – she manipulated existent literary genres as a way of articulating and negotiating her contrary, triply debarred situation. Her polemic stems from her experiences of exile, witnessing from across the English Channel acts of precisely the 'monumental stupidity and violence' which Ingram describes. For Ingram women are additionally alienated by male discourse: 'For some ... the ambiguities and paradoxes inherent in finding a place to write are at least partly resolved by finding a "home" in writing itself'.[36]

In one of her 1650s publications, *A True Relation*, Cavendish defines her relationship with the men closest to her in terms of exile and dispossession, telling how her father, after killing a man in a duel, had to flee, his exile lasting 'from the time of his misfortune to Queen *Elizabeths* death'.[37] Some pages later, she talks of her husband's own exile. Her use of the term 'exile' in talking of her father's case, and her preferred expression of William's exile as a 'banishment' may be deliberate (it is the same word William used on the Cavendishes' tomb), the former implying a necessitous and pragmatic self-removal, the latter being indicative of an involuntary, enforced experience. 'Though my Lord hath lost his Estate', she writes,

> and banish'd out of his Country for his Loyalty to his King and Country, yet neither despised Poverty, nor pinching Necessity could make him break the Bonds of Friendship, or weaken his Loyal Duty to his King or Country.[38]

It is in her *Life* of William, written, significantly, after their return from exile, that Cavendish differentiates between William's initial departure – 'he went voluntarily out of his Native Country' – and his subsequent official banishment.[39] The specific nuances to 'exile' in Cavendish's discussion echo the specific nuances it had in her life, and serve to underline the importance of dealing with it, in a project such as this, not only as an abstract concept but also as an actual set of historical events. The milieux Cavendish inhabited in the 1650s provided her with a very specific impetus to write, and her writing, in turn, served as both an escape from and a critique of that very specific period in her life.

Those historical circumstances meant that literary forms other than drama were also being appropriated by vying political sides. Further, as Steven Zwicker has observed, literary forms do not remain unscathed by conflict but come out 'brilliantly charged, freighted with convictions and urgencies quite different from those that animated literary forms before the civil wars'.[40] Other 'literary systems' such as the 'ballad and the emblem', as Lois Potter writes, 'because of their associations with the popular sentiment', were hotly contested.[41] To adopt a genre, then, was to make a political commitment, and drama was not the only genre which the Puritan administration tried to control. Cavendish's apparent political subversion was staged in the face of various Acts which had been passed to control the circulation of literature and ideas. In March 1642 it was deemed compulsory to license newsbooks, and on 14 June 1643 a Parliamentary Ordinance was passed controlling all book and pamphlet publication. By September 1647 the army had press control, and in October 1649 an Act of Parliament led to the control of the press until the Restoration, and the suppression of blatantly subversive literature. The placatory tones of parts of the 1652 Act of Oblivion extended to anti-government literature, too, which, for the sake of avoiding a royalist rebellion, might have a parliamentary blind eye turned towards it.

The answer to such authority, then, was to make sure, as Cavendish did in her manipulation of generic conventions and expectations, that one's work did not appear blatantly subversive.[42] Her clever generic play acted like a code, without drawing to itself the attention which might have led to its interception either at the ports or in London.[43] Like allegory or fable, genre functioned as a literary cipher, arousing certain readerly expectations which, whilst being fulfilled on some levels, were profoundly challenged on others.

Who and where, then, were the circumstances and people amongst whom Cavendish, the romance heroine of whom I wrote in my introduction, found herself in the 1650s, the years which she spent largely in exile, and during which she began to publish her writing?[44] The decade marks a distinctive conjunction of personal and political circumstances in the writer's life. Cavendish's self-consciousness as 'a writer' is pronounced throughout her work, and she provides the reader with an account of the circumstances surrounding her decision to begin to publish her writing, a decision expressly necessitated by the political conditions of the 1650s. She attributes her inception as a writer to an earlier period in her life, referring to her juvenilia, sixteen 'Baby-Books', written because *it pleased God to command his Servant Nature to indue me with a Poetical and Philosophical Genius, even from my Birth; for I did write some Books in that kind, before I was twelve years of Age*'.[45] She makes clear her motivations, and her techniques, declaring that 'I pass my time rather with scribling than writing, with words than wit ... when I am writing any sad fain'd Stories ... I am forc'd many times to express them with the tongue before I can write them with the pen'.[46] The specific circumstances which led Cavendish to publish her work read (not so coincidentally, as will be seen) like those from the lives of her imagined protagonists in her writing.

In 1644 Cavendish, then Margaret Lucas, accompanied Queen Henrietta Maria (to whom she was a Maid of Honour) and her court from Oxford to France, where they took up residence in the Louvre in Paris, and the palace of Saint-Germain-en-Laye.[47] It was here that she met the aristocratic military commander William Cavendish, Marquis of Newcastle, who had come to France after the royalist defeat at Marston Moor.[48] Despite William being thirty years Margaret's senior, and the differences in social rank between the two, by December 1645 they had married in the private chapel of Sir Richard Browne in Paris.[49] Together they moved into William's Parisian lodgings, and then to a furnished house, where they began an exilic existence of vicissitude and uncertain credit. Here Cavendish met for the first time her brother-in-law, Charles, for whom she maintained a deep-seated affection, later writing that 'he was nobly generous, wisely valliant, naturally civill, honestly kind, truly loving, vertuously temperate'.[50]

During the years in exile Cavendish made many intellectual contacts through her brother-in-law and her husband. She dined with both Thomas Hobbes and René Descartes, and she struck up an acquaintance with Walter Charleton, with whom she was to exchange ideas about atomism.[51] Charles Cavendish established an acquaintanceship with Pierre Gassendi and Marin Mersenne, and William dined with the poet Edmund Waller.[52] The charged atmosphere of intellectual enquiry in Cavendish's immediate circle during the 1640s, and throughout the 1650s, can scarcely be overstated.[53]

In May 1647 a naval mutiny led to the defection of some parliamentary warships to the Netherlands, where they were joined at Helvoetsluys by the Duke of York. Henrietta Maria requested William Cavendish to accompany Princes Charles and Rupert from Saint-Germain to Helvoetsluys. The Cavendishes and their household consequently departed for Helvoetsluys via Rotterdam. It was at this time that Cavendish received news of the executions at Colchester of her brother, Sir Charles Lucas, 'being shot to death for his Loyall Service', and of Sir George Lisle, and also news of the desecration of the tomb of her mother and sister.[54] Discovering that the fleet and the princes had already sailed, the Cavendishes went to Antwerp, where they were to remain until the Restoration, despite, and remaining apparently largely unaffected by, the First Dutch War of 1652–54.[55] Here, they rented the mansion which 'belonged to the Widow of a famous Picture-drawer, *Van Ruben*'.[56] The 1640s, then, were for Cavendish a time of deep personal grief, dispossession, financial insecurity and itineracy; they were also the years during which she was in the midst of a flourishing intellectual milieu.

Shortly after the execution of Charles I, William Cavendish learned that a similar fate awaited him should he return to England, and that his estates had been confiscated.[57] In one of the poems William wrote to Margaret during their courtship he expressed with bitter irony his position as a traitor. In 'The Savinge Love' he wrote that 'To love me, tis high treason / Against your State and reason'.[58] By 1651, following Prince Charles's flight to France after the Battle of Worcester, the Cavendishes were running out of credit, and any optimism they might have had about an early restoration was severely dented. William therefore sent his wife and his brother to England to raise revenue, and so began the 'interregnum in Margaret's married life'.[59]

In November 1651 Cavendish and her brother-in-law settled at lodgings in Covent Garden, and on 10 December she appeared before the Committee for Compounding at Goldsmith's Hall.[60] Because William was regarded as a traitor, she was refused funds. 'I found their hearts as hard as my fortune', she later wrote, 'and their Natures as cruell as my miseries, for they sold all my Lords Estate … and gave me not any part thereof.'[61] Sophie Tomlinson has described Cavendish's performative appearance before the Committee as 'one of the few occasions in her life when she had the chance to make effective use of public speech', and I would argue that Cavendish's inability at that time to orate successfully, tied in as it is with her effective political status as a non-citizen, was later to undergo a fantastic transformation in the shape of her fictional characters.[62]

Cavendish had written 'Baby-Books' before, and now, '*to delude* Melancholy Thoughts, *and avoid* Idle Time', she began to write once more.[63] After eighteen months, 'part of which time I writ a Book of

Poems, and a little Book called my Phylosophicall Fancyes ... [I] became very Melancholy, by reason I was from my Lord', and so she returned in March 1653 to Flanders.[64] At the same time, her first volume, *Poems, and Fancies*, was published, followed two months later by *Philosophical Fancies*. This latter had been intended as a supplement to *Poems, and Fancies*.[65]

In commercial terms the Antwerp to which Cavendish returned was not thriving. For the Cavendishes, however, life at the magnificent Rubenshuis was comfortable, largely due to William's skilful handling of his creditors. Increasing numbers of exiled royalists, forced from France by the Fronde, had made the city their home. Edward Hyde visited the Rubenshuis, and the Queen of Sweden briefly met with the Cavendishes.[66] Cavendish's *CCXI Sociable Letters* is a semi-autobiographical account of much of her life at that time, wherein she records her delight in the dramatics of an Italian mountebank troupe, going so far as to hire a room overlooking the stage, in order to watch them daily.[67] Whilst this may or may not be an authentic autobiographical detail – *CCXI Sociable Letters* occupies an anomalous generic position between fiction and autobiography – the passion expressed for the exiled genre, 'drama', shows how clearly politicised such an activity could be, since acting and public performance of this kind were specifically banished from Puritan England. The mountebank troupe's performance thus becomes royalist by association, and, despite its uncertain status as autobiographical fact, Sophie Tomlinson has identified the incident as constituting a key moment in Cavendish's self-creation as a writer whose plays were to feature a 'use of performance as a metaphor of possibility for women'.[68]

The continued enjoyment of public performance becomes, then, an expressly royalist, exilic act. Although the royalists were in exile from their native land, and exiled from dominant discourses and power, associated practices or activities continued unabated, becoming in themselves charged with an almost compensatory political significance. Thus the 1658 publication by William Cavendish, 'never without hopes of seeing yet ... a happy issue of all his misfortunes', of his lavish *La Methode et Invention Nouvelle ... de dresser les Chevaux*, may be understood as 'a moving expression of his loyalty to the crown and of his love for England'.[69] William's nostalgia for public plays, spectacles, and festivities is also conveyed in his *Advice* to Charles II, in the sections on 'The Devertismentes For Your Ma[tie] People Both In The Citeye, & Counterye', and 'For The Countreye Recreations'.[70] 'All the olde Holedayes, with their Mirth, & rightes' should be reinstated, according to William, as he longingly details a bucolic idyll with:

> Caralls & wassells att Christmas, with good Plum Porege & Pyes which nowe are forbidden as prophane ungodlye thinges ... The Countereye People with their fresher Lasses to tripp on the Toune Greene aboute the Maye pole.[71]

Such activities have both a social function, since 'the devirtismentes will amuse the peoples thoughts, & keepe them In harmles action which will free your Ma[tie] frome faction & Rebellion', and a political significance.[72] They are linked intrinsically not with the present, restrictive regime but nostalgically with the Stuarts, since 'Kinge James off Blessed Memorye writt a litle Booke nott onlye In defence off dansinge, butt comanded thatt his good People Shoulde reioyce them selves with dansinge after Eveninge Prayer'.[73] William's *Advice*, in its overall recommendation of the establishment of an elite oligarchy, functions to demonstrate that such a system of government actively relies upon public spectacle. Davenant, too, in his *Proposition* of 1654, expressed a similar belief in the social amelioration drama might bring about.[74] William's determination to maintain a dramatic tradition in exile is demonstrated also by his publication in 1648 of his plays *The Country Captain* and *The Variety*.[75] Cavendish herself did not publish drama until after the Restoration, but it appears that she was writing plays much earlier, first drafts of some of them being lost during the sinking of the boat conveying the manuscripts from Antwerp to England to be printed.[76] For a short while in the late 1640s there was in Paris a dramatic company which performed for the émigré community.[77]

Much of this information about Cavendish's life comes from her own autobiography. Douglas Grant's assessment of this text, the '*true Story at the latter end* [*of 'Natures Pictures'*], *wherein there is no Feignings*' as serving 'in effect, though not in intention, to show that all her tales were essentially autobiographical ... Each story has its heroine and each heroine is Margaret in disguise', is an astute one.[78] However, it does not allow for other permutations of Cavendish's presentation of the autobiographical, in peritextual material, or in sections, for example, such as the first book of *Natures Pictures*, where there is no one single 'heroine' to be identified with, but where autobiographically motivated political comment is present in a generically disguised way. Cavendish's actual autobiography, her *True Relation*, like her *Life* of William, is in itself an example of how an established genre could become highly politicised to the point of subversion. The overall impression given by the autobiography is of a woman with a fantastically busy creative mind, a singularity in dress and, in counterpoint, a delight in the quiet, passive life of the country, and a natural tendency towards melancholy – 'not crabbed or peevishly melancholy, but soft melting solitary, and contemplating melancholy' – and bashfulness.[79] She exploits the vehicle of autobiography to express vindications of her own and her husband's wretchedness during the Civil War years, and widens her focus to embrace a critique of the Interregnum. Her explicit impetus for writing her autobiography is clearly conveyed in its concluding paragraph, where she ensures against the eventual effacement of her identity, and vindicates herself in the face of imputations of vanity, emphasising the work's function not as entertainment but as historical document:

> I hope my Readers, will not think me vain for writing my life … I write it for my own sake, not theirs; neither did I intend this piece for to delight, but to divulge; not to please the fancy, but to tell the truth, lest after-Ages should mistake, in not knowing I was daughter to one Master *Lucas* of *St. Johns* neer *Colchester* in *Essex*, second Wife to the Lord Marquiss of *Newcastle*, for my Lord having had two Wives, I might easily have been mistaken, especially if I should dye, and my Lord Marry again.[80]

This assertion conflicts with her declaration some few lines before that she is 'so vain, if it be a Vanity, as to endeavour to be worshipt, rather than not to be regarded'.[81] Such hyperbolic language is immediately and paradoxically deflated by its apparently unaffected frankness.

These seemingly unresolvable tensions between extreme and apparently arrogant hyperbole and painfully introverted shyness or modesty epitomise much of Cavendish's work, and are the key to her wish to make public that contradictory artefact – the autobiography. The self-conscious woman wants to make the public readership conscious of her self. This is the complex dilemma which lies at the heart of this work (indeed, all her work), which depicts a remarkably bashful woman, uneasy in most social situations ('I durst neither look up with my eyes, nor speak, nor be any way sociable'), yet one who can declare 'I am very ambitious, yet 'tis neither for Beauty, Wit, Titles, Wealth or Power, but as they are steps to raise me to Fames Tower, which is to live by remembrance in after-ages'.[82] Twenty years later, the *Life* of William was written as much for the assurance of the author's own fame as for that of her husband, and Cavendish's post-Restoration *Blazing World* has been read as affording the author compensation for the fact that her autobiography was so much shorter than the biography of her husband. That fiction, argues Mary G. Mason, is where Cavendish experiments with self-portrayals which do not belong in her autobiography.[83]

In the spring of 1658 'all the Royal Race' had assembled at the Rubenshuis for a banquet and party.[84] Given the Prince's own near-poverty, the celebration was extreme in its performative ostentation. By the end of 1658 Cromwell was dead, and on 8 May 1660 Charles was proclaimed King of England, Scotland, France and Ireland. William accompanied him to England, Cavendish herself remaining in Antwerp, a 'Pawn for [her husband's] ... debts'.[85] After a short time Cavendish followed her husband into rural seclusion in Welbeck Abbey in Nottinghamshire, where she could continue with her writing whilst, to a degree, living out her fantasy: 'I could most willingly exclude my self, so as Never to see the face of any creature, but my Lord, as long as I live, inclosing my self like an Anchoret, wearing a Frize-gown, tied with a cord about my waste.'[86] The wish of the 'Anchoret' for the companionship not of Lord God but of her own 'Lord' serves to highlight the idea that, although she defends her right as a writing woman in, and by the very production of, all her works, Cavendish frequently calls upon the support of her male relatives, especially in prefatory material. The opening words of her autobiography – 'My Father was a Gentleman' – are echoed in its concluding preoccupations with the possibilities that William might remarry should she die. Her self-definition is ultimately in terms of her relation to her father and husband. Implicit in the work's last paragraph is the assumption that Cavendish will be remembered not for her oeuvre but for her familial (and specifically male) connections. However, when such self-presentation is not labelled with, and consequently confined by, the generic signifier of a 'True Relation', with all the cultural expectations of a woman which that entails, but rather is present elsewhere in Cavendish's works, in her prefaces and fictions, it is more audacious and experimental. In portraying her life, as in all else she does, Cavendish is a wily manipulator of generic codes, making them work for, and not on, her writings.

In her preface to her *Life* of William, Cavendish suggestively offers an indication of the stage her perception of genre had reached by 1667, almost the end of her writing career. 'When I first Intended to write this History', she declares, she was:

> no Scholar, and as ignorant of the Rules of writing Histories, as I have in my other Works acknowledg'd my self to be of the Names and Terms of Art ... Many Learned Men, I know, have published Rules and Directions concerning the Method and Style of Histories.[87]

This professed ignorance does not, however, preclude her from entering into a little taxonomic play of her own, which in itself is highly politicised. As Hobbes did in his comments on *Gondibert*, so Cavendish here establishes a trinity of classifications, in this instance of history. She identifies general, national and particular sorts of historical account, and at once politicises them by comparing them with 'the three sorts of Governments, Democracy, Aristocracy, and Monarchy'.[88] The distinctions and classifications continue throughout the volume, as when she discusses her husband's literary works. She claims that William is 'the best *Lyrick* and *Dramatick* Poet of this Age', going on to praise the mimetic and didactic qualities of his comedies, 'for they are composed of these three Ingredients, viz. *Wit, Humour*, and *Satyre*' (p. 146). Even though the rule-books of 'Many Learned Men' are represented as being unread, Cavendish evidently is not without her own sense of taxonomic divisions and literary classifications.

Cavendish's person and her voice were both exiled in the 1650s, then. Further, whole aspects of royalist culture were analogously sent into exile on the Continent. The House of Commons which legislated against stage plays on 2 September 1642 was predominantly Puritan, few royalists remaining among its ranks. The Order advocated:

> all possible Means to appease and avert the Wrath of GOD ... Public Sports do not well agree with Public Calamities, nor Public Stage-plays with the Seasons of Humiliation ... being Spectacles of Pleasure, too

commonly expressing lascivious Mirth and Levity ... Public Stage Plays shall cease, and bee forborn, instead of which are recommended to the People of this Land the profitable and seasonable Considerations of Repentance, Reconciliation and Peace with GOD.[89]

As Philip Edwards has suggested, the Order is a curious mixture of moral indignation and a sense of political pragmatism in a time of national crisis. The political and religious objections expressed in it are barely separable, and Edwards claims that 'the central motivation' behind them 'was antagonism to the monarchy'.[90] In 1633 the Puritan William Prynne had published his *Histriomastix: The Players Scourge*, a volume of more than a thousand pages condemning '*popular Stage-playes (the very Pompes of the Divell)*'.[91] Prynne had exemplified an earlier tradition of Puritan opposition to theatre, his emphasis being religious, characterising playacting as both symptom and cause of 'paganism and idolatory'.[92] Piety and performance, then, had long been incompatible. 'It is too well knowne to divers Stage-customers' declared Prynne,

that the most notorious Panders, Bawdes, and Strumpets ... the most branded Adulteresses, Adulterers, Whore-masters, Brothel-house-haunters, and the like, are the chiefest Admirers, Patrons, Spectators, Supporters of; the most beneficiall Customers and Contributors to our Stage-playes.[93]

Puritan opposition to theatre, whilst ostensibly being motivated by moral concerns, contained an element of religious partisanship too, since aspects of both Catholicism and Anglicanism were, in their explicit performance, arguably like playacting. Other public ceremonies could be designated as being immorally akin to theatre, whilst Puritan rites, by contrast, could be set apart by their relative simplicity and spontaneity. The rhetoric in William Cavendish's *Advice* is interlocutory, almost dialogic, for example, as he discusses the centrality of 'seremoneye' to his political plans. He writes that:

withoute seremoneye whatt Is our church off Englande Coumde to nothinge whatt Is our late kinge Coumde to murtherde withoute Seremoneye whatt Is our Lordes coumde to dispisde & nothinge, withoute seremoneye the Genterye Loste, & Everye thing In Confution.[94]

Objections to drama, therefore, were not simply objections to immorality, but had complex religio-political bases. Upon the outbreak of the civil wars many players had fought on the King's side, and public stage plays became politically subversive activities, covertly continuing throughout the 1640s and 1650s. Records of 'dramatic activity' at the time, then, 'show only sporadic and usually hasty play-acting in an extremely hostile environment'.[95] The Red Bull, mentioned by William Cavendish in his *Advice*, was the location for evenings of extracts from assorted plays, and seems to have held out the greatest resistance against the ordinances against acting, being raided right through the 1650s.[96] The movement against the playhouses appears to have been fairly concerted, a manuscript addition to Stowe's *Annales* telling how, on one day, 24 March 1649, for example, 'a company of souldiers, set on by sectuaries of these sad times' pulled down both the Phoenix and Salisbury Court theatres.[97]

Charles I and Henrietta Maria ensured on various levels that the association between performance and royalism was maintained, and their court has been described as 'London's "third theatre"'.[98] The Queen's pastoral masques, in which she and other female members of the court participated, were famed, and in 1629 a visiting company of French actors with women among its ranks may have been one of the factors provoking Prynne.[99] Through the 1640s the court masques became, with their largely pastoral themes and in their pointed evocation of halcyon edenic days, implicitly politicised themselves. Prynne's subsequent punishment of a year's imprisonment, a hefty fine and having his upper ears cut off, for what was widely regarded as his indirect censure of Henrietta Maria, serves to emphasise the interconnectedness between the court and drama – to criticise the latter was seen as a criticism of the former.[100]

Cavendish, according to Catherine Gallagher, identified as much with the King as the Queen, defining her '*moi absolu*', through her writing, in terms of Charles's '*roi absolu*', and being, because of her political banishment as a royalist, and crucially as a woman, 'in miniature what Charles II was on a grander scale during the years of their shared exile'.[101] The Stuarts became strongly associated with the dramatic genre of romantic tragi-comedy, not just in their performances but in wider cultural representations of their lives. *Mercurius Politicus*, for example, the republican newspaper, described Charles II's flight after the Battle of Worcester as 'a very pretty Romance'.[102] Such pejorative attitudes could play right into the hands of the royalists, whose work, if regarded as mere romancical nonsense, could reach a far wider audience without suspicions being aroused that it might, in fact, contain subversive ideas.

Charles I and Henrietta Maria positively encouraged their representation within the discursive framework of romance. Annabel Patterson has identified how the royal couple benefited from their maintenance of the myth of their 'Caroline romance'.[103] Charles I cultivated an image of himself as the patriotic and chivalric St George, and this was seized upon by his political adversaries. Patterson cites a poem written in the late 1650s by Richard Lovelace called *A Mock Song*.[104] The poem, a rallying cry for the revolutionaries after the regicide, recalls Livy's fable of the Belly and the Members in its reversal of Charles's romantic self-appellation:

> Now the Thighs of the Crown
> And the Arms are lopped down,
> And the Body is all but a Belly;
> Let the Commons go on,
> The Town is our own,
> We'l rule alone;
> For the knights have yielded their Spent-gorge;
> And an order is tane
> With *HONY SOIT* profane,
> Shout forth amain
> For our Dragon hath vanquish'd the St. George.[105]

Cavendish's attitude to the romance genre, as examined in later chapters of this study, when read in terms of such strategic appropriation may function as a generic double-bluff. That is, if she professes a distaste for romance, she might distance herself from courtly culture and so not be associated with the suspicions which would inevitably fall on publications by the close-knit members of Henrietta Maria's coterie.[106]

The connection between royalism and performance, then, permeated the courtly culture with which the Cavendishes had contact in the 1640s and 1650s. Throughout his reign King Charles I was represented in a series of iconographic images, such as that on the frontispiece to his *Eikon Basilike*, criticised by Milton in a phrase which encapsulates the affiliation of royalism with drama, for looking like a 'Masking Scene'.[107] The *Eikon Basilike* itself seems to defy classification – it is at once a deeply personal work, yet destined for a public audience, and it is part religious meditation, part political treatise.

However, it had a massive political impact, buoying up Charles's public image. A plan for Inigo Jones's Cockpit in Court has the enthroned King effectively on his own little stage opposite the Proscenium.[108] Even Charles I's execution has been seen as a carefully staged performance – directed not by Parliament but by the King himself who took on the role of actor, concerned lest his words might not be heard by his audience.[109] In the late 1650s Davenant was organising operas in London, despite the continuation of prosecutions of actors. In order to stage his 1656 *The First Day's Entertainment at Rutland House* successfully, he played the subversive potential of the drama for Parliament's benefit, taking care to 'incorporate into his "entertainment" anti-French propaganda and songs in praise of Cromwell'.[110] In the 1650s Davenant held entertainments at his home, and eventually in 1658, with permission from the Protectorate, put on a production of *The Cruelty of the Spaniards in Peru* in the revamped Phoenix in Drury Lane.[111]

Performance, ceremony and spectacle, therefore, were constructed and perceived as inherently royalist activities which had explicitly to demonstrate parliamentarian sympathies before being acceptable. They were activities which the royalists took into exile with them, this continuity between royalism and performance being underscored after the Restoration with the almost immediate granting of permission to establish theatre companies to Davenant and Killigrew.[112] Taken into exile, the genre of drama had never gone away, and the rapidity of its reinstatement under the Restoration regime as a facet of cultural life emphasises the idea that, like its royalist proponents, it 'had never been totally suppressed'.[113]

Lois Potter, however, has attempted to move away from a too simplistic association of theatre with royalism, illustrating, for example, how the very language of the stage could be manipulated to have political implications, with royalists accusing 'Parliament of acting a *Comedy of Errors* or *A King and No King*', and how the publication of plays became in itself an inherently political activity.[114] The 1647 publication of Beaumont and Fletcher's *Comedies and Tragedies*, for example, has been seen as 'a symbol of an idealized aristocratic culture', and Fletcher's plays have been characterised as functioning like 'a talisman, a means for the Cavalier supra-society of defining itself and reasserting its values in a time of social and political upheaval'.[115] The publisher of drama Humphrey Moseley used prefatory material from a range of contributors to express certain political opinions, introducing into his texts 'extra levels of meaning' in much the same way that Cavendish arguably did.[116]

The motivation behind this construction of a text with multi-generic meanings was, then, primarily political, and directly informed by Cavendish's experience of the triple exile. I have shown how her peritextual material registered this experience, and in the next chapter I demonstrate how, intratextually, she utilised genre to facilitate her initial movement into print, that is, to negotiate one of the triple binds. In publishing *Poems, and Fancies* in 1653, Cavendish presented her work for the first time to an unpredictable readership. She attempted to defuse this unpredictability through recourse to ancient literary forms and paradigms. An analysis of this attempt constitutes the subject matter of the next chapter.

Notes

1 Thomas Hobbes, 'Answer' to Davenant's preface to *Gondibert*, in David F. Gladish, ed., *Sir William Davenant's 'Gondibert'* (Oxford: Clarendon Press, 1971), p. 55. In March 1650 Davenant sent his commander, William Cavendish, the bound preface and Hobbes's reply, some months before the eventual publication of the entire volume in 1651. See Grant, *Margaret the First*, p. 114. Cavendish herself praises 'Sir *W. Ds* ... Heroick Poem' in *CCXI Sociable Letters* (London, 1664), Letter CXXVII, p. 258. *Gondibert* has been read as royalist propaganda which, in the anticipation of the regicide in the Third Book, offers a severe critique of clericalism. See Lois Potter, *Secret Rites and Secret Writing: Royalist Literature, 1641–1660* (Cambridge: Cambridge University Press, 1989), pp. 93–7.

2 Hobbes, 'Answer', p. 55.

3 Steven Zwicker goes even further, wryly suggesting of Hobbes's reply that the 'affinity with Davenant is so close that it sounds like a concerted program'. Steven N. Zwicker, *Lines of Authority: Politics and English Literary Culture, 1649–1689* (Ithaca: Cornell University Press, 1993), p. 25.

4 Hobbes, 'Answer', p. 45. Hobbes's theory of genre marked an important shift from an Aristotelian system of classification dependant on rules followed, to a system with more emphasis on the temperaments being expressed.

5 At least one other text was sent into England for publication, but was lost when the ship conveying the manuscript from Antwerp was sunk. See Grant, *Margaret the First*, p. 159.

6 My thanks to Deborah Taylor-Pearce for helping me with this information, and for directing me to Leona Rostenberg, *Literary, Political, Scientific, Religious and Legal Publishing, Printing and Bookselling in England, 1551–1700: Twelve Studies*, 2 vols (New York: Burt Franklin, 1965), II, p. 240.

7 Cavendish, *Natures Pictures*, p. 103.

8 Gérard Genette, *Seuils* (Paris: Éditions du Seuil, 1987). For the purposes of this chapter, the translation by Jane E. Lewin will be that to which reference is made, and to which page numbers refer. See Gérard Genette, *Paratexts: Thresholds of Interpretation*, trans. Jane E. Lewin (Cambridge: Cambridge University Press, 1997).

9 Genette defines the peritext as the 'spatial category' composed of 'such elements as the title or the preface and sometimes elements inserted into the interstices of the text, such as chapter titles or certain notes'. The epitext comprises 'distanced elements ... interviews, conversations ... private communications' about a text. As Genette summarises, 'for those who are keen on formulae, *paratext* = *peritext* + *epitext*'. *Ibid.*, pp. 4–5.

10 Genette is careful to draw a distinction between readership and public. The *public* may only ever encounter parts of the paratextual material of a publication, whereas only a *reader* develops a familiarity with it all. See Genette on 'Addressees', pp. 74–5. He also persuasively argues, as I attempt to here, that 'the effect of the paratext lies very often in the realm of influence – indeed, manipulation – experienced subconsciously. This mode of operation is doubtless in the author's interest, though not always in the reader's' (p. 409).

11 Cavendish, *The Worlds Olio*, sig. Av.

12 Genette, p. 17.

13 On onymity, see *ibid.*, pp. 39–42.

14 Cavendish, *Poems, and Fancies*, title-page.

15 Cavendish, *Natures Pictures*, title-page.

16 Grant suggests how the change from 'Fancies' to 'Opinions' marks 'the greater seriousness of her intentions'. Grant, *Margaret the First*, p. 143. What I am identifying, which is implicit to Grant's assertion, is a concomitant and enabling change in Cavendish's confidence. She has the ability and right to project herself into the world as a writer with just those opinions which deserve to be taken seriously.

17 Cavendish, *Natures Pictures*, title-page.

18 Grant, p. 151. The reasons behind this title's apparent inclusivity are explored later.

19 Genette, p. 94.

20 I discuss this epistle and its topicality in more detail in Chapter 4.

21 Genette, p. 124.

22 On dedication as a performative act see *ibid.*, pp. 134–5.

23 See Cavendish, *The Philosophical and Physical Opinions* (London, 1655), unnumbered prefatory material.

24 As Genette writes, '"For So-and-So" always involves some element of "By So-and So"', and 'on the threshold or at the conclusion of a work, one cannot mention a person or a thing as a privileged addressee without invoking that person or thing in some way ... and therefore implicating the person or thing as a kind of ideal inspirer'. Genette, p. 136.

25 Cavendish, *The Philosophical and Physical Opinions*, unnumbered prefatory material.

26 *Ibid.*, pp. 26–7, 51–3, 99, 100–1, 171. On intertitles see Genette, pp. 294–318.

27 Cavendish, *The Philosophical and Physical Opinions*, pp. 168–9.

28 Genette, p. 161.

29 *Ibid.*, p. 178.

30 Cavendish, *Poems, and Fancies*, unnumbered prefatory material.

31 This dedication, '*To The Lady of* Newcastle, *upon her Book Intituled, The* WORLD'S OLIO', is not attributed to William, but is almost certainly by him. Page unnumbered.

32 Genette, p. 275.

33 See James Fitzmaurice, 'Front Matter and the Physical Makeup of *Natures Pictures*', *Women's Writing*, 4 (1997), 353–67 (p. 354).

34 For more on the frontispieces see *ibid.*

35 Angela Ingram, 'Introduction: On the Contrary, Outside of It', in Mary Lynn Broe and Angela Ingram, eds, *Women's Writing in Exile* (Chapel Hill: University of North Carolina Press, 1987), pp. 1–15 (p. 4).

36 *Ibid.*, p. 5.

37 Cavendish, *A True Relation* (London, 1656), pp. 368–9. When one writes of the Cavendishes' 'dispossession', it should be remembered that all things are relative, and that a court, even in exile, is none the less still a court with a degree of the social advantage which that implies. William Cavendish appears repeatedly to have utilised this fact in his negotiations with creditors.

38 *Ibid.*, p. 376.

39 Cavendish, *The Life of William Cavendishe* (London, 1667), unnumbered prefatory material.

40 Zwicker, *Lines of Authority*, p. 201.

41 Potter, *Secret*, p. 73.

42 The dates in this paragraph are from *ibid.*, p. 4. Potter makes the important point that, since royalists did not recognise Parliamentary authority, they could characterise themselves less as being subversive than as in fact maintaining an assumed right. See *ibid.*, p. 6. This idea is also Potter's concluding caveat, as she emphasises that for a reader to share a writer's point of view, and to understand a writer's allusions, leads to an interpretation of the text in question as rather supportive – because it accords with the reader's perspective – than subversive. See *ibid.*, pp. 209–10.

43 On such interceptions see *ibid.*, p. 39.

44 The best source for details of Cavendish's life is her own writing, in particular her autobiography of 1656, *A True Relation of My Birth, Breeding, and Life*, which is appended to the first edition of *Natures Pictures*. Modern biographies include Grant, *Margaret the First*; Sara Heller Mendelson, *The Mental World of Stuart Women: Three Case Studies* (Brighton: Harvester, 1987) and Kathleen Jones, *A Glorious Fame: The Life of Margaret Cavendish, Duchess of Newcastle, 1623–1673* (London: Bloomsbury, 1988).

45 Cavendish, epistle dedicatory to *Life*, n.p. In Letter CXXXI of *CCXI Sociable Letters*, Cavendish writes of these 'Baby-Books' that they have 'neither Beginning nor End, and [are] as Confused as the Chaos, wherein is neither

Method nor Order, but all Mix'd together without Separation'. Cavendish, *CCXI Sociable Letters* (London, 1664), p. 267.

46 Cavendish, *A True Relation*, p. 384.

47 Grant, *Margaret the First*, p. 71.

48 Historians and biographers since Clarendon have been eager not to represent William Cavendish's flight as cowardice. Geoffrey Trease, for example, in his discussion of the rout of Cavendish's 'Lambs', and Prince Rupert's troops by Cromwell and Fairfax, emphasises that 'we may imagine with what anguish Newcastle saw the annihilation. There was no more he could do'. Geoffrey Trease, *Portrait of a Cavalier: William Cavendish, First Duke of Newcastle* (London: Macmillan, 1979), p. 138.

49 Grant, *Margaret the First*, pp. 85–6. Sir Richard Browne (1605–83) was effectively ambassador in Paris for both Charles I and Charles II, his chapel being a focus for exiled Anglicans. See Robert Latham and William Matthews, eds, *The Diary of Samuel Pepys*, 11 vols (London: Bell & Hyman, 1983), X, 48.

50 Cavendish, *A True Relation*, p. 378. Clarendon wrote in scarcely less hyperbolic terms of Charles's 'mind and … soul … that was very lovely and beautiful'. Quoted in Grant, *Margaret the First*, p. 91.

51 Hobbes had been connected with the Devonshire branch of the Cavendish family since the early years of the seventeenth century, and by the 1630s was also well acquainted with William and Charles. See Richard Tuck, *Hobbes* (Oxford: Oxford University Press, 1992), pp. 118–32. Grant, *Margaret the First*, p. 117.

52 Grant, *Margaret the First*, p. 92.

53 The composition of and circumstances of this group are examined in Clucas, 'Cavendish Circle'.

54 Cavendish, *A True Relation*, p. 377.

55 Grant, *Margaret the First*, pp. 98–100; Trease, p. 158.

56 Cavendish, *Life*, p. 63.

57 Grant, *Margaret the First*, p. 103.

58 Douglas Grant, ed., *The Phanseys of William Cavendish* (London: Nonesuch Press, 1956), p. 16. This ironic language is echoed by Thomas Killigrew in his *Thomaso, or the Wanderer* (c. 1654). He describes the characters of his play as 'Remnants of the broken Regiments; Royal and Loyal Fugitives, highly guilty all of the Royal Crime'. Killigrew, *Thomaso*, quoted in Potter, 'Closet Drama', p. 275.

59 Lilley, *Blazing World*, p. x.

60 Grant, *Margaret the First*, p. 108. Other royalist women involved in the highly performative act of petitioning included Elizabeth, Viscountess Mordaunt, Anne Verney and Lady Isabella Twysdale. See Jones, p. 90.

61 Cavendish, *A True Relation*, p. 379.

62 Tomlinson, p. 146. The connections between performance and oration, female agency and citizenship, are further discussed in Chapter 4, below.

63 Cavendish, *CCXI Sociable Letters*, Letter CXXXI, p. 267; *Poems, and Fancies*, p. 122. Geoffrey Trease avers that Cavendish was writing before her

departure for London, caustically remarking that 'She was dashing off little essays of varied lengths on whatever occurred to her. Some might have done very well for women's magazines, had such publications then existed' (p. 164). Cavendish's use of the word 'melancholy' may be read as a conscious adoption of a royalist trope akin to Burton's attribution of his internal melancholy to the turmoil of external events, in his *Anatomy of Melancholy*. See Potter, *Secret*, p. 151.

64 Cavendish, *A True Relation*, p. 382.

65 Grant, *Margaret the First*, p. 130.

66 Jones, p. 102.

67 Cavendish, *CCXI Sociable Letters*, Letter CXCV, pp. 405–8. The mountebank show was soon closed down by the magistrates 'for fear of the Plague ... although some said, the Physicians through Envy to the Mountebank, Bribed them out'. Cavendish, *CCXI Sociable Letters*, p. 407.

68 Tomlinson, p. 137.

69 Cavendish, *Life*, pp. 75–6; Grant, *Margaret the First*, p. 148. The full title of this huge and beautiful volume is: *Methode et Invention Nouvelle de dresser les Chevaux par le Tres-Noble, Haut, et tres-Puissant Prince GUILLAUME Marquis et Comte De Newcastle*. As I suggested in my introduction, Cavendish's expression of being 'never without hope' is a caveat to the post-Restoration reader of the potential pitfalls of hindsight. Writing the texts which form the main object of this study during the 1650s, Cavendish's audacity is emphasised because she did not know when or if a restoration would occur, nor whether she could ever return to England on a permanent basis again. This should be borne in mind throughout this book.

70 William Cavendish, *Advice to Charles II*, in S. Arthur Strong, ed., *A Catalogue of Letters and Other Historical Documents Exhibited in the Library at Welbeck* (London: John Murray, 1903), pp. 173–236 (pp. 226–7). William lists the playhouses he recalls from before the Interregnum – 'Black-Friers, the Cock-Pitt, Salsburye Courte, the Fortune, & the Redd Bull' – and nostalgically recalls the boy actors 'att Black-Friers, & Paules', and the 'kinges Players ... att the Globe – which is nowe Calde the Phenixe' (p. 226).

71 *Ibid.*, pp. 226–7.

72 *Ibid.*, p. 227.

73 *Ibid.*

74 See Jacob and Raylor whose article includes the full text of Davenant's *Proposition* (pp. 242–8). As Simon Trussler has pointed out, some Puritans, too, shared a belief in the possible didactic benefits of a reformed theatre, most notably among them Milton. See Simon Trussler, *The Cambridge Illustrated History of British Theatre* (Cambridge: Cambridge University Press, 1994), p. 117.

75 Trease, p. 164. Of *The Variety* it has been written that William dared in his play 'not only to satirize courtiers but even to parody that last resort of Caroline self-deception, the court masque'. Trussler, p. 113.

76 See Grant, *Margaret the First*, p. 159.

77 See Trease, p. 154; see also Potter, 'Closet Drama', p. 274.

78 Grant, *Margaret the First*, p. 154.
79 Cavendish, *A True Relation*, p. 388.
80 *Ibid.*, pp. 390–1. Such confusions between the Duke's two wives indeed appear to have arisen: 'This mistake, as Brydges points out, was actually made. In *The Loungers Common Place Book*, vol. ii. p. 398, there is a notice of the Duchess wherein this passage occurs. "This lady, the first of characters, a good wife, as well as a sensible and accomplished woman, was the daughter of William Basset, Esquire, of an ancient family in the county of Stafford". Edward Jenkins, ed., *The Cavalier and his Lady: Selections from the Works of the First Duke and Duchess of Newcastle* (London: Macmillan, 1872), p. 77.
81 Cavendish, *True Relation*, p. 390.
82 *Ibid.*, pp. 374, 389.
83 Mason described Cavendish as a 'double-focus' writer. It is a construction which is reminiscent of the unified, autonomous self proposed by Catherine Gallagher in 'Embracing the Absolute'. A key word in Gallagher's argument is 'singularity', but it is a singularity which, in its need for subjects, paradoxically embraces and necessitates multiplicity. See Gallagher, pp. 24–39.
84 Cavendish, *Life*, p. 80.
85 *Ibid.*, p. 86.
86 Cavendish, *A True Relation*, p. 390.
87 Cavendish, *Life*, unnumbered prefatory material. Significantly, to Cavendish there is no formal division between 'history' and 'biography'. This serves to underline the importance of a diachronic approach to genre, which treats it as a flexible and contingent phenomenon.
88 *Ibid.*, unnumbered prefatory material.
89 Quoted in Philip Edwards, 'The Closing of the Theatres', in Edwards, *et al.*, *The Revels History of Drama in English*, IV (London: Methuen, 1981), pp. 61–7 (pp. 61–2).
90 *Ibid.*, p. 63.
91 William Prynne, *Histriomastix: The Players Scourge* (London, 1633; facsimile repr. New York: Garland, 1974), title-page. Prynne's text had a wide audience, and even Charles II had a copy bound in morocco leather. See Arthur Freeman, 'Preface' to *Histriomastix*, p. 6.
92 Edwards, p. 63. Somewhat ironically, Prynne's text is structured as an 'Actors Tragædie, *Divided into Two Parts*' (title-page). Prynne's outspoken treatise was, in generic terms, structurally as well as in terms of content, his downfall. He might have been saved, argues Patterson, had he elected more openly 'to make use of the structural protection of the play' (p. 91). The anti-theatrical Puritan campaigner himself 'became a tragic actor in the live theater of politics'. See Patterson, p. 91. Trussler makes the point that the theatres, as sites of assembly, had been closed in times of plague, prior to 1642. They were shut, for example, in Charles I's accession year, 1625. See Trussler, p. 106.
93 Prynne, *Histriomastix*, p. 389.
94 William Cavendish, *Advice*, p. 189.

95 Gerald Eades Bentley, 'The Period 1642–60', in Edwards, *et al.*, pp. 120–24 (p. 120).

96 See *Ibid.*, p. 123.

97 A. M. Nagler, *A Source Book in Theatrical History* (Sources of Theatrical History) (New York: Dover, 1952), p. 158.

98 Trussler, p. 108.

99 On Henrietta Maria's masques see Erica Veevers, *Images of Love and Religion: Queen Henrietta Maria and Court Entertainments* (Cambridge: Cambridge University Press, 1989). On the visiting French troupe see Trussler, p. 108.

100 Of Prynne's libel trial Patterson has written that it was 'about how the state functions as a "reader" of texts, about the role and status of ambiguity in the reading process'. Patterson, p. 10. Prynne attempted to argue against such ambiguity by appeal to intentionality: he claimed that a direct critique of Henrietta Maria could not have been his purpose because he had started to write *Histriomastix* in 1624. See Patterson, p. 105.

101 Gallagher, pp. 25, 28.

102 See Potter, 'Closet Drama', p. 270.

103 Patterson, p. 166.

104 *Ibid.*, p. 170.

105 *Ibid.* For more on the political signifcance of Livy's fable see Chapter 5, below.

106 The particular fluidity of the romance form is examined by Potter, who demonstrates how it could be characterized as either pejorative or serious, even didactic. See Potter, *Secret*, pp. 74–5.

107 For an analysis of this frontispiece, and the reference to Milton, see Potter, 'Closet Drama', p. 268.

108 See Trussler, p. 109.

109 See Potter, *Secret*, pp. 169, 189–90.

110 Bentley, p. 123.

111 Trussler, p. 116.

112 Charles II arrived in London on 29 May 1660. Killigrew received his grant to set up a theatrical company on 9 July, just six weeks later. See Edwards, p. 67.

113 *Ibid.*, p. 67.

114 Potter, 'Closet drama', p. 264. Elsewhere, Potter argues that 'Given these shifting alignments [as was the case with Edmund Waller], it is only with reference to a specific date that one can safely describe a writer as belonging to one party or the other'. Potter, *Secret*, p. xiii. No evidence suggests that any such ambiguity inhered in the Cavendishes' political allegiances. Another historian who warns against a too simplistic equation of hostility to the theatre with Puritan sentiment is Simon Trussler. He makes the point that playhouses of the late 1620s, 'when Charles began his ill-fated eleven-year experiment in personal rule', could be anti-monarchy, and in 1640 players at Salisbury Court were imprisoned by the Crown for staging Richard Brome's *The Court Beggar*, which Charles I felt was critical of his Scottish policies. See Trussler, pp. 108, 113.

115 Robert Markley, '"Shakespeare *to thee was dull*": the Phenomenon of

Fletcher's Influence', in Robert Markley and Laurie Finke, eds, *From Renaissance to Restoration: Metamorphoses of the Drama* (Chagrin Falls: Bellflower Press, 1984), pp. 88–125 (p. 95).

116 Potter, 'Closet Drama', p. 267.

2

'Sweet Honey of the Muses':
Lucretian resonance in
Poems, and Fancies

We with *Ignorance* about do run,
To know the *Ends*, and how they first begun.
(Margaret Cavendish, '*Of the* Subtlety *of* Motion',
Poems, and Fancies (1653), p. 19)

Following her return from exile in 1660 Cavendish sought a scholar
to translate her philosophical works into Latin. It was a desire which
she had expressed as early as 1655 when, in *Philosophical and Physical
Opinions*, she wrote:

> *I fear me my book will be lost in oblivion, or condemned by ignorance, unlesse
> some generous disposition which hath a genius in natural Philosophy, and
> [is] learned and eloquent in the Latine tongue, will translate my work.*[1]

At the Restoration, Jasper Mayne, canon of Christ Church, Oxford,
directed the chosen translator 'to read Lucretius ... who having
softened the most stubborn parts of natural philosophy, by making
them run smoothly in his tuneable verses, by an easy imitation will
teach him, to do the like'.[2] The project was never completed, but the
anecdote serves to emphasise the pre-eminence accorded to Lucretius
in the middle of the seventeenth century, and suggests, in Mayne's
union of philosophy and poetry, something of the generically complex
nature of Cavendish's poetical philosophical texts. For Mayne, Lucretius's 'tuneable' work was possessed of an expediently curative
character, the effects of which could be only of benefit when applied
to Cavendish's own often 'stubborn' writing.

There are two ways of characterising Cavendish's relationship to Lucretius in her first published work, *Poems, and Fancies* (1653). Firstly, both engage with Epicurean atomism. Secondly, in a structural sense, Lucretius provided for Cavendish a generic model for presenting her work to the world. It is on the second of these two engagements with Lucretius that this chapter will focus primarily, but reference to the shared doctrine of atomism will also be made. It is not Cavendish's choice of subject matter so much as its mode of presentation – in verse – which is of key importance. As will be shown, a specifically Lucretian approach to poetry is fundamentally political, in that it grants unpopular or subversive ideas the possibility of a public platform. These subversive ideas are of two kinds. Firstly, by publishing her own writing, Cavendish is breaking that aspect of her triple exile which I earlier termed as prohibiting a woman's 'promiscuously transgressive' movement into print. Secondly, the grip of the political arm of the triple exile is weakened by her use of poetry to critique the Interregnum or Protectoral regime. Both of these unpalatable facets of the triple exile could be addressed, and therefore implicitly challenged, in mellifluous verse. In this Lucretius may be understood to be Cavendish's generic model. The relationship of the two writers in this modal sense is a suggestive one. That is, Cavendish does not mention the Roman poet directly, and any familiarity she had with him was conveyed to her through her male acquaintances; she did not have the classical education necessary for reading *De rerum natura* herself. This 'suggestive' relationship warrants further investigation, before engaging in a close reading of sections of *Poems, and Fancies*.

De rerum natura, the Imperial Roman Lucretius's 'bible of Epicurean atomism', was written in the first century BC and depicts an unteleological, mechanistic universe, composed of innumerable imperceptible atoms pitched about in the void, composing themselves into myriad combinations to create every natural phenomenon.[3] It is a non-providential universe in which the gods have no involvement and religion functions as a force which, through fear and superstition, keeps human beings in thrall. Through his atomic explication of phenomena such as illness and natural disaster, Lucretius aims, with his 'honeyed tongue', to enable human beings 'to stand aloof in a quiet citadel ... and to gaze down ... on others wandering aimlessly in a vain search for the way of life'.[4] He was versifying

Epicurus's thought at a time which he typifies as involving a 'brutal business of war by sea and land … this evil hour of my country's history', an opinion which Margaret Cavendish might well have held of England in the 1650s.[5]

Lucretius's use of verse to convey his philosophy suggested to Cavendish a genre which she adopted, carefully and deliberately constructing the rendering of scientific theory in poetry as a culturally acceptable literary activity for a woman. Further, Lucretius's generic influence may be traced throughout the whole of *Poems, and Fancies*, not being confined to Cavendish's explicitly atomist poems.[6] My concern here, however, as I stated above, is not to map in precise detail how like to Lucretius's philosophy Cavendish's is, but rather to demonstrate that the genre and structure of his work facilitated her own imaginative incursions into a print culture which, in being both male and anti-Royalist, reflected and was a product of the multiple exiles under which Cavendish wrote in the 1650s.[7]

Cavendish's interpretation of *De rerum natura* is characteristically eclectic. This means that at times she appears to be writing intentionally against the grain of Lucretius's argument, whilst still using his images as material for her own work.[8] In this suggestive relationship, form is as important as substance. Frequently, she picks up on notions which Lucretius rejects, exploring them with as much enthusiasm and reverence as she demonstrates for his positive hypotheses.[9] This intensely speculative understanding of Lucretius's doctrine (she is not, after all, rewriting his work) manipulates the rhetorical and generic boundaries he erects between science fiction and science fact, between possibility and impossibility.[10] In her poems and in her fancies Cavendish writes in a Lucretian mode, even when, substantively, her philosophy is at odds with his. One compelling reason for the idiosyncratic nature of Cavendish's engagement with Lucretius lies in how his doctrine was mediated to her, since, in the absence of any means of reading it first-hand, she had to rely on adaptations and interpretations as provided by other members of the émigré community, Hobbes in particular.[11]

Several versions and critiques of parts of Lucretius's doctrine were available to Cavendish, notably Robert Greville's *Nature of Truth* of 1640, and Kenelm Digby's *Two Treatises*, which followed four years later.[12] Du Bartas's *Holy Days and Weeks*, to which Cavendish had indirect access, is a sixteenth-century adaptation of Lucretian style and phrasing.[13] George Sandys's 1615 work *A Relation of a Journey begun Anno Domini 1610* contained five translated quotations from *De rerum natura*, and more excerpts appeared in Hakewill's *Apologie* of 1635, the mid-century Epicurean revival continuing with the publication in 1656 of John Evelyn's partial translation of *De rerum natura*, and Walter Charleton's *Epicurus's Morals*.[14] Charleton's 1654 work *Physiologia Epicuro-Gassendo-Charltoniana* has been termed 'the first major presentation in English of the atomic doctrine'.[15] Wolfgang Fleischmann makes the point that so great was Lucretius's impact in the middle of the seventeenth century that even self-professed enemies of the ideas of Epicurus and Hobbes, such as the Cartesian Boyle, and the Anglican Glanvill, were not above borrowing his atomist theories.[16] Thus there is a strong argument for the inference that what may perhaps be best defined as cultural osmosis was as responsible for Cavendish's understanding of Lucretius as a more direct or formal engagement could be. In *Philosophical and Physical Opinions*, she was to offer her reader her own explanation of this intellectual transmission:

> as I have said of the names and tearms of art, and the several opinions of the Antients, and the distinguishment of the sciences, and the like, I learned them from my neerest and dearest friends as from my own brothers, my Lords brother, and my Lord.[17]

The key to her suggestive relationship to Lucretius's text lies less in the complex intricacies of his philosophical exposition than in the very mode of that exposition. His alluring versification of science suggests a dexterity of genre which seduced the aspiring woman writer.[18]

The potency of atomism as a cultural image is manifold and contradictory. Whilst the unalterable nature of its immutable constituent elements may allow it to be constructed as representative of stability, the vertiginous fragmentation of Lucretius's universe suggests quite the reverse. In the 1640s Cavendish's personal world disintegrated. Institutions and conventions were atomised, and her holistic universe was rendered chaotic by what she perceived as anarchic acts, chief among them, of course, the regicide. Her decision to versify scientific theories, employing an illustrative mode for making sense of the imperceptible and fantastic, becomes in itself an implicitly political act.[19] The exiled royalist finds in Lucretius's rendering of his atomist doctrine a genre both explicative and subversive.[20]

Poems, and Fancies has a multifaceted generic construction – scientific treatise; work of fantasy; political commentary – which is made possible by, and yet, in its particulars, occasionally directly contradicts, *De rerum natura*. This is not to suggest, however, that *De rerum natura* itself operates within simplistic genres. Epicurean philosophy offered its adherents salvation through common-sense, originating in a systematic understanding of previously misinterpreted natural phenomena. 'When human life lay grovelling in all men's sight, crushed to the earth under the dead weight of superstition', writes Lucretius of his mentor, 'a man of Greece was first to raise mortal eyes in defiance, first to stand erect and brave the challenge'.[21] A common-sense philosophy is prima facie one which is objective, that is, which is constituted of verifiable truths.[22] However, in *Poems, and Fancies*, Cavendish's 'common sense' conforms to a rigidly royalist agenda, being open to subjective vicissitude. Similarly, Lucretius claims to uncover the objective nature of things, but the very opening words of *De rerum natura*, addressed to Venus – 'Mother of Aeneas and his race' – locate his argument firmly in a particular time and suggest a specific political agenda.[23] Both Cavendish and Lucretius, then, exploit their apparently neutral, fact-finding explorations of the natural world simultaneously to convey their very subjective political sympathies. The potential aggressiveness of this exploitation is extenuated by its presentation in verse.

Lucretius's text, whilst resisting facile generic classification itself, is characterised by a careful organisation of its material, which, in turn, is full of categorisations and classes of phenomena.[24] The atom, key to Lucretius's universe, is the most basic classificatory element, lowest common denominator of all things, connecting them at the most fundamental level, and yet, in its numerous combinations and variations, making them discrete. In presenting this radically naturalistic philosophy, the invisible nature of the atom demands of the reader a considerable leap of faith. In loosely Baconian terms, Lucretian atomist doctrine in the mid seventeenth century is a philosophy which must remain unable to be proved, since it is experimentally unverifiable.[25] It is the language of poetry which can make the invisible understood.[26] In the opening book of *De rerum natura* Lucretius explicates his decision to use verse. 'My art is not without a purpose', he declares, making his didactic intent clear, going on to explain his methods thus:

Physicians, when they wish to treat children with a nasty dose of wormwood, first smear the rim of the cup with a sweet coat of yellow honey. The children, too young as yet for foresight, are lured by the sweetness at their lips into swallowing the bitter draught. So they are tricked but not trapped, for the treatment restores them to health. In the same way our doctrine often seems unpalatable to those who have not sampled it, and the multitude shrink from it. That is why I have tried to administer it to you in the dulcet strains of poesy, coated with the sweet honey of the Muses.[27]

The apparent contradiction in Lucretius between his austere philosophy and its rich and beautiful mode of expression has been commented on by critics.[28] Further, in sections of *De rerum natura*, Lucretius actually inveighs against the excesses of poetry, since philosophy should halt delusions, not be expressed in a misleading manner.[29] Lucretius's skill in this persuasive passage has been remarked upon by Monica Gale: 'The use of poetic artifice as a vehicle for the argument that poetic artifice is an appropriate vehicle for argument means that the passage is simultaneously an explanation and an illustration'.[30] Although Cavendish is not rewriting Lucretius, it is noticeable at this point that in *Poems, and Fancies* she demonstrates an acute awareness of the seductive power of verse, occasionally characterising it in notably erotic terms:

> *Verse* must be like to a *Bounteous Face*,
> Both in the *Eye*, and in the *Heart* take place.
> Where *Readers* must, like *Lovers*, wish to be
> Alwaies in their *Deare Mistris* Company.[31]

The opening section of *Poems, and Fancies*, where Cavendish sets out her atomist doctrine, is also in verse. In the prefatory material, she characterises her verse as operating less as a Lucretian mollifier than as obliterative camouflage. 'The Reason why I write it in *Verse*', she maintains, 'is, because I thought *Errours* might better pass there, then in *Prose*'.[32] She continues: '*Poets* write most *Fiction*, and *Fiction* is not given for *Truth*, but *Pastime*'. This is an important distinction which she expands upon up by constructing a direct comparison between her subject-matter and her chosen mode of expression: 'I feare my *Atomes* will be as small *Pastime* ... for nothing can be lesse then an *Atome*'. There is an ambiguity in this last statement which has implications for the self-effacing tone of the prefatory material as a whole, for indeed, in this milieu 'nothing can be less than' an atom, but, by extension, nor can anything be greater, or more important, than it in fundamental terms. When she writes, 'so shall I remaine an unsettled *Atome*, or a confus'd heape', the process of comparison has reached its logical conclusion – the body of the author herself.[33] Such complex image-systems are distinctly Lucretian in tone. Taken at their basal level, the statements work not as literary comparisons but as literal statements of fact: 'nothing *can* be lesse then an *Atome;*' the author *is* 'a confus'd heape' of atoms.[34] The comparisons also work on an imagistic level, and so the hiatus between poetic expression and scientific statement is narrowed.[35]

Much the same effect occurs in the second book of Lucretius's work where, in his attempt to describe atomistic motion, the poet grows increasingly didactic, his language correspondingly increasingly poetic. 'It is', he begins, 'for you to devote yourself attentively to my words'.[36] He goes on to describe a shaft of sunlight in a dusty room where there are 'a multitude of tiny particles mingling in a multitude of ways in the empty space within the light of the beam, as though contending in everlasting conflict, rushing into battle rank upon rank'.[37] Of the didactic power of the image he writes: 'To some extent a small thing may afford an illustration and an imperfect image of great things', and it is in the next phrase that the regressive, ultimately self-referential nature of the image is evident, since 'these particles that are seen dancing in a sunbeam [... are] an actual indication of underlying movements of matter that are hidden from our sight'.[38] The dust dances like and because of atoms. Their choice of mode of expression has led both Lucretius and Cavendish to a point where there can exist 'no analogical relationship between visible phenomena and invisible atoms which does not involve an ontological connection as well'.[39] This position raises a challenge to notions that science and verse are altogether separate entities in the seventeenth century. Science may be understood less as 'fact' than as one more discourse expedient for describing the world. In the pre-Newtonian universe of Imperial Rome, or 1650s Europe, hypothesis may have equal status with scientific 'fact'. In these intensely heuristic environments such hypotheses would, of necessity, border on the fictional or fantastic. Cavendish, then, is free to blur the boundaries between factual and fictional discourse, between scientific treatise and verse, and this is precisely what she achieves in *Poems, and Fancies*.[40]

Although Cavendish occasionally uses her text as a vehicle for the expression of partisan views on matters such as monarchical rule, which go against the dominant political discourses of the 1650s, *Poems, and Fancies* is not didactic in the same way as *De rerum natura*. Indeed, in her conclusion to the volume, Cavendish writes that 'My *intention* was, not to teach *Arts*, nor *Sciences*, nor to instruct in *Divinity*, but to passe away *idle Time*', a statement in itself calculated to deflect criticism.[41] Cavendish does share with Lucretius the status of a pioneer engaged in a controversial and unpopular project: in his case, the dissemination of a radical philosophy; in hers, the publication of a woman's work.[42] For Lucretius, poetry renders his doctrine more palatable; for her it is a mode of expression which can be gendered as specifically, and safely, feminine, and so can facilitate her first entry into print. Since poetry relies on imagination, Cavendish argues in her preface 'To All Noble, and Worthy Ladies', it is especially suited to women because 'their *Braines* work usually in a *Fantasticall motion*', and such activity actually guarantees female self-control, since if '*Wives, Sisters, & Daughters*, may imploy their time no worse then in … *Fancies* … *Men* shall have no cause to feare … their *loose Carriages*'.[43] Both writers must, for public consumption, coat with poetic honey the bitter pills of their respective projects.[44]

Occasionally, Cavendish seizes on notions which Lucretius posits then rejects, and derives imaginative stimulus from them, as is evident in her apparent adaptation of the discussion of hybridity in Book II of *De rerum natura*. Lucretius's hypothesis is that there cannot be an infinite variety of combinations of atoms: 'If that were so, you would see monsters coming into being everywhere. Hybrid growths of man and beast would arise. Lofty branches would sprout here and there from a living body.'[45] The *poetic* possibilities of such speculation are not lost on Cavendish, whose texts are inhabited by just such monstrosities. Conventional personification of the inanimate or abstract is taken to a fantastic extreme in *Poems, and Fancies* as, for example, an oak tree is characterised as possessing a range of emotions such that it does seem to sprout 'from a living body'. In '*A Dialogue between an* Oake, *and a* Man *cutting him downe*', the tree's agonies stem precisely from its hybridity. It is significant that it is specifically an oak, since the tree had strongly royalist associations which had entered the popular consciousness following Charles II's refuge in an oak tree at Boscobel after the Battle of Worcester.[46] The very choice of tree to some extent guides royalist readerly sympathies.

Existing apart from the human world, yet possessing highly developed sensitive faculties, the tree pleads for leniency. Although it is the hybrid which Lucretius denied as a possibility, the oak, paradoxically, is intensely Lucretian in its being and logic. Just as atoms do not die but are reassembled into new entities, so felling does not imply death for the tree. The woodcutter promises a variety of new existences, as a ship, or as part of a house, for example, all of which the oak rejects. Further, the oak is pervaded by Epicurean sagacity: '*He* nothing loves', the tree declares, 'but what he cannot get', recalling Lucretius's warnings against fretting life away in permanent dissatisfaction: 'to be for ever feeding a malcontent mind ... surely exemplifies the story of those maidens in the flower of life for ever pouring water into a leaking vessel which can never by any sleight be filled'.[47] Cavendish's poem, initially appearing simply to be one in a series of nature dialogues, may also be read as a debate on monarchical succession. A political point may be made because of the judicious use of genre. The oak, argues the woodcutter (significantly the character with whom the reader has not been led to identify), must succumb to his axe in order to allow the acorns their turn, and because 'all *Subjects* they in *Change* delight, / When *Kings* grow *Old*, their *Government* they slight'.[48]

The possibilities for the existence of other civilizations which Lucretius allows in *De rerum natura* – 'You are bound ... to acknowledge that in other regions there are other earths and various tribes of men and breeds of beasts' – provides Cavendish with an opportunity for escape from the necessitous confines of exile.[49] This is manifest in poems such as '*Of many* Worlds *in this* World'.[50] If poetry, as characterised by Lucretius, functions as a placatory medium, Cavendish's highly speculative, and, in terms of its bleak eschatology, unorthodox philosophy makes full use of its permissible expression in verse. At times, however, the utility of the genre outweighs its appropriateness, and the poet's authoritative expression collapses under the demands of metre. This happens in '*What* Atomes *make* Vegetables, Minerals, *and* Animals' thus: 'in all *Stones*, and *Minerals* (no doubt,) / *Sharpe* points do lye, which *Fire* makes strike out'.[51] The interpolative nature of the expression 'no doubt', actually raises more uncertainty than it dispels, and the occasionally stilted mode of expression throughout the volume is something Cavendish is aware of and seeks to justify: 'I found it difficult, to get so many *Rhythmes*, as to joyn the *sense* of the *Subject*', she writes at the end of the volume, continuing, 'I rather chose to leave the *Elegance* of *words*, then to obstruct the *sense* of the *matter*'.[52] Her understanding of poetry is once again characterised as being a proper vehicle for her imaginative creativity, consisting 'not so much in *Number, Words*, and *Phrase*, as in *Fancy*', unlike '*elegant Prose*'.[53] Further, she too has recourse to the imagery of the hive in a discussion of poetic originality. Some, 'just as the *Bees*', she writes:

> by their *Stings Industry* do they get,
> That *Honey* which the *Stinglesse Droanes* do eat.
> So *Men* without *Ambitious Stings* do live,
> Upon th' *Industrious Stock* their *Fathers* give.
> Or like to such that steals a *Poets Wit*,
> And dresse it up in his owne *Language* fit.[54]

The honey represented here is not only the mellifluous genre of verse but has substantive resonances, too. It functions not merely as a superficial and deceptive device, but has an intrinsic, qualitative value all its own.

De rerum natura provides for Cavendish not only justification for her self-presentation as writer, but also a paradigm for the representation of Nature and Creation as feminocentric phenomena. The poetic mediation of a distinctly maternal universe which Lucretius achieves in *De rerum natura* also suggested creative and imaginative possibilities to Cavendish. Having carefully established her work as fictional, almost irrational, in her prefatory material, a status supported by her reasons for its being in verse, Cavendish, like Lucretius, has constructed generic permission not only for her pioneering foray into print but also for the audaciously feminised and mechanistic universe of her poems. Such a universe is instituted by the two poems which open the entire atomist sequence, and which figure Nature as feminine: '*Nature calls* a *Councell, which was* Motion, Figure, Matter, *and* Life, *to advise about making the World*', and 'Deaths *endeavour to hinder, and obstruct* Nature'.[55] Once more, the model for this poetic rewriting of the creation myth along potentially highly impious lines may be seen to be Lucretius's eulogistic construction of Venus as source of all life, at the opening of *De rerum natura*.[56] The sensuality of several of the later poems in the volume also echoes the eroticised natural world of *De rerum natura*. In Cavendish's series of culinary allegories, the poem '*A Tart*', for example, is explicit in its delight in '*Cherry Lips* that's red, / And *Sloe-black Eyes* from a *faire Virgins Head*. / And *Strawbery Teats* from high *Banks* of white *Breast*'.[57] Lucretius, then, offers a paradigm which Cavendish, perhaps on account of the second-hand mode of her reception of his text, manipulates for her own polemical ends. Whereas the female in *De rerum natura* does not extend to include the reader, and is figured primarily in generative terms, Cavendish does allow for, even welcome, the female reader, thus figuring the female in an intellectual as well as eroticised fashion.[58] Her ingenious manipulations of the Lucretian mode have enabled her not only to express her own intellect but also to condone the existence of the cerebral in other female figures, through her initial construction of verse as a non-rational, fictional genre.

Cavendish's careful justification for her activities as a writer is apparent throughout the volume, markedly in the prefatory material to the third part, 'To Poets'.[59] Her apologia for her self-characterisation as a poet stems directly from her prior establishment of herself as an authority in atomism. Atomic structure, she argues, might explain the scarcity of women writers, were men's and women's brains differently constituted: 'Mens Braines *with more of the* Sharp Atomes … *and* Womens *with more of the* round'.[60] However, the scarcity is '*rather a* Dishonour, *not a* Fault *in* Nature'.[61] Scientific language allows Cavendish to show that social condemnations of writing women lack physiological justification. If women's writings are dishonourable, she argues, it is as a result of cultural inculcation, not atomic composition, and what are perceived as Nature's 'Inferiour Workes', women, may indeed '*move towards* Perfection'.[62] As in Lucretius's work, so here, atomism is central to an enabling, radically didactic, discourse.[63]

Reading *Poems, and Fancies* in terms of Lucretian genre need not be confined to the atomist writings, but facilitates analysis of other parts of the work, too. In the prefatory material to the second part, 'To Morall Philosophers', Cavendish establishes a series of comparisons between the apparently incompatible discourses of moral philosophy and arithmetic.[64] In so doing, she is arguably producing a microcosmal analysis of her own text, where equally incongruent discourses are juxtaposed in order, paradoxically perhaps, to increase the reader's understanding. Moralists, she argues, can control their emotions as though they were the most exact arithmeticians, in order to increase their happiness, being 'like powerfull *Monarchs*, which can make their *Passions* obedient at their pleasure'.[65] In characterising human beings as desiring contentment and true knowledge, Cavendish is writing in an Epicurean vein, but she takes this one step further and transgresses Lucretius's advocation of the quiet, unexceptional, private life, in addition to denying his mortal soul.[66] '*Fame*', she writes, 'is like a *Soule*, an *Incorporeall Thing*'.[67] In the dialogues which follow this statement Cavendish espouses both Lucretian and non-Lucretian possibilities, representing both sides of a debate, a rhetorical posture which adumbrates her *Orations of Divers Sorts* of 1662.

In '*Of* Fame. A Dialogue *between* two *Supernaturall Opinions*' Cavendish constructs two interlocutors, each of whom believes in the immortality of the soul, their differences arising in their discussion of the properties of this soul: 'may not *Soules*', asks one in a moment of anti-Epicurean superstition, 'as well as *Angels*, know, / And *heare* and *see*, what's done i'th' *World* below?'[68] In the apparently more straightforwardly Epicurean '*Of* Fame. A Dialogue *between* two Naturall Opinions', the conviction is initially that 'when men do dye, all Motion's gone', but this forthright position is retracted, perhaps as the poet considers the bleakness of that vision: 'The *Motion* of the *Mind* may live on high; / And in the *Aiery Elements* may lye'.[69] These 'Naturall Opinions' in fact revert to a supernatural explication. Elsewhere in the volume Cavendish's opinion of the relationship between body and soul is radically idiosyncratic. In 'Soule, *and* Body', for example, Death removes the flesh of the deceased, and cleans and stores it before reuniting it with the soul.[70] Cavendish, despite her eclectic engagement with Lucretian topics, is by no means an unreserved Epicurean convert. Rather, she has recognised in *De rerum natura* an appealing generic model wherein poetic structure and philosophical and scientific vocabulary converge.

This is really an intellectual purloining of Lucretian conceits which continues throughout the dialogues, taking the form more of an eclectic echo than of an uncomplicated imitation. As was the case with Cavendish's monstrous oak, the echo is occasionally the antithesis of an idea in *De rerum natura*, but, in his rejection of such ideas, Lucretius nevertheless conjures up their possibility for Cavendish. In creative or imaginative terms they operate as forcibly as if they had received Lucretius's acceptance. '*There may be more* Earths *then one*, *for all we know'*, writes Cavendish, appearing to accord with Lucretius's 'it is in the highest degree unlikely that this earth and sky is the only one to have been created'.[71] However, Cavendish's very assertion appears in '*A* Dialogue *betwixt* Earth, *and* Darknesse', a form of personification which in itself contradicts Lucretius's declaration that 'the earth is and always has been an insentient being'.[72] In this same dialogue, ghosts are adduced as actual phenomena, a possibility which negates Lucretian anti-superstition, as do the fairy-kingdom poems of the fourth section of the volume.[73] In the speculative world of the 1650s, however, their existence was no less verifiable, and hence no more fantastic, than that of the minuscule atom upon which the entirety of *De rerum natura* is founded.

The less explicitly scientific dialogic poems of the second part of *Poems, and Fancies*, then, are as informed by Cavendish's idiosyncratic adaptation of *De rerum natura* as are the atomist verses with which the volume opens. In her personification of Mirth in '*A* Dialogue *between* Melancholy, *and* Mirth', the poet implicitly critiques the popular, libertine conception of Epicureanism, favouring the pragmatically Lucretian presentation of the Epicurean doctrine as articulated by Melancholy.[74] Mirth's proposition of a lighthearted, bacchanalian existence, 'I shall make you happy all your *Life*', is undercut by the solemn self-characterisation of a distinctly Lucretian Melancholy:

> I search the *depth*, and *bottome of Man-kind*,
> Open the *Eye* of *Ignorance* that's blind.
> I travell far, and view the *World* about,
> I walk with *Reasons Staff* to find *Truth* out.[75]

This didacticism continues in the 'Moral Discourses' which constitute the third part of Cavendish's volume. The dialogic format of the second section is abandoned, but the same themes recur. Again, the universe of these poems results from a highly eccentric interpretation of *De rerum natura*. It is a universe, like that of Lucretius, where tranquillity is sought, but it is also one where direct, providential intervention is allowed as a possibility. This quest for tranquillity and stasis could be seen to evolve directly from Cavendish's traumatic exilic experiences, and its intensely autobiographical basis is indicated by recurrent images of sea travel. The perturbed life, writes Cavendish, '[is] as a *Barque*, made of a *rotten* Tree. / Where every

Wave indangers it to split'.[76] Her adoption of Lucretian genre is palliatory. The honeyed first taste is what facilitates the administration of the bitter autobiographical discourse, which is of necessity politicised. The polemic, Cavendish's 'oblique communication', is made palatable by the overall impression created by a volume of verse, the mellifluous genre.[77] As the overt appearance of a volume of poems and 'fancies' is a non-threatening one, within its pages political critique of the most explicit kind may flourish. The 'Discourse *of a* Knave' is ostensibly one more in a series of didactic sketches, but the severe language suggests that Cavendish may have had a specific figure, presumably Cromwell, in mind as she wrote:

> A *Prosperous Knave*, that *Mischiefes* still doth plot,
> Swels big with *Pride*, since he hath power got.
> Whose *Conscience*, like a *Purse*, drawne open wide,
> *False hands* do cast in *Bribes* on every side.
> And as the *Guts* are stuft with *Excrement*,
> So is his *Head* with *Thoughts* of ill intent.[78]

Less explicitly political is the promised land which Cavendish constructs in one of several sections entitled 'The Claspe'.[79] By framing *'Of an* Island' in Classical terms, she is harking back to a golden age of fertility and plenty. In an expressly Lucretian tone she writes of flowers, that 'Their *Mother* the *Island*, they her *Children* sweet, / Born from her *Loines*', recalling the fecund earth of *De rerum natura*.[80] The prosperity of the island, however, leads to vanity and idolatry which only the Fates can halt. The Fates are subordinate to 'the *Gods*', who are curiously Lucretian in their otiose lack of true omniscience and involvement: 'why do Gods complaine against them so, / Since *Men* arc made by *them* such waies to go?'[81] As with the horrific scenes at the conclusion of *De rerum natura*, so too in Cavendish's poem plague is constructed as the only solution since it ultimately promises regeneration for the just. It is, however, at this point that the poet reverts to a more conventional tenet, which none the less has at its core a desire for Epicurean *ataraxia*: '*those* that keep the *Lawes* of *God* on high, / Shall live in *Peace*, in *Graves* shall quiet lie'.[82]

The autobiographical content of *Poems, and Fancies* is always politicised. Cavendish's adoption of Lucretian generic techniques allows her to make such political statements. The obliquity of genre means that she receives, from some quarters, censure, but not censorship of her work. Arguably, a poem such as 'The *Temple of Fame*' could be read as having allegorised anti-censorship sentiment.[83] The Puritan regime had banned the ringing of church bells. In portraying the voices of the eminent inhabitants of the Temple as being like church bells, Cavendish may obliquely be arguing against authoritarian silencing. In the 'Claspe', '*Phantasmes* Masque', autobiographical elements once again come to the fore in '*Similizing a young* Lady *to a* Ship'.[84] Here the ship sails through 'nineteen *Degrees*', and is wrecked by '*Rebellious Clouds*' and '*Showers* of *Blood*'.[85] In a direct response to Cavendish's experiences of financial insecurity in 1651, the same ship is threatened in the next poem by '*Thundring Creditors*'.[86]

The masque is generically intended for private performance, for the illustration of abstract qualities through concrete representation. Significantly, in Cavendish's text, the masque is staged in the poet's brain, as she manipulates genre to suit her own autobiographical needs, the text becoming abstracted, remaining an imaginary construct. This generic manipulation derives from the isolating experiences of dispossession and exile, in addition to being necessitated by the practical demands resulting from the closure of the theatres. The masque is a suitably detached genre in which to offer a partisan critique of the Cromwellian regime, and her experiences of exile. Further, so that her decision to use a dramatic genre may not be criticised, it is abstracted still further, and its interiority emphasised so that 'The Scene *is* Poetry. *The Stage is the* Braine *whereon it is Acted*'.[87] Her highly stylised masque, then, functions as Lucretian honey, sweetening the bitter message of her polemic.

The subject matter of *De rerum natura* veers from the microcosm to the macrocosm in a vertiginous series of images and illustrations. Atomist doctrine facilitates this because of the commonality of the constituent atom to all phenomena, be they inside the human body, or out in the wider universe. In *Poems, and Fancies*, too, in poems such as '*Similizing the* Head *of* Man *to the* World', there are examples of a similar movement from individual consciousness to universal cosmos: 'The *Braine* [is] *as Earth*', writes Cavendish, 'from whence all *Plants* do spring'.[88] This imaginative process also allows for subtle polemic, as in '*Similizing the Body to many Countries*', where '*Britanny*' is ironically characterised as 'The *Liver*', seat of melancholy or choler.[89] It is the poetic medium which expedites such transitions, and which figuratively aids understanding of invisible or abstract principles and concepts, being precisely the generic stratagem which Lucretius exploits in his own text. Such profoundly ruminative verses as '*The* Fairies *in the* Braine, *may be the* causes *of many* thoughts', thus may be understood as Lucretian not in their content but in their form, that is, they focus on supernatural entities which they render concrete, even possible, through the poetic medium.[90]

The poetic representation of abstract qualities continues into the final section of Cavendish's text in allegorical poems such as '*A Battel* between *Courage, and Prudence*'.[91] Cavendish's gory descriptions of war where 'heads are cleft in two parts, *braines* lye masht, / And all their *faces* into slices hasht', recall Lucretius's descriptions of 'the heat and indiscriminate carnage of battle'.[92] Further, the '*Fort, Or Castle of Hope*', constructed to keep Doubt's factions at bay, perhaps, in its moral and intellectual superiority, suggests Lucretius's 'quiet citadel', inhabited by the contented followers of Epicurean teaching.[93] At its most fundamental level, poetry has allowed Cavendish to write of phenomena outside her direct experience, appropriating masculine discourses and activities.[94] '*These* Armies', she writes, '*I mention, were rais'd in my* braine, *fought in my* fancy, *and registred in my* closet'.[95]

The last poem in Cavendish's volume is 'Of the *death* and *buriall* of *Truth*', and in its bleak mapping of the decline of civilization from a golden age, through a silver and a bronze age, up to 'the last *hard Iron Age*', it may be read as a bitterly ironic, figurative, reversal of Lucretius's literal account of the development of human society in the fifth book of *De rerum natura*.[96] In Lucretius's work, 'the circling years bring round reversals of fortune', so that gold becomes more prized, although not as useful as, copper, and iron is more valuable on the battlefield.[97] As was true in Cavendish's experience, even when a society has attained its most civilised state, ambition and greed may lead to civil strife. With startling clarity, and in terms which would have had particular relevance for the exiled royalists, Lucretius describes how:

> the kings were killed. Down in the dust lay the ancient majesty of thrones, the haughty sceptres. The illustrious emblem of the sovereign head, dabbled in gore and trampled under the feet of the rabble, mourned its high estate ... So the conduct of affairs sank back into the turbid depths of mob-rule.[98]

Cavendish, too, portrays an anarchic society wherein '*Controversies* within the *Church* shall rise, / And *Heresies* shall beare away the *prize'*, concluding her poem with the acrimonious assertion that 'now this *Iron Age*'s so *rusty* grown, / That all the *Hearts* are turn'd to hard *flint-stone*'.[99] The pessimistic representation of civilization debased and deluded continues into the final book of Lucretius's text, where he describes the devastation of plague. The dispiriting conclusion of *De rerum natura* marks its most effective didactic moment, suggesting that human beings must recognise as misguided their reverence for the gods, turning instead to Epicurus's teaching. Lucretius's text thus concludes with a promise of a cyclic narrative renewal, the Venus of the first book once more predominating. Correspondingly, following the sombre vision of 'Of the *death* and *buriall* of *Truth*', Cavendish's volume ends in the regenerative, microcosmal *Animall Parliament*, with its audaciously affirmatory conclusion: 'God save the King, God save the King'.[100]

Lucretius's text then, didactic to the last, becomes in its reformative narrative structure what it preaches.[101] Cavendish's ultimately optimistic text similarly promises regeneration at its conclusion. For Cavendish, however, Lucretius's text, its poetic structure and the powerful suggestiveness of its atomist doctrine, provided not only a form and subject matter fundamental to her first published work but also the generic justification for that very act of publication. By the end of the volume she has established herself as a writer, and need make no further apology for her desire to venture away from honeyed verse into the less sweet discourses of philosophical prose. 'Reader', she concludes, 'I have a little *Tract* of *Philosophicall Fancies* in *Prose*, which will not be long before it appear in the *world*'.[102] In this seemingly trivial advertisement, Cavendish in fact asserts a new, confident self-identity, constructing herself as a legitimate writer with a constant readership, and recording the next step in her artistic movement into prose, a genre which she has already typified throughout *Poems, and Fancies* as being superior.[103] It is to a prose work that this book now turns.

Notes

1 Cavendish, *Philosophical and Physical Opinions*, sig. a2r.
2 The title for this chapter, 'Sweet Honey of the Muses', is taken from Lucretius, *De rerum natura*, ed. Ronald Latham (Harmondsworth: Penguin, 1968),

p. 54. All further quotations from *De rerum natura* are from this edition. The same quotation appears later too, p. 130. This repetition may in itself be understood to be a deliberate generic ploy, thus establishing the potential of genre and form for purposive uses. See Monica Gale, 'Lucretius 4.1–25 and the Proems of the *De Rerum Natura*', *Proceedings of the Cambridge Philological Society*, 40 (1994), 1–17. See also Alessandro Schiesaro, 'The Palingenesis of *De Rerum Natura*', *Proceedings of the Cambridge Philological Society*, 40 (1994) 81–107. Schiesaro argues that 'Repetition is the essence of learning, and befits a didactic poem' (p. 98). For Mayne's statement see Grant, *Margaret the First*, pp. 218–19.

3 Wilson L. Scott, *The Conflict Between Atomism and Conservation Theory 1644–1860* (London: Macdonald, 1970), p. 11.

4 Lucretius, pp. 39, 60.

5 *Ibid.*, p. 28.

6 Several studies attempt an identification of the exact nature of, and sources for, Cavendish's atomism. See, for example, Robert Kargon, *Atomism in England from Hariot to Newton* (Oxford: Clarendon Press, 1966), and Clucas, 'Cavendish Circle'.

7 For an analysis of Cavendish's use of 'the skeptical methodology of the new science not only to attack traditional natural philosophy, but also as a weapon in her battle for the recognition of female intellectual equality', see Sarasohn, p. 289. What I have referred to as radical speculation or intense heurism Sarasohn would characterise as scepticism.

8 Stephen M. Wheeler gives an account of Ovid's discovery of his own genre as a *via media* between Lucretius and Virgil. This has resonances for Cavendish's highly idiosyncratic generic adaptation. See Stephen M. Wheeler, 'Ovid's Use of Lucretius in *Metamorphoses* 1.67–8', *Classical Quarterly*, 45 (1995), 200–3.

9 The complex relationship in terms of generic influence and imitation which Cavendish has with Lucretius echoes that explored by Charlotte Goddard in her examination of the writing of the fifteenth-century Italian Giovanni Pontano. Identifying the apparent contradictions which may inhere in such a relationship (as I here attempt with Cavendish's writing), Goddard writes that 'Pontano imitates Lucretius in order to reject him, and his rejection emphasises his own religious orthodoxy'. See Charlotte Goddard, 'Pontano's Use of the Didactic Genre: Rhetoric, Irony and the Manipulation of Lucretius in *Urania*', *Renaissance Studies*, 5 (1991), 250–62 (p. 257).

10 It is just such fluidity which, according to Bazeley, has given rise to 'a strong prejudice within mainstream historiography against Cavendish's philosophical predilections'. Bazeley, p. 12.

11 Kargon and Scott suggest that the Cavendish circle's attitudes to atomism were influenced predominantly by Pierre Gassendi, the French philosopher. More recent studies, among them that of Stephen Clucas, have cast doubt on Kargon's hypothesis. Clucas argues that 'While it is apparent ... that Gassendi was a philosopher whose views were recognised by the circle, and indeed discoursed with members of the circle when they were in Paris,

it is not so easy to find evidence of the importance or priority of his ideas amongst the group'. Clucas, 'Cavendish Circle', p. 252. Focusing on 'fire atomism', Clucas goes on to demonstrate Gassendi's debt to Lucretius, and Cavendish's divergence from Gassendi. He also discusses the development of Cavendish's atomism after *Poems, and Fancies* as 'a refinement of the crudities of an updated Democritean-Lucretian atomism'. *Ibid.*, p. 261. Richard Kroll characterises Gassendi as the age's single most important catalyst in the neo-Epicurean revival and Boyle and Evelyn as its propagandists, responsible for its cross-Channel communication. See Richard W. F. Kroll, *The Material Word: Literate Culture in the Restoration and Early Eighteenth Century* (Baltimore: Johns Hopkins University Press, 1991), p. 15. Donald Williams Bruce's article, 'The Thwarted Epicurean: Abraham Cowley', serves as more evidence that it would have been very difficult for a member of the Oxford court, and later, of the émigré community, to avoid the influence of Epicurean thought through mediators such as Walter Charleton. See Donald Williams Bruce, 'The Thwarted Epicurean: Abraham Cowley', *Contemporary Review*, 254 (1989), 139–45. Whilst it cannot be unequivocally ascertained that Cavendish had access to Lucretius's text first-hand, what is certain is that Lucretius's text nevertheless would have been conveyed to her sufficiently to offer a substantial stimulus to her creative output.

12 See Wolfgang Bernard Fleischmann, *Lucretius and English Literature 1680–1740* (Paris: A. G. Nizet, 1964), pp. 19–20.

13 See *Ibid.*, pp. 20–1. See also Douglas Bush, *English Literature in the Earlier Seventeenth Century, 1600–1660* (Oxford: Clarendon Press, 1962), p. 294. Cavendish's probable familiarity with Sylvester's Du Bartas is recorded in Grant, *Margaret the First*, p. 113. In *Philosophical and Physical Opinions* Cavendish warns of the damage translation may do to a text, contrasting this with the fact that 'Ovid *and* Dubartus *were so happy as to meet a* Sylvester *and a* Sands'. Cavendish, *Philosophical and Physical Opinions*, sig. a2.

14 See Fleischmann, pp. 86–90, 21. See also Kroll, pp. 147–51. Fleischmann also mentions an undated manuscript translation of part of the first book of *De rerum natura*, attributed to Sir Edward Sherburne (1618–1702), who was in the court at Oxford in the early 1640s. Fleischmann, however, supposes the translation to have been executed after the Restoration (p. 50). Reid Barbour traces the influence of Epicureanism on the Stuart court in the first four decades of the seventeenth century in 'The Early Stuart Epicure', *English Literary Renaissance*, 23 (1993), 170–200. See also Reid Barbour, *English Epicures and Stoics* (Amherst: University of Massachusetts Press, 1998).

15 See Robert Kargon, 'Introduction' in Walter Charleton, *Physiologia Epicuro-Gassendo-Charltoniana: Or a Fabrick of Science Natural, Upon the Hypothesis of Atoms* (New York: Johnson Reprint Corporation, 1966), p. xx.

16 Fleischmann, p. 34.

17 Cavendish, *Philosophical and Physical Opinions*, sig. Br. It is outside the scope of my present study to examine in depth the nature of the relationship of

Cavendish with her husband and *éminence grise*, William. However, it is an area which gives rise to many interesting questions of influence and originality which have yet to be fully investigated.

18 Cavendish was not alone among women writers in finding Lucretius 'alluring'. On Lucy Hutchinson's changeable relationship with *De rerum natura*, see the Appendix, below.

19 On how a writer's choice of ancient paradigm indicated the nature of their own political discontent see Kroll, p. 9. Kroll explains how the Epicurean model of the world may be made to account for both stability and change. Kroll, p. 10.

20 It would be wrong, however, to suggest that only republicans rejected atomism in the 1650s. Royalists and republicans alike adopted both pro- and anti-atomistic stances and arguments expediently. See Stephen Clucas, 'Poetic Atomism in Seventeenth-century England: Henry More, Thomas Traherne and "Scientific Imagination"', *Renaissance Studies*, 5 (1991), 327–40. Clucas describes how both Dryden and Milton exploited the image of atomization (pp. 330–1). In the case of Cavendish in the 1650s, however, attitudes to Lucretian atomism are indeed dependant on politico-religious sympathies. For an analysis of Cavendish's atomist poems and the different, if not inconsistent, stances she adopts in them see Stevenson, pp. 533–5. Stevenson maps how Cavendish's attitude to atomism changed as her writing career progressed.

21 Lucretius, p. 29.

22 For an investigation of the tensions between empirical and theoretical methodologies, and the processes by which certain discourses may attain the status of scientific 'fact' see De Santis, who asks: 'Is objectivity a matter of method, rhetoric, or sleight-of hand?'. De Santis, p. 12.

23 Lucretius, p. 27. His opening words are patriotically Roman. See James H. Nichols, Jr, *Epicurean Political Philosophy: The* De rerum natura *of Lucretius* (Ithaca: Cornell University Press, 1976), p. 51, and J. L. Penwill, 'Image, Ideology and Action in Cicero and Lucretius', *Ramus: Critical Studies in Greek and Roman Literature*, 23 (1994), 68–91. Of the poem's opening Penwill writes: 'Venus and Mars are important in the Roman pantheon because these are the two deities who in terms of current belief were literally the ancestors of the Roman people ... to evoke these two is to advertise a poem with a distinctly nationalistic flavour'. Penwill, p. 76. Elsewhere in *Poems, and Fancies*, Cavendish enjoys a good-natured nod to the eulogistic opening of *De rerum natura*. '*Venus* is a *Tinkers Wife*, we see', she declares in '*The Fairy Queen*', continuing: 'Not a *goddesse*, as she was thought to be; / When all the world to her did offerings bring, / And her high praise in prose, and verses did sing'. Cavendish, *Poems, and Fancies*, p. 150. The paradoxical implication is that, having taken on Lucretius's anti-superstition, she may dismiss his very reverence for Venus as superstitious in itself.

24 For the debate as to whether *De rerum natura* should be read as a predominantly didactic or rather as an epic poem, in the light of the Ancients' classifications of poetry see Monica Gale, *Myth and Poetry in Lucretius*

(Cambridge: Cambridge University Press, 1994), pp. 99–101, 127. Gale argues that 'Lucretius clearly would have been regarded as an epic poet, simply because the term epos included didactic hexameter poetry ... however, it seems quite legitimate to speak of his use of epic themes and stylistic features without the danger of tautology'. Gale, *Myth*, p. 104.

25 For the claim that 'Bacon abandoned atomism and the void, but it cannot be said that he ever got Epicurus off his mind' see Barbour, 'Early Stuart', p. 177. Bazeley argues that the anti-Baconian character of Cavendish's empiricism may have resulted from necessity, since she did not have access to an experimental laboratory. Bazeley, p. 196. Hayden White usefully encapsulates the hypothesising of Baconian empiricism, arguing that 'when it is a matter of seeking knowledge of the believed world, an erroneous hypothesis is better than none at all. It at least provides the basis for any intended action, a praxis in which the adequacy of the proposition to the world of which it speaks can be tested'. White, p. 20.

26 See Gale, 'Lucretius', for the effectiveness of poetry in making the unseen understood: 'The clarity of poetry consists in its ability to concretize abstract ideas, to provide a *simulacrum et imago* of the invisible by the use of imaging and figurative language, enabling the reader to "see" the nature of the universe in his mind's eye'. Gale, 'Lucretius', p. 17, n. 59.

27 Lucretius, p. 54.

28 See for example, Nichols, p. 7.

29 See *Ibid.*, p. 26.

30 Gale, *Myth*, p. 141.

31 Cavendish, *Poems, and Fancies*, p. 143.

32 The notion that Cavendish's choice of Lucretian genre and tenor for her first publication was pragmatic is emphasised by her publishing *Philosophical and Physical Opinions* just two years later. In this (prose) work not only does she have 'A Condemning Treatise of Atoms', but also declares that she '*would have turned [... her] Atomes out of verse into prose*' had it not involved turning her thoughts from their '*natural course*', that is, interrupting the flow of new ideas. Cavendish, *Philosophical and Physical Opinions*, sig. a2. In *Natures Pictures*, she elaborates on this position, not only declaring that '*Verse [is] not so proper for Philosophy*' but also offering short prose versions of some parts of the opening book of *Poems, and Fancies*. Cavendish, *Natures Pictures*, p. 157. More confident by 1656 in her place and right as a writer, she need no longer honey these ideas with verse.

33 In discussing the noble associations of the atom in the early decades of the seventeenth century, Barbour quotes the poet Thomas Carew's reference to the deceased Count of Anglesey as a 'heape of atoms'. Barbour, 'Early Stuart', p. 172.

34 All quotations in this paragraph are from Cavendish, *Poems, and Fancies*, unnumbered prefatory material. The emphatic '*can*' is my addition.

35 Kroll examines the repercussions of this for the scientific observer who has to function as a textual reader, renouncing postulates in favour of intuitions (p. 13).

36 Lucretius, p. 61.

37 Ibid., p. 63.

38 Ibid. For an analysis of the necessity of poeticising atoms 'whose activities and constructure had to be imagined rather than perceived' see Clucas, 'Poetic', p. 327. De Santis discusses the problem of 'transdiction', that is, the extension of scientific reasoning to non-observable phenomena. De Santis, p. 112. She focuses on Cavendish's opinion of the science of optics as a way out of the transdictive problem, as expressed in her *Observations Upon Experimental Philosophy* (London, 1666) and *Blazing World* (in *Observations*, London, 1666), and places Cavendish in relation to her contemporaries as 'defend[ing] a more complex relationship between our experience, rational imagination, and artistic fancies'. De Santis, pp. 123–7, 144.

39 Schiesaro, p. 87. He argues that there can thus be no independent analogue for atoms, and that the very words used in a search for one constitute 'not only an image of the atomic reality, but a part thereof'. *Ibid.*, p. 87. See Roy Dreistadt, 'An Analysis of the Use of Analogies and Metaphors in Science', *The Journal of Psychology*, 68 (1968), 97–116, for an account of how analogies may actually be the genesis of the circumstances which they subsequently describe.

40 According to Bazeley: 'There is a strong prejudice within mainstream historiography against Cavendish's philosophical predilections, her confessional tone, her unstructured method of discourse, and against her continual melding of the discourses of fact and fiction'. Bazeley, p. 12.

41 Cavendish, *Poems, and Fancies*, p. 212.

42 Cavendish's pioneer status is characterised in the prefatory material as operating on two levels, one being in terms of her being a woman, the second in terms of her originality. This latter, certainly the less veracious of the two, functions as a conventional trope signifying natural wit and denial of influence. Cavendish is '*the first* English Poet *of* [her ...] Sex', and '*the first that ever wrote this way*'. Cavendish, *Poems, and Fancies*, n.p. Cavendish herself expands on this trope in the subsequent '*To Naturall* Philosophers', where she claims that '*Ignorance* of the *Mother Tongues* makes me ignorant of the *Opinions*, and *Discourses* in former times'. Cavendish, *Poems and Fancies*, n.p. Lucretius is characterised as 'an originator in poetry while a follower in philosophy' by Albert Cook, in 'The Angling of Poetry to Philosophy: The Nature of Lucretius', *Arethusa*, 27 (1994), 193–222 (p. 204). Cook's focus is on Lucretius's ability to reconcile the use of poetry with Epicurus's condemnation of it.

43 Cavendish, *Poems, and Fancies*, sigs A4r, A4v.

44 Cavendish's longing for approbation is marked in her epistle to Charles Cavendish, whom she figures as capable of conferring acceptability '*by the* favour *of* [... his] Protection'. Cavendish, *Poems, and Fancies*, sig. A2r. For more on this epistle see Chapter 4, below.

45 Lucretius, p. 80.

46 On the Boscobel incident see Richard Ollard, *The Escape of Charles II After the Battle of Worcester* (London: Hodder and Stoughton, 1966), p. 38.

47 Cavendish, *Poems, and Fancies*, p. 70; Lucretius, pp. 126–7. In Cavendish's poem, the woodcutter attributes the oak's sagacious contentment to its satisfaction with its existence, unlike man's *'Wit'*, which 'runs about / In every *Corner*, to seeke *Nature* out'. Cavendish, *Poems, and Fancies*, p. 70.

48 *Ibid.*, p. 67.

49 Lucretius, p. 92. Although *Poems, and Fancies* was largely composed whilst Cavendish was in England in the first years of the 1650s, effectively, legally, she was still in exile.

50 Cavendish, *Poems, and Fancies*, pp. 44–5. Placed as it is alongside *'It is hard to beleive, that there are other* Worlds *in this* World', and '*A World in an* Eare-Ring', this poem may be understood as one in a series in which Cavendish experiments with rhetorical self-positioning and philosophical speculation. *Ibid.*, pp. 43–4, 45–6.

51 *Ibid.*, p. 12.

52 *Ibid.*, p. 212.

53 *Ibid.*

54 *Ibid.*, p. 149.

55 *Ibid.*, pp. 1–4, 5.

56 For an examination of Lucretius's construction of the feminine see S. Georgia Nugent, '*Mater* Matters: The Female in Lucretius's *De Rerum Natura*', *Colby Quarterly*, 30 (1994), 179–205. Deborah Bazeley also writes on Cavendish's pre-eminent Nature, writing that 'despite the requisite paeans to God the Father in her works, the supreme deity did not free Cavendish's imagination in quite the same way that nature did'. Bazeley, p. 164. For an interpretation of the concept of 'piety' in Classical terms see Gale, *Myth*. She describes piety as 'a correct relationship with the gods', who, in their tranquil existence, their state of *ataraxia*, provide mortals with a perfect example of how to live pleasurably. A lesser detachment from human affairs would be 'incompatible with *ataraxia*'. Gale, *Myth*, p. 45.

57 Cavendish, *Poems, and Fancies*, pp. 131–2.

58 For Cavendish's recognition of female audience and intellect see 'To all Noble, and Worthy Ladies', and '*To all Writing Ladies*' in *ibid.*, sig. A3.

59 *Ibid.*, p. 121–3. The section of the work for which this constitutes the prefatory material is clearly delineated, by a large intertitle, as consisting of 'Fancies', a generic distinction which is introduced in 'To Poets', as Cavendish asks that her readers should '*read this part of my* Book *very slow ... because in most of these* Poems, *every word is a* Fancy'. *Ibid.*, pp. 126, 123.

60 *Ibid.*, p. 122.

61 *Ibid.*

62 *Ibid.*

63 Lucretius, however, is distinctly misogynist throughout *De rerum natura*. Women are not figured as his readers, but, further, in the fourth book, they are represented in grotesque terms. The (male) lover does not see his beloved rationally: 'She has an impediment in her speech – a charming lisp, of course ... A waspish, fiery-tempered scold – she "burns with a gem-like flame" ... Her breasts are swollen and protuberant: she is "Ceres suckling

Bacchus" ... She is driven to use foul-smelling fumigants'. Lucretius, pp. 166–7. For an incisive interpretation of this passage from *De rerum natura* see Nugent, pp. 187–94. Nugent places particular importance on the 'fumigants' passage, concluding that 'what is true of the female body seems to be true of the earth's body on a much grander scale ... At the lowest common denominator, the female is simply a stench in the nostrils of the male'. Nugent, pp. 195–6. For Lucy Hutchinson's uncharacteristic delight in this passage see the Appendix below.

64 Cavendish, *Poems, and Fancies*, pp. 51–2.

65 *Ibid.*, p. 51.

66 *De rerum natura* constitutes in part Lucretius's attempt to persuade his addressee, Memmius, not to succumb to the lures of *res publicae*. The Lucretian universe does not reward public ambition: 'Burning fevers flee no swifter from your body if you toss under figured counterpanes and coverlets of crimson than if you must lie in rude home-spun ... The fears and anxieties that dog the human breast do not shrink from the clash of arms or the fierce rain of missiles. They stalk unabashed among princes and potentates'. Lucretius, p. 61. This stance does not, however, prevent Lucretius from declaring his own desire for fame: 'high hope of fame has struck my heart'. Lucretius, p. 54.

67 Cavendish, *Poems, and Fancies*, p. 52.

68 *Ibid.*, p. 53. This vital soul, antithetical to Lucretius's mortal *anima*, is also found in Cavendish's '*A* Dialogue *of* Birds', where a very specific eschatology is established: 'Although the *Life* of *Bodies* comes from *Nature*, / Yet still the *Soules* come from the great *Creator*. / And they shall live, though *wee* to *dust* do turne, / Either in *Blisse*, or in *hot flames* to burne'. *Ibid.*, pp. 70–5, 73. These poems appear in a section of *Poems, and Fancies* clearly generically delineated as 'DIALOGUES'. *Ibid.*, p. 53. Cavendish's eclectic thinking about the soul sporadically approaches the Christianised mediation of Epicurean theories by Pierre Gassendi, popularised by Walter Charleton. See Merchant, pp. 200–2.

69 Cavendish, *Poems, and Fancies*, p. 53.

70 *Ibid.*, p. 135.

71 *Ibid.*, pp. 64–6. Lucretius, p. 91. Lucretius also personifies the earth, however: 'showers perish when father ether has flung them down into the lap of mother earth'. Lucretius, p. 34. For an exploration of Lucretius's use of personification or, more properly, 'deification' see Gale, *Myth*, p. 3. Lucretius and Cavendish are anti-Platonic in considering the possibility of a multiplicity of worlds. 'This Heaven', wrote Plato, 'has come to be and is and shall be hereafter one and unique'. See Plato, *Timaeus*, ed. and trans. John Warrington (London: Dent Everyman, 1965), p. 21.

72 Lucretius, p. 79.

73 For more on these poems see Chapter 5, below.

74 Cavendish, *Poems, and Fancies*, pp. 76–80.

75 *Ibid.*, pp. 77–8. Such Lucretian concerns are apparent in other of the dialogues, such as '*A* Dialogue *betwixt* Joy, *and* Discretion': '*Feare*, being a *string*,

bindes hard; when once tis crackt: / *Spirits* find *Liberty*, strait run about'. *Ibid.*, p. 80.

76 *Ibid.*, p. 97. For Cavendish's suspicion of sea travel see Grant, *Margaret the First*, pp. 175–6. Lucretius, too, uses maritime images to represent the human condition. See, for example: 'The human infant, like a shipwrecked sailor cast ashore by the cruel waves, lies naked on the ground'. Lucretius, p. 177. For an analysis of the symbolic importance of the sea voyage in the literature of the Ancients see Gale, *Myth*, pp. 122–6. She writes that 'The Epicurean who has attained *ataraxia* has ... both metaphorically and literally escaped from these storms'. Gale, *Myth*, pp. 120–1.

77 On 'oblique communication' see Patterson, p. 45, and my introduction, above.

78 Cavendish, *Poems, and Fancies*, pp. 106–7.

79 Sections of *Poems, and Fancies* entitled 'The Claspe' begin on pp. 47, 110, 155, 162. Immediately prior to or following each of the first three 'Claspe[s]' comes the poet's comment on her poetic style, often invocatory in tone. In the first 'Claspe', the poet characterises her brains as impatiently wanting to expel fancies to allow room for new ones to breed. *Ibid.*, p. 47. 'Give *Mee* the *Free*, and *Noble Stile*', and 'Give me that *Wit*, whose *Fancy's* not confin'd', writes Cavendish. *Ibid.*, pp. 110, 154.

80 *Ibid.*, pp. 116–18, 117. Page 117 is misnumbered as '177'. See Lucretius: 'The name of mother has rightly been bestowed on the earth'. Lucretius, p. 195. For a more specialised analysis of what the Ancients may have understood by the concept of a 'golden age' see Gale, *Myth*, pp. 161–82.

81 Cavendish, *Poems, and Fancies*, p. 119.

82 *Ibid.*, p. 120.

83 *Ibid.*, pp. 146–7.

84 *Ibid.*, p. 155.

85 *Ibid.*, pp. 155–6. The 'nineteen degrees' perhaps refer to Cavendish's age at the onset of civil war.

86 *Ibid.*, p. 156.

87 *Ibid.*, p. 155. For an analysis of the relationship between atomism and the Platonic court masques of the 1620s and 1630s, see Barbour, 'Early Stuart', p. 173. Cavendish's abstract masque could similarly be read as an ideational refinement of grosser elements into pure or platonic constituent forms. See also Tomlinson.

88 Cavendish, *Poems, and Fancies*, p. 148.

89 *Ibid.*, p. 165. '*Britanny*' presumably refers to Britain, and is indeed changed to '*Brit'n*' in the second edition of *Poems, and Fancies* (London, 1664).

90 Cavendish, *Poems, and Fancies*, pp. 163–4. In this poem Cavendish attributes dreams to the activities of fairies in the brain, and avers that a belch can consequently cause a terrible storm in fairyland.

91 *Ibid.*, pp. 171–3.

92 *Ibid.*, p. 173. Lucretius, p. 115.

93 Cavendish, *Poems, and Fancies*, pp. 169–70. Lucretius, p. 60.

94 Such appropriation, with its concomitant implications for the activity of

writing for publication, renders the female-authored text less exclusive than that of Lucretius, where 'the reader is invited to undertake ... thought experiment[s] nonsensical for a woman'. See Nugent, p. 181. Nugent emphasises precisely such military images as those which Cavendish here arrogates.

95 Cavendish, *Poems, and Fancies*, p. 167.

96 *Ibid.*, p. 196.

97 Lucretius, p. 210. The trope was also used by Ovid, in whose *Metamorphoses* Justice leaves the earth because of her disgust with civilization's decline. 'Last of all arose the age of hard iron', writes Ovid, 'all manner of crime broke out; modesty, truth, and loyalty fled ... War made its appearance'. See Ovid, *Metamorphoses*, ed. and trans. Mary M. Innes (Harmondsworth: Penguin, 1955), pp. 32–3.

98 Lucretius, p. 206.

99 Cavendish, *Poems, and Fancies*, p. 198.

100 *Ibid.*, p. 211. Significantly, in terms of a Lucretian reading, the Parliament recognises the need to do away with superstitious beliefs, replacing them with new ones. These approach Epicurean rationality, such as *'That Death is only a privation of Motion, as Darknesse is a privation of Light. That the Soule is a thing, and nothing'*. *Ibid.*, p. 204. Ostensibly a political allegory, *The Animall Parliament* is informed by Cavendish's autobiographical experiences. See Chapter 5, below.

101 See Schiesaro for the argument that the text stages *'in rebus* the concepts it teaches *in uerbis'*. Schiesaro, p. 103. See also Gale, *Myth*, for the reader's role upon finishing *De rerum natura*: 'to find consolation he has to close the circle and turn back again to the beginning'. *Ibid.*, p. 228. Penwill suggests that 'the whole poem, representing in its overall structure the progress from birth (Venus) to death (plague), is an *imago* of the world it portrays: an *imago mundi* generated by words'. Penwill, p. 81.

102 Cavendish, *Poems, and Fancies*, p. 214.

103 The advertisement also conveys an acute sense of moment, and of the physicality of the book, since it is absent from the second edition of *Poems, and Fancies* of 1664. It is 'the next step' because, although the volume is to be 'in *Prose*', it is still composed of '*Fancies*'.

3

Heavens Library:
Platonic paradigms
and trial by genre

But let us strive to build us Tombs while we live, of Noble, Honourable,
and good Actions, at least harmlesse;
That though our Bodies dye,
Our Names may live to after memory.
(Margaret Cavendish, 'To All Writing Ladies',
Poems, and Fancies (1653))

He pleads not guilty, but refus'd
By Histriomicke Poëts to be try'd ...
Shakespear's a Mimicke, *Massinger* a Sot,
Heywood for *Aganippe* takes a plot:
Beaumont and *Fletcher* make one poët, they
Single, dare not adventure on a Play ...
Plato refus'd such creatures to admit
Into his Common-wealth, and is it fit
Parnassus should the exiles entertaine
Of *Plato*? [1]

Thus the editor of the *Post* refuses to accept the jurors' judgement in
this imaginary trial published by George Wither in 1645. In *The Great
Assises Holden in Parnassus* civil war newspapers such as the republican *Kingdom's Weekly Intelligencer* and the royalist *Mercurius Aulicus*
are arraigned before Apollo. Other classical and literary figures have
courtroom functions. It is Tasso, for example, acting as a court usher,
who brings in 'alive, or dead, each one / That had discovered been,
or to defile / The Press with Pamphlets scarrilous, and vile'.[2] The

sentences which Apollo hands down are witty and imaginative: the editor of 'Britannicus' is to be shot with porcupine quills and that of the 'Scout' must guard beehives naked, armed only with a feather.[3] The paper from the 'Occurrances' is to serve 'Cloaca's', and the editor of the 'Scottish Dove' must never again cross the River Tweed and journey outside Scotland.[4] It is Phoebus who intervenes and reprieves both 'Aulicus' and 'Britanicus'.[5]

The text gives prominence to issues of modernity and genre and, as the opening epigraph demonstrates, the poets' credentials as judges are called into question, and their claims to paradigmatic literary and historical status scrutinised. Whilst in Cavendish's 1656 text Heavens Library there is a separation between mythical gods and mortal defendants, and her poets are not, even nominally, the judges, her concern is, like Wither's, with propagating contemporary political critique through a mock-judicial discourse. Further, Plato's relationship with Wither's 'creatures' (in other words, poets) is one which operates as a guide to the generic motivation behind Natures Pictures as a whole.

The full title of Natures Pictures indicates the extent of Cavendish's fascination with literary classification, and its seemingly infinite potential for manipulation and subdivision.[6] A concern with forms or types is suggested by the title which, as was seen in Chapter 1, promises the 'Comical, Tragical, and Tragi-Comical, Poetical, Romancical, Philosophical, and Historical, both in Prose and Verse'. Cavendish invokes, and subverts for personal and political ends, Platonic theories of generic ideals and literary structure. Central to this strategy is the short prose passage apparently randomly appended to Book X, called Heavens Library, which is Fames Palace purged from Errors and Vices. Once Heavens Library has been analysed in terms of Cavendish's ideas about the uses of genre, it serves to explain not only its own anomalous position in the volume but the generic nature of other sections of Natures Pictures too. Heavens Library is the key which unlocks Natures Pictures, revealing it to be something quite other than the work it at first appears. This chapter is an examination of the generic play in which Cavendish engages in order to fashion this key, and will focus on what it unlocks. The focus here is on Cavendish's manipulation of generic expectations for political means, and her witty adaptation of Platonic conceptions of genre and the social utility of the literary, in the construction of the collection of ideal forms found in *Heavens Library*. An understanding of this process illumines Book I of *Natures Pictures*, where Socratic dialogic structure is utilised in an ultimately subversive manner. That elements of *Natures Pictures* are polemical in their condemnation of the Interregnum regime is suggested once generic similarities between Cavendish's text and Plato's are recognised. Through her idiosyncratic reworking of Plato's ideas Cavendish generates in *Natures Pictures* a vertiginous effect of constantly shifting genres. Ostensibly straightforward generic categories are redefined in provocative and imaginative ways for political purposes which run counter to what Cavendish would have perceived to be dominant 'Puritan' ideologies. In terms of this subversion a textual slippage occurs from what appear to be discussions of modernity, to a critique of dominant anti-royalist ideological discourses. Genre facilitates this subversive literary manoeuvre, and the reader is made alert to this possibility only after having read *Heavens Library* carefully since, as I have already argued, it is the whole volume's key. Further, and to return to the formulation of the triple exile, Cavendish's generic commutations may have as much to do with her anxieties about her status as an exiled royalist writer with, in reality, minimal control over her destiny and her text as they have to do with her confident and deliberate forays into literary experimentation.

Although couched in ancient Parnassian lore, *Heavens Library* is astounding in its contemporaneity. Concise, learned and acerbic, it is the most pointed polemic in Cavendish's oeuvre. For the exiled Cavendish, the library is an edenic Albion, beguiled by the serpent of Puritan doctrine and rebellion. It possesses properties at once abstract and concrete, divine and mundane, textual and corporeal. More than a repository for books or manuscripts, it is a location for generic ideals, quasi-Platonic Forms, a hall of fame where great men or their works are elected to reside. This election, or trial, centres on the intellectual contribution each man has made to a specific activity. Presided over by Jove, the trial is undertaken by the assembled gods.

Cavendish's models in *Heavens Library* are not only classical, as its engagement with, for example, *Don Quixote* makes clear. Once the reader of her text is alerted to her attitude towards Plato, the way is clear for identifying how a clever deployment of genre is at work elsewhere in *Natures Pictures*. Her witty interpretation of Cervantes's text is one example of this. What Plato and the character Don Quixote have in common is their recourse to modes of generic censorship, a trope to which Cavendish subscribes precisely in order to make, from her own position of exile, contentious political statements without her words being censored.[7] In what ways, then, does Cavendish identify with Plato and his ideas?

The Athens in which Plato grew up was an unsettled place ravaged by the Peloponnesian War and finally falling in 404 BC.[8] Drawn to politics, Plato was repelled by the corruption he beheld around him which culminated in the execution of his mentor, Socrates, whose rigorous scepticism had not been welcomed by the state. *The Republic*, probably written in 375 BC, represents Plato's attempt to define how a just society might be brought about through 'true philosophy', having come to the conclusion that all existing states were badly governed.[9] Central to his ideas was the importance of education, especially rhetoric, and how this connected with a wider social morality. It was a morality which poets threatened. In *The Republic*, Socrates tells Adeimantus:

> So if we are visited in our state by someone who has the skill to transform himself into all sorts of characters and represent all sorts of things, and he wants to show off himself and his poems to us, we ... shall tell him that he and his kind have no place in our city, their presence being forbidden by our code.[10]

In Cavendish's text the exiled author resorts to her own Socratic disingenuousness, banishing Plato's 'Commonwealth ... by reason it was so strict'.[11] The irony of the writer exiled from the Puritan republic adopting the generic characteristics of the philosopher who exiled the poets in *The Republic*, is apparently not lost on Cavendish. Plato's emphasis on democracy over oligarchy would have offended Cavendish's political sensibilities, and this is one reason behind her own banishment of *The Republic*. Further, her act of literary revenge evokes the paradox that Plato, banishing the poets, was himself a poet, a predicament addressed by John Milton. 'Surely you will recall the poets exiled from your State', Milton wrote, 'for you are the greatest fabler of them all; or, founder though you be, you must yourself go forth'.[12] In the 1650s Plato's theorisation of literature created the opportunity for a commonality of opinion among writers from opposite ends of the political spectrum, and on different sides of the English Channel. Whilst Cavendish and Milton are political opponents, a Platonic conception of universal Truth mediated through poetry is mutual. Where Cavendish departs from this common ground of opinion is in her political manipulation of the Platonic construct of poet as social arbiter. Taking to its logical conclusion the notion that genre should be regulated in order to represent and increase true virtue, Cavendish reinterprets Plato's socio-literary theories. The result, as demonstrated in *Heavens Library*, is that monarchical rule becomes constituted as 'truth', and the Cromwellian regime is condemned, apparently with ancient justification.

The pantheistic context of *Heavens Library* evokes Plato's writing, as does the dialogic structure of the piece, but Cavendish asserts her own, contemporary, reading through her explicit disavowal of Plato's 'too strict' rules concerning representation of the divine.[13] The advocation in *Heavens Library* of the establishment of a just and profitable society which aspires to virtue through literature, science and philosophy is on occasion undermined, as Cavendish's depictions border on the mundane. The library's ideal, abstract qualities vie with descriptions of a commonplace physicality, and intermittently the gods' responses are far from divine. When Cupid pleads for the inclusion of '*Tibullus* and his son', Jove decrees that they 'be placed in some out corner of the Library; at which sentence *Cupid* frown'd, knowing his Mother *Venus* would grieve'.[14]

'*Tibullus* and his son' narrowly escape exclusion because of their standing as 'Naturall Poets', a dignity which itself has political nuances in Cavendish's text. To have 'natural' status is, in the consciousness of the exiled, to occupy the moral high ground. In cavalier rhetoric the only true aristocracy is that which is inherent; natural poetic wit is superior to Puritan inspiration, and the natural, monarchical social structure surpasses the new state constructed as the result of unnatural usurpation.[15] Aligned with the issue of the precedence Cavendish accords to the 'natural' is that of the disapprobation which she reserves for the 'modern' in *Heavens Library*. Modernity thus becomes a highly politicised notion, being applicable to sanctioned, that is, Puritan, discourses. Cavendish herself, writing in exile, does not construct herself as a sanctioned author *per se*, and so, excluded from that category, is free to criticise contemporary writers. Of these, the gods 'could find not one true Naturall Poet, not amongst five hundred'.[16] The imagery Cavendish employs to portray 'the Moderns' is grotesque in its virulence: they are 'like a company of Ravens, that live upon dead carckasses ... like Maggots, that have been bred in their dead flesh ... like Hornetts, and some like Bees'.[17] Cavendish's generic framework grants to statements like these an obliquity which deflects the censure they might attract if expressed in a different generic register. Her earlier witty and irreverent treatment of Plato's *Republic* would alert the careful reader to such obliquity later in the piece. The specific narrowness of Cavendish's understanding of modernity is further emphasised by her inclusion in the library and, therefore, her exclusion from the category of 'modern', of sixteenth- and seventeenth-century figures. The gods spare Cervantes (d. 1616) and Galileo (d. 1642), Machiavelli (d. 1527) and Lyly (d. 1606).[18] Her attitude to the Ancients was to remain constant through to one of her last publications, *Observations upon Experimental Philosophy*, in which she not only positions her own natural philosophy in relation to that of Plato but also stresses the importance of reverence for the Ancients. Her objections to the 'Moderns', and the basis of her self-separation from them, are politically motivated, and this is made quite explicit in the same treatise. Modern writers 'are like those unconscionable men in Civil Wars', she writes in *Observations*, 'which endeavour to pull down the hereditary Mansions of Noble-men and Gentlemen, to build a Cottage of their own'.[19]

In *Heavens Library*, just as war and political ambition have ravaged England, so '*Mars, Venus* and *Fortune*' have introduced 'vices ... as Serpents, and Errors as Wormes' into the library.[20] It is significant, therefore, that among the first resolutions of the council is that 'all those Records that were of Usurpers, and Invaders should be cast forth'.[21] Undeserved fame and corruption are so rife in the library that the proposition in favour of the rejection of 'obstructive controversy ... also tedious Disputes, and Sophistry' is met with the protestation that 'if all these Records should be cast forth, the famous library would be very empty'.[22] Jove's response, that only acts which 'supprest vice, and advanc't vertue ... chiefly those that glorified the Gods' recalls the Socratic injunction that 'the only poetry that should be allowed in a state is hymns to the gods and paeans in praise of good men'.[23] Such echoes of *The Republic* emphasise its pervasive influence, and accentuate the witty irony which accompanies that text's uncontested banishment by the council. The exiled Cavendish's revenge on Plato is subtle and faultlessly logical, but no less sweet for that: Socrates' desire to exile poets must ultimately lead to Plato's own expulsion.

Plato is not the sole object of Cavendish's attack, and the anger she learnedly directs towards his *Republic* is temperate in comparison to that which she reserves for the Puritan one. In the central section of *Heavens Library* the divine council turns its attention from 'Phylosophers ... Phisicians', mathematicians, and 'Astronomers', to 'Law-makers ... Orators', and politicians, finally discussing 'Heroick Records' at length.[24] The deliberation over politicians is not expanded beyond this phrase: 'for Politicks only *Achitophell* and *Machiavell*', whereas the debate over heroism extends over more than sixty lines.[25] This debate functions as the locus of Cavendish's most intense anti-Puritan rhetoric. Here genre has a function which surpasses the purely literary, as the boundaries of the classification 'heroic' are drawn. Rightful heroism, and just wars, are carefully distinguished from unlawful military and political arrogation. Whereas '*Tamberlain*' is cast out 'for he had no right to the Turks Empire', 'the Records of the Jewes Heroes' may remain because Canaan 'was given them by the Gods'.[26] The critique of the Cromwellian regime is unmistakable:

> *Jove* said, that all the Records, that were of the actions of those they call the *Heroes*, most of them ought to be cast out, being violators of Peace, and destroyers of Righteous Laws and Divine Ceremony, Prophaners of our Temples, breaking down our Altars and Images, Robbing us of our Treasures, therein to maintain their ill gotten power, or to get that power they have no right to, having no Justice but strength to make their Titles good, besides they are the greatest troublers of Mankinde, Robbers and Theeves, disposing the right of antient Possessions, and defacing the Truth of antient times.[27]

The moral register is quite clear. The old, monarchical regime was just, right and true; the usurpers are 'violators ... destroyers' and 'Prophaners'. The references to Cromwell's iconoclasm are explicit, as is the notion of usurpation as the political equivalent of theft. '*Jove*' may begin the sentence, but this ventriloquism is no disguise as Cavendish completes it. Pallas answers Mars's interjection that lawyers and priests support the usurping regime. She demonstrates how Jove has been claimed by them as justification for their acquiescence. Textual exegesis has been manipulated for political ends, intimidating the lawyers and priests into compliance. 'Those two professions',

86

Pallas declares, 'plead always for the stronger side . . . and makes the Text and Laws, as a nose of wax, which will take any Print'.[28] Again, Cavendish's excoriation of Puritan rule leads her to move beyond the Classical context she has constructed into a contemporary arena. The weight of ancient rhetoric and justification behind her critique lends it a strength and authority which, written solely in the author's own voice, it might have lacked.

At times, the virulence of Cavendish's attack leads her plot to be sacrificed to polemic. The polytheistic framework, for example, is momentarily let slide as Cavendish targets the regicides, Jove declaring that 'Kings are Gods Deputies and Viceregents, and therefore sacred, and ought not to be injured, but when they are, their injurers are to be severely punished'.[29] The gods' choice of writers to reside in the library also suggests as much about Cavendish's own culture as it does about the establishment of a timeless hall of fame. As careful distinctions between rightful, just occupation and unlawful usurpation were made in the discussion of heroes, so the literary contenders must demonstrate natural rights before taking up their places. The contenders are usually the authors themselves, but at times they are individual texts.[30]

The criteria for grouping and assessing the writers and their works are distinctly Platonic, with social influence and utility being at the top of the agenda, but co-existing with this Platonic paradigm are Cavendish's archetypal seventeenth-century literary opinions. The romance genre, regarded as void of verisimilitude and individual restraint, and hence potentially corrupting, is condemned. Such condemnation was not unusual in the 1650s. In the preface to Madeleine de Scudéry's *Ibrahim*, for example, the relationship of verisimilous writing to romance is discussed and characterised as 'like the foundation stone of the building . . . And if its enticing deception does not deceive in the romances, to read them can only disgust the mind instead of pleasing it'.[31] Cavendish is less conciliatory, as Jove casts out all romances which 'corrupt Mortalls thoughts, and ma[k]e them neglect their divine Worship, causing them to spend their time, vainly, idly and sinfully'.[32] Her antipathy to the romance genre is apparent elsewhere in *Natures Pictures*, where, with characteristic specificity, the volume is differentiated from 'Romancy Writing' of which 'the most . . . [she] ever read . . . was but part of three Books, as the three parts of one, and the half of the two others'.[33]

Cavendish's rejection of romance may also be read as an implicit critique, which she expressed more fully after the Restoration, of the exiled court's modish adaptation of romance discourses under the tutelage of Henrietta Maria. In Cavendish's *Playes* of 1662 the author's own materialism, sharply in contrast to the platonic love espoused by the exiled court, is reflected by a depiction of incorporeal love as ultimately absurd.[34] Another exiled royalist, William Davenant, had also satirised Henrietta Maria's platonic love cult in *The Platonick Lovers*, treating the theme with rather more seriousness in the popular tragicomedy *Love and Honour*.[35] Indeed, Davenant may be characterised as the channel connecting England with European generic developments, particularly that of heroic drama, and his connections with the Cavendish family were close.[36] Davenant's influence on Cavendish was considerable, and his lengthy preface to *Gondibert* illumines contemporary theories about genre (as seen in the quotation at the start of Chapter 1 above). Pertinent to this analysis of Cavendish's Platonic paradigms is Davenant's defence of Plato, which comes towards the conclusion of his preface. Addressing 'the Enemys of Poesy', who cite Plato's *Republic* as their justification, Davenant claims that '*Plato* says nothing against Poets in generall', but restricts his critique to Homer and Hesiod, and 'not against Poesy, but the Poems then most in request'.[37] Such a critique is depicted as justifiable, even necessary, in the context of misrepresentation of gods and heroes, and the socially detrimental potential this possesses. Davenant's interpretation of Socrates' statements is narrower than Cavendish's, and attributes to Plato a clarity which *The Republic* does not have.[38]

I touched in Chapter 1 on the various ways in which the romance genre was contested by vying political sides, and suggested that Cavendish's professed rejection of it may be understood as a pragmatic and self-defensive dissociation from the courtly pretensions of Henrietta Maria and her followers. The remarkable fluidity which characterised the term 'Romance' has been commented on by Margaret Doody, who provides credible seventeenth-century contexts for regarding the genre, which she identifies as a direct progenitor of the novel, as either monarchical or bourgeois.[39] It is this latter association, with its concomitant implications for civic power and status, which Cavendish suggests in her remarks. As Doody expresses it, 'The Novel is an enemy of the civic, in short – whether the civic represents itself as monarchical or republican'.[40] The generic flexibility Doody identifies is what Cavendish exploits, and it explains in part her apparently inconsistent attitude to romance which leads her to condemn it, as here, or rework it, as demonstrated in the analysis of *Assaulted and Pursued Chastity* in my next chapter.

In *Heavens Library*, aware of the possibilities of generic experimentation and play, Jove acquits '*Don Quixot*, by reason he hath so wittily abused all other Romances', but in an ironic, intertextual reversal, *Amadis de Gaule*, saved in *Don Quixote* from the flames, is summarily 'cast out, by reason it was the originall of all the rest'.[41] Indeed, the legalistic tone of *Heavens Library* owes much to the episode in Cervantes's text in which the curate and the barber set about Don Quixote's library. Here, '*Amadis of Gaule'* is acquitted because it is the first of its genre, 'and all the others have had their beginning and originall from this'.[42] As in *Heavens Library*, there are three varieties of sentence which the texts may receive: acquittal, that is, leave to remain included in the library; conditional discharge, being in Cavendish's text, banishment to a dusty antechamber of Heaven's Library, or being deposited in a 'drie Vault' in *Don Quixote*; or, ultimately, execution, that is, destruction on the curate's bonfire in Cervantes's text, or perpetual torment or death by drowning in 'the River of *Stix'* in Cavendish's.[43]

In *Don Quixote* genre operates in a way similar to that in which Cavendish establishes generic expectations which allow her to publish apparently seditious material. This is especially true of Book I of *Natures Pictures*, where the generic expectation aroused is of an ostensible *Symposium*-based, round-the-fire discussion of love, but the text turns into a blatant critique of Puritan involvement in the civil wars. In Cervantes's text it is genre which sets up expectations in the censor which predispose him to a volume even before it has been opened. Of 'these little bookes that remaine', the curate decides to keep all of them because they 'are not bookes of Knighthood, but of Poetry ... [which cannot] doe so much hurt as bookes of Knighthood, being all of them workes full of understanding and conceits'.[44] Overall, the episode in Don Quixote's library is far less reverential than Cavendish's, within which, as has been shown, there operates a sophisticated level of allegory. As the barber and the curate grow bored and tired, authors are allowed to remain because they are acquaintances, and a translation of Ovid narrowly escapes being burned when the curate 'grew wearie to see so many bookes, and so he would have all the rest burned at all adventures'.[45]

Edifying or intellectually witty texts such as *Don Quixote*, then, are given leave to remain in Heaven's Library. Mercury, paradigm of aspiring intellect, 'joy[s]' when Jove decrees that the morally didactic Aesop's *Fables* should not be cast out, and that '*Lucian* and *Rablas* shall be kept, both for their huge wit and judgment, rectifying Schollars understandings'.[46] The social impact of the literary, as was the case in *The Republic*, is at the fore of the writer's concerns. This attitude chimes with that expressed by William Cavendish in his *Advice* to Charles II where civil strife is blamed indirectly on increased literacy: 'The Bible in Englishe under everye wevers & Chambermaydes Arme hath dun us much hurte'.[47] Such attitudes contradict those expressed by, among others, William Davenant, who believed that 'Ignorance is rude, censorious, jealous, obstinate, and proud'.[48]

Homer is considered at some length in *Heavens Library*. The generic and social differences between his role as historical chronicler and that as poet are accentuated. In the gods' debate concerning the category of 'heroic', Homer's place in the library is secured because of his function as 'Heaven['s] Chronologer'.[49] When their attention turns to poets, the gods place '*Homer, Pindar*, and *Anacrion* ... as the three first'.[50] By the 1650s the individual works of these three were rarely read, but their supposed types of writing were emulated, namely Homer's epic, the Pindaric ode and Anacrion's convivial, erotic style, which was in keeping with the exiled Cavaliers' ethos. Where the gods debate in greater depth the work of a writer such as Ovid it suggests, on Cavendish's part, a deeper familiarity with that writer.[51] As with '*Tibullus* and his son', so Ovid escapes exclusion (proposed in this instance by Jove for 'divulging his severall Amours'), on account of being a 'Naturall Poet'.[52] This criterion also saves Virgil and Horace, whose works signified much to the exiled Cavaliers, and who, in addition, were representative of genres, namely the Virgilian epic, the Arcadian pastoral epitomised by Virgil's *Georgics* and the Horatian ode.[53]

The selective nature of the gods' decision in *Heavens Library* to reject Plato's 'Commonwealth' indicates that his other works are regarded as rightful occupants. Of these *The Symposium* has particular relevance in a consideration of the content and structure of much of the rest of *Natures Pictures*, specifically Books I, 'Her Excellencies Tales in Verse', and X, *The She Anchoret*. The complex narrative structure of *The Symposium*, in addition to its ambiguous generic status as part philosophy, part fiction, is significant for an understanding of Cavendish's project, as is the notion that Plato, alienated by Athenian politics, set his work in what he regarded as a more contented past.[54] In *The Symposium*, Apollodorus recounts to an unnamed companion what Aristodemus told him about the drinking party which took place some years earlier. Within Apollodorus's report, Eryximachus, Phaedrus, Pausanias and others each speak in the first person, as does Diotima within Socrates' long speech. Structurally, then, the multi-layered narrative is highly complex, and Cavendish attempts to evoke a similarly Platonic heteroglossia in Book I of *Natures Pictures*, where characters gathered around a fire relate stories to one another. These verse stories, apparently about love, are linked one to the next by a series of semi-dramatic exchanges between the characters. Unlike in Plato's text, the company described at the start of *Natures Pictures*, of 'Both Men and Women by the Fire set', is not exclusively male.[55] The first story of the series is told by a man who, commencing 'when he had spit and blow'd his Nose', recalls by this noisy physical act Aristophanes' hiccups.[56] Within his tale, already folded deep within a narrative structure which has Cavendish the writer on the outside, her narrator, and her male character within, a further layer is added as a female character, a widow, speaks: 'Give leave, you Gods, this loss for to lament, / Give my soul leave to seek which wayes he went'.[57] Such a multipartite narrative recalls Socrates' delineation of three modes of poetic discourse, being diegesis, mimesis and a mixture of the two, 'the fountainhead of generic classification'.[58] Further, Diotima's explanation of the theory of universal Forms has resonance for notions of literary types.

Cavendish's attempts at figural or mimetic representation in the 1650s, however, were merely foreshadowings of the authorial ventriloquism which she attempted in post-Restoration works such as *Orations of Divers Sorts* (1662) and *CCXI Sociable Letters* (1664). Whereas in his *Symposium* Plato's characters spoke in individual and revealing voices (the pedantic Eryximachus; the venerable, yet flirtatious Socrates), in the first book of Cavendish's *Natures Pictures* the characters' utterances are only nominally differentiated. At first, poetry is constructed as a literary form best suited to men, as the female characters, in response to their own protestations, are permitted to make their contributions 'both out of time, and non-sensly', that is, without metre, or even sense.[59] In actuality most of the verse-tales are written in identical metrical style; iambic pentameters marshalled into occasionally tortuous rhyming couplets.[60] Further, most follow the same narrative patterns and preoccupations, being inquiries into the nature of true love and the soul, featuring the recurrent, and fairly conventional, motif of a weeping woman. Rarely are the speaker's characteristics or gender apparent independently of authorial indication. Cavendish herself is the only clearly defined character in the first book of *Natures Pictures*, and her interventions are polemical.[61] Unlike the finely judged and astute critique of the Puritan regime which is found in *Heavens Library*, however, that of the first book lacks subtlety or refinement.

Plato's nostalgic choice of time-frame for his *Symposium* allowed him tacitly to critique the Athenian regime under which the text was produced, and Cavendish too constructs a congenial assembly where, in terms of genre, the anticipated discourse is quite neutral. However, the verses, mostly ostensibly love-poems of a didactic, moralistic nature, are sometimes political. The generic expectations inspired by a recognition of the structural similarities between Cavendish's text and Plato's are subverted by the presence in both texts of a political dimension, and genre has provided an expedient literary disguise for the exiled royalist wishing to condemn the Interregnum regime.[62] The last six poems of Book I are unequivocally autobiographical, and consequently partisan, set apart by the title of the first, 'A Description of Civil Wars', which marks the shift in theme.[63]

These six poems serve as a vehicle for Cavendish to offer her own interpretation of recent events. The Puritans are depicted as iconoclastic and tyrannical, their lack of enjoyment of life the immediate result of the unjustifiable way in which they seized power. They do not relish their political success 'because their Conscience did them so torment, / For all their Plenty they were discontent'.[64] As in *Heavens Library*, Cavendish here invokes a polytheistic surety, rendering natural and expiable the royalist cause. 'No mercy can they hope from Gods on high' she writes, 'O serve the Gods, and then the Minde will be / Allways in peace, and sweet tranquillity'.[65] Tranquillity, nobility, justice, even history itself, are repeatedly associated with what Cavendish perceives as the natural, monarchical order. In another of the civil war poems in which England is represented

by a stone cross, 'pull'd down quite, the fault was onely Age', inno-
vation is equated with anarchy and tyranny.[66] Again, as in *Heavens
Library*, censure of modernity is, by logical extension, criticism of the
contemporary Puritan administration. Cavendish emphasises the
preternatural repercussions of parliamentarian activities in another
poem, in an account of the execution of her brother, Charles Lucas,
following the surrender of Colchester in August 1648. In highly
emotive language reminiscent of that in pamphlets such as 'The
Loyall Sacrifice', Cavendish writes:

> Vollyes of Shot did all his Body tear,
> Where his Blood's spilt, the Earth no Grass will bear.
> As if for to revenge his Death, the Earth
> Was curs'd with Barrenness even from her Birth.[67]

The time before the civil wars is depicted as being edenic in another
partisan, nostalgic poem. In language peppered with Biblical resonances, England is constructed as a land full of 'Chrystal Brooks
[which] run every Field between ... And fatted Beasts, two inches
thick with Tallow'.[68] The last of the civil war poems is told by a
'*Ladye*' and is strongly suggestive of the experiences Cavendish under-
went in 1651 at Goldsmith's Hall. England, once Cavendish's secure
and ordered native land, is now bitterly dubbed 'happ'land', a remote
place of contingency and hazard.[69] The Committee members are
personified as being devoid of pity: 'Hard were their Hearts, and cruel
every Minde'.[70] In effect, then, to Cavendish's tendentious and pragmatically selective memory, the land she has been forced to leave
was, before the wars, as perfect a state as even Socrates could have
envisioned.

Book X of *Natures Pictures* is *The She Anchoret*, the opening of
which, in structure and tone, has similarities with Book I. As *The She
Anchoret* progresses, however, the narrative undergoes a dialectic
shift, from a model which, in its dialogic form and selection of themes,
recalls *The Symposium* to a form reminiscent more of *The Republic*.
This shift to some extent explains the classically *ex abrupto* presence
of *Heavens Library* at the end of Book X. The resistance of *The She
Anchoret* to simple generic classification is suggested by its dedicatory
title, wherein Cavendish, with her customary distinction-drawing
and desire for inclusiveness, addresses eighteen types of reader, from
'*Naturall Philosophers, Physicians*', and '*Married-men, and their Wives*',

to 'Virgins ... Aged Persons, and Souldiers'.[71] This suggestion that such a mélange of an audience could read the text echoes the prefatory remarks at the beginning of Natures Pictures. Here The She Anchoret is recommended as being 'solid and edifying', Natures Pictures itself characterised as a work to 'quench Amorous passions ... beget chaste Thoughts, nourish love of Vertue ... forwarne youth, and arme the life against misfortunes'.[72]

Such prefatory avowals are Socratic in their assumptions about the culturally beneficial potential of the literary, as is the structure of The She Anchoret, which masquerades as a moral tale of youthful virtue preserved in the face of violation but which is actually a series of short philosophical and moral essays and aphorisms.[73] The anchoret is like 'Diogenes in his tub', receiving in turn each of the same categories of people that Cavendish delineated as the potential readership of the book.[74] The author's self-identification with the anchoret is explicit.[75] The overtly pedantic philosophical differentiations which are drawn within the dialogues the anchoret conducts expose the weakness and superficiality of the story, which is reduced to a vehicle for the dry and prosaic ideas Cavendish wishes to explore. 'Fortune', she writes in one discussion, is 'a sufficient cause to produce such an effect, for a conjunction of many sufficient causes to produce such an effect, since that effect could not be produced, did there want any of those causes'.[76] The author's drive for clarity leads the framing narrative to suffer, then, and the will to inclusiveness borders on the neurotic. In the perplexing world of Cavendish's text the generic mixture undermines the status of much of what she states, as fact becomes uncomfortably blended with fiction, the figural with the actual. In her discourse glow-worms' tails glow because they are transparent, and, were the human skull transparent, it too would glow with the light of knowledge.[77] The reader's frustration with the text was shared by B. G. MacCarthy, who writes of the anchoret's untimely demise: 'She makes an oration to a convenient multitude, and swallows poison before anyone can prevent her, whether they would have done so being a controverted point'.[78] Denise Riley, with rather more reverence, characterises the suicide as an incident of 'nympholepsy'.[79]

Reminiscent, then, in its question and answer format, of Socrates' discussions in The Republic, yet ostensibly framed by a standard romance format, The She Anchoret possesses a highly anomalous generic status. Neither wholly philosophical tract nor romance nor dramatic dialogue, it fails to achieve the equilibrium between didacticism and entertainment which typifies its generic model. This failure is in part attributable to the author's anxieties about a loss of control over her text once it has passed into the printer's care. Such unease is not unfounded, for structurally the 1656 edition of *Natures Pictures* is highly illogically organised, with an epistle intended to be read before *The She Anchoret* appearing more than thirty pages after its conclusion. Overall in *Natures Pictures* there are nine prefatory pieces; twelve 'Parts' or 'Books' (of which Books I and X are especially pertinent to this analysis); Cavendish's autobiography (the 'true Story ... wherein there is no Feignings'); and then, at the end of the volume, various passages and epistles which are, according to accompanying instructions, to be read at certain points in the main body of the text. The eccentrically located *She Anchoret* epistle divulges much about Cavendish's preoccupation with genre, in addition to accentuating the degree to which she hopes that her text will not be misread. 'I Shall intreat those Readers that reade this feigned Story of my she Anchoret' writes Cavendish, 'that when they read those parts ... which treat of the Rational and Sensitive Spirits, that they will compare those to my Book of Philosophical and Physical Opinions, being parts that should be added thereto'.[80] As *Philosophical and Physical Opinions* had already been published, however, 'wherein they should be placed, I put them into this Book'.[81]

The concrete realities of literary production have frustrated Cavendish's control over her text, as *Natures Pictures Drawn ... to the Life ...* have had to accommodate a 'feigned Story'. She has encountered the impasse between reality and representation. It is the same impasse she perceives in *The Republic*, Socrates' state theory being characterised in *Heavens Library* as 'so strict, it could never be put in use, nor come into practise'.[82] Through her epistle Cavendish has attempted classification and control, but the attempt is frustrated by the very *position* of the epistle, itself a reminder of the author's impotence. The positioning of this and other verses and epistles at the end of the volume serves to highlight Cavendish's desire for the physical book to take on some of the fluid qualities with which she, throughout the 1650s, characterised herself. The book, however, is a fixed physical entity, escaping its finitude and taking on new meanings only in the process of interaction with the readers' minds.

It is her inability to have any control over precisely this interaction, this interpretative activity, which so troubles Cavendish. Her last-minute prefaces; her desire for inclusiveness; her generic play, all mark the author's attempt at control over her text and her reader. The fluidity she wants for her text must be, paradoxically, controlled. The author wants her volume to go to the printer, but continues to desire an input.[83]

In my last chapter I described how Cavendish had very specific reasons for presenting her first publication in verse. *Heavens Library* may be read as a prose version of some of the ideas which its author had explored in poetic form in *Poems, and Fancies*. In this earlier work the poem '*Fames Library* within the *Temples*' may be read as a direct, poetic precursor of *Heavens Library*, particularly in its successful synthesis of the allegorical and the contemporary; the eternal and the immediacy of political cynicism:

> *Fames Library*, where old Records are plac'd,
> What acts not here unto *oblivion* cast.
> There stands the *skelves* of *Time*, where books do lye,
> Which *books* are tyed by *chaines* of *destiny*.
> The *Master* of this *place* they *Favour* call,
> Where *Care* the *door-keeper*, doth lock up all:
> Yet not so fast, but *Bribery* in steals,
> *Partialities, cousenage truths* not reveals.
> But *Bribery* through all the world takes place,
> And *offerings* as a *bribe* in heaven findes grace.
> Then let not men disdaine a *bribe* to take,
> Since *gods* do blessing give for a bribes sake.[84]

The bitterness of the concluding couplet recalls that which permeated Cavendish's vision of the decline of civilisation in *Poems, and Fancies* when she described the '*last hard Iron Age*'.[85] Read in such a light, *Heavens Library* is as much a fantastic vision of a repository for Platonic forms or ideals, as an allegorical interpretation of human society's futile and frenzied attempts to preserve some sense of order, culture, and history. In exile, powerless and dispossessed, Cavendish must resort to Socratic guile, and generic ruse in order to retain some small degree of control over her work, and obliquely to propagate a partisan voice which spoke contrary to dominant political discourses. The figure of a fictional woman adopting just such a voice is the subject of my next chapter.

Notes

1 George Wither (attrib.), *The Great Assises Holden in Parnassus by Apollo and his Assessors* (1645; repr. Oxford: Luttrell Society/Blackwell, 1948. Wing W3160), pp. 25–6.

2 *Ibid.*, p. 4.

3 *Ibid.*, pp. 30–1.

4 *Ibid.*, pp. 32, 34.

5 *Ibid.*, p. 35.

6 The multipartite nature of Cavendish's title recalls the second act of *Hamlet*, in which the loquacious Polonius announces the arrival of the players: 'The best actors in the world, either for tragedy, comedy, history, pastoral, pastoral-comical, historical-pastoral, tragical-historical, tragical-comical-historical-pastoral, scene individable, or poem unlimited'. Shakespeare, *Hamlet*, ed. Harold Jenkins (London and New York: Routledge, 1982), II.ii. 392–6. The title-page of *Mel Heliconium*, Alexander Rosse's poetical reference book of the early 1640s, is suggestive in its generic inclusivity, too: '*The first Book*: Divided into VII Chapters, according to the first VII Letters of the Alphabet: Containing XLVIII FICTIONS, Out of which are extracted many Historicall, Naturall, Morall, Politicall, and Theologicall Observations, both delightfull and usefull'. See Alexander Rosse, *Mel Heliconium: Or, Poeticall Honey, Gathered Out of the Weeds of Parnassus* (London: L. N. and J. F. for William Leak, 1642. Wing R1962).

7 It is in her *Orations* that Cavendish perhaps most explicitly deals with issues of censorship. One speaker tries to convince the crowds in the market-place of political writings that: 'all such Books should be Burnt, and all such Writers Silenced' apart from state-sanctioned ones. His oratorial adversary argues that such punishment 'may advance their Authors Fame, but not advance the Publick Good'. See Cavendish, *Orations of Divers Sorts* (London, 1662), pp. 63, 66.

8 The historical information in this paragraph is derived from Plato, *The Republic*, ed. Desmond Lee (Harmondsworth: Penguin, 1987), pp. xi–xxii.

9 *Ibid.*, p. xvi.

10 *Ibid.*, p. 98.

11 Cavendish, *Heavens Library, which is Fames Palace purged from Errors and Vices*, in *Natures Pictures*, pp. 357–62 (p. 358). In Milton's *Areopagitica*, a Puritan text concerned with censorship and the social effects of the literary, Plato's 'commonwealth' refers to his *Laws*. Milton writes: 'Plato [was ...] a man of high authority, indeed, but least of all for his commonwealth, in the book of his Laws, which no city ever yet received'. See Gordon Campbell, ed., *John Milton: Complete English Poems* (London: Everyman, 1993), p. 593. It is unclear whether Cavendish is referring to *The Laws* or *The Republic*. Both deal with literary matters, but as the exilic theme is foregrounded in the better-known *Republic*, that is the text I have taken Cavendish to mean. Further, the epigraph to this chapter implies that Wither identified *The Republic* as the 'Common-wealth'.

97

12 John Milton, *De Idea Platonica*, quoted in Irene Samuel, *Plato and Milton* (Ithaca: Cornell University Press, 1965) p. 45. Milton himself went into exile after the Restoration, declaring in 1666 that 'one's country is wherever it is well with one'. See Louis L. Martz, ed., *Poet of Exile: A Study of Milton's Poetry* (New Haven: Yale University Press, 1980), p. 79. Martz identifies a double exile for Milton, occasioned not only by his political exclusion but also by his blindness.

13 See Plato on secondary or literary education, *Republic*, Books II and III. In Book II Socrates declares that 'the worst fault possible' is 'misrepresenting the nature of gods and heroes, like a portrait painter whose portraits bear no resemblance to the originals'. *Ibid.*, p. 73. This comparison of writer with portraitist is echoed in the very title of Cavendish's *Natures Pictures*. On how *Heavens Library* 'anticipates Dryden's "An Essay of Dramatic Poesy" because it is written in the form of a Socratic dialogue', see Philip Bordinat, 'The Duchess of Newcastle as Literary Critic', *The Bulletin of the West Virginia Association of College English Teachers*, 5 (1979), 6–12 (p. 9).

14 Cavendish, *Heavens Library*, p. 361.

15 For an analysis of the political connotations of 'wit' and 'inspiration' in the 1650s and 1660s see Zwicker, pp. 28–34. Here Zwicker identifies, for example, only one appearance of the term 'wit' in Milton's *Paradise Lost*, where it is associated with falsity and deceit. He also sets up in opposition 'the politics and aesthetics of conviviality' and Puritan sobriety. Zwicker, p. 35. In his preface to *Gondibert*, William Davenant discusses '*inspiration*; a dangerous word ... a spirituall Fitt'. See Thomas Hobbes, 'Answer' to Davenant's preface to *Gondibert*, in David F. Gladish, ed., *Sir William Davenant's 'Gondibert'* (Oxford: Clarendon Press, 1971), p. 22. Here Hobbes characterises 'inspiration' as derivative. He describes 'a man enabled to speake wisely from the principles of nature, and his owne meditation', who 'loves rather to be thought to speake by inspiration, like a Bagpipe'. See Hobbes, 'Answer', p. 49.

16 Cavendish, *Heavens Library*, p. 361.

17 *Ibid.*, p. 361.

18 Cavendish writes of keeping 'for Grammer *Lilly*', which could refer to either William Lily, the early sixteenth-century Greek scholar, or, more probably, to John Lyly (1554–1606), poet, and romance and comedy writer. *Ibid.*, p. 359.

19 Cavendish, *Observations*, n.p.

20 Cavendish, *Heavens Library*, p. 357.

21 *Ibid.*, p. 358.

22 *Ibid.*

23 *Ibid.*; Plato, *Republic*, p. 375.

24 Cavendish, *Heavens Library*, pp. 358–9. Cavendish's discussion of the relative merits of astronomers is especially interesting because of her inclusion in 'Fame's Palace' of '*Copernicus, Ticobrach, Ptolomey & Galleleo*'. *Ibid.*, p. 359. She does not indicate that she realises how Ptolemaic astronomy had been overtaken by new methodologies. The absence of such an indication points

either to her desire to depict an ageless hall of fame, or – less likely – to a surprising gap in her erudition.

25 The brevity with which Cavendish dismisses politicians, and her careful classification of them as being quite distinct from orators and law-makers, is a highly politicised authorial action. Implicitly this distinction is damning of the contemporary political situation in England, about which the gods can find nothing positive to say. The act of classification is in itself a political statement. See *ibid.*, pp. 359–60.

26 *Ibid.*, p. 360.

27 *Ibid.*, p. 359.

28 *Ibid.* The vivid image of someone with 'a nose of wax' suggests one who is pliable or complaisant.

29 *Ibid.*, p. 360.

30 This conflation of texts and authors, men and works, suggests much about Cavendish's use of the term 'library'. Socrates, for example, is elected to occupy a place in the library, yet he does not have his own body of texts, other than those mediated by Plato. It is in such a context that that part of the title of *Heavens Library* which refers to *Fames Palace* is informative.

31 Allan H. Gilbert, *Literary Criticism: Plato to Dryden* (Detroit: Wayne State University Press, 1962), p. 582. On de Scudéry's emphasis on '*vraisemblance*' see Lennard Davis, *Factual Fictions: Origins of the English Novel* (New York: Columbia University Press, 1983), p. 28.

32 Cavendish, *Heavens Library*, p. 360.

33 Cavendish, *Natures Pictures*, n.p. For an analysis of the attitude of the heroine of *Assaulted and Pursued Chastity* to romance see Chapter 4, below.

34 Cocking writes of Cavendish's acute dislike for court Platonism, and draws parallels between Mistress Troublesome of *The Lady Contemplation* and the playwright herself. See Cocking, especially Chapter II, 'Platonic Influences and Their Treatment in Margaret's Writing; The Concepts of Love, Fame and Imagination'. However absurd Cavendish thought the incorporeal was in 1662, her ideas were rather revised by 1666, as the 'platonic seraglio' of *New Blazing World* suggests. See Cavendish, *Blazing World*, p. 194.

35 In *The Platonick Lovers*, Buonateste, the physician, tells Sciolto that Plato's own desires were far from purely incorporeal, as he had 'a wench'. He says, 'My Lord, I still beseech you not to wrong / My good friend Plato, with this Court calumny; / They father on him a fantastic love / He never knew, poor gentleman'. Davenant, *The Platonick Lovers* (II, 38), quoted in Howard S. Collins, *The Comedy of Sir William Davenant* (Paris: Mouton, 1967), p. 111. Collins writes of the play, 'Neither supporting the Platonic theory entirely, probably because he himself found it unsympathetic, nor ridiculing it completely because of the Queen's sentimental attitude, Davenant equivocates throughout and thus weakens its dramatic force'. *Ibid.*, p. 109. Also on the subject of Davenant's Platonism see Sophia B. Blaydes and Philip Bordinat, *Sir William Davenant: An Annotated Bibliography 1629–1985* (New York: Garland, 1986), Introduction. For an analysis of the relationship between

Henrietta Maria's Catholicism and her cultivation of a courtly Platonic cult see Veevers.

36 See Allardyce Nicoll, 'The Origin and Types of the Heroic Tragedy', *Anglia*, 44 (1920), 325–36. For the Davenant–Cavendish connection see Grant, *Margaret the First*, pp. 113–15.

37 Gladish, pp. 42–3. In his *Apology*, Sidney makes a similar point, taking care to separate the 'abuse' of poetry from the 'thing' itself. Sidney, *Apology*, pp. 129–30. Plato banished the former, he argues, thereby giving deserved pre-eminence to the latter.

38 Of the dangers of so narrow an interpretation Julia Annas writes that 'there is uncertainty over whether Plato does in the end allow there to be any good, imitative poetry in the ideally just state ... he is very sure what is bad, but less sure about what is good. He is caught between the idea that imitation is all right as long as only morally certified models are imitated, and the idea that there is something morally fishy about imitation as such'. Julia Annas, *An Introduction to Plato's 'Republic'* (Oxford: Clarendon Press, 1981) p. 99.

39 Margaret Anne Doody, *The True Story of the Novel* (London: Harper Collins, 1997), pp. 264–6.

40 *Ibid.*, p. 267.

41 Cavendish, *Heavens Library*, p. 360. That Cavendish's antipathy to *Amadis de Gaule* is politically as well as aesthetically motivated is suggested by a remark made about her husband by Fairfax. Early in 1643 William Cavendish challenged Fairfax to act in a more heroic fashion. 'Lord Fairfax replied by a refusal "to follow the rules of Amadis de Gaule, or the Knight of the Sun, which the language of the declaration seems to affect in offering pitched battles".' See Cavendish, *The Life of William Cavendish, Duke of Newcastle*, ed. C. H. Firth (London: Routledge, n.d.), p. x.

42 See Miguel de Cervantes, *The History of Don Quixote of the Mancha, Translated from the Spanish of Miguel de Cervantes by Thomas Shelton, Annis 1612, 1620*, ed. James Fitzmaurice-Kelly, 4 vols (London: David Nutt, 1896), I, 57.

43 *Ibid.*, p. 59; *Heavens Library*, p. 362.

44 Cervantes, p. 61.

45 *Ibid.*, pp. 62–3. Patterson offers a reading of Cervantes's treatment of and attitude towards the romance genre in *Censorship*, pp. 163–6. She briefly discusses Thomas Shelton's 1612 and 1620 translations of *Don Quixote* into English, and recounts how Ben Jonson's library burned down in 1623, prompting the poet wryly to complain that his lack of engagement with romances, as either a reader or a writer, should have spared his books. See *Ibid.*, p. 166.

46 Cavendish, *Heavens Library*, pp. 360–1.

47 William Cavendish, *Advice*, ed. Strong, p. 179. See also Thomas P. Slaughter, ed., *Ideology and Politics on the Eve of the Restoration: Newcastle's Advice to Charles II* (Philadelphia: American Philosophical Society, 1984). Slaughter dates the *Advice* to 1658–59.

48 Gladish, p. 39.

49 Cavendish, *Heavens Library*, p. 360.

50 *Ibid.*, p. 361.

51 Cavendish's description of Ovid's 'curious intermixing and ... subtill inter-weaving of ... severall discourses, Theams, Arguments, or Transmigrations' echoes Ovid's own characterisation of his style and purpose in writing *Metamorphoses*, as 'to tell of bodies which have been transformed into shapes of a different kind. You heavenly powers ... spin an unbroken thread of verse'. See *ibid.*; Ovid, *Metamorphoses*, ed. and trans. Innes, p. 29.

52 Cavendish, *Heavens Library*, p. 361. Presumably, too, Cavendish could not condone the banishment of Ovid, himself a poet and victim of involuntary exile.

53 Horace's proportion and balance would have appealed to the dispossessed royalist exiles seeking to make sense of a disordered world. For the importance to the sequestered Cavaliers of Virgil's pastoral writing, and its influence on Walton's *Compleat Angler*, see Zwicker, pp. 60–89.

54 Cavendish, similarly alienated by contemporary politics, also sets her tales in a pre-Interregnum, halcyon time. *The Symposium* was written after 385 BC; the drinking party which is its focus has been dated to about 416 BC, and the Apollodorus narration is set c. 400 BC. See introduction to Plato, *The Symposium*, ed. Walter Hamilton (Harmondsworth: Penguin, 1951), pp. 9–10.

55 Cavendish, *Natures Pictures*, p. 1. Another possible model for the narrative structure of this part of *Natures Pictures* is Boccaccio's *Decameron*, where the story-tellers are exiled from the Florentine plague. Chaucer's *Canterbury Tales* are also evoked. Both men and women speak in each text. It must, however, be remembered that in Plato's text a woman, Diotima, does effectively speak and, in her explication of the concept of universal Forms, is constructed as both articulate and intelligent. It has been commented upon that the frontispiece to the 1656 edition of *Natures Pictures* represents the company seated around the fire in its first book and has political and autobiographical significance for Cavendish. See Fitzmaurice, 'Fancy and the Family', pp. 198–209.

56 Cavendish, *Natures Pictures*, p 1; Plato, *Symposium*, p. 53. Such interruptions of the narrative flow are integral to the overall aporetic structure of *The Symposium*, and the hiccups anticipate Alciblades' drunken intrusion later in the text. As he is invited by the company to offer his own narrative to the proceedings, so too in Cavendish's text there enters '*a Lady young, that had not been / In that Society*'. Cavendish, *Natures Pictures*, p. 67. This character prefaces her 'Tale of the four Seasons of the Year' with a short passage about representative art. She declares that that which the imagination conjures forth is '*Lifes Quintessence*', and is immortal. *Ibid.*, p. 67. This analysis of mimetic art appears to reinterpret the Platonic notion of permanent Forms which Diotima articulates, and which, in their supreme immutability, can only ever be approximated.

57 *Ibid.*, p. 2.

58 Plato, *Republic*, Book X. This is described as 'the fountainhead' in Paul Hernadi, *Beyond Genre: New Directions in Literary Classification* (Ithaca:

Cornell University Press, 1972), p. 153. Hernadi proposes a fourth category to encompass 'discourse in which poet and character speak simultaneously or, more precisely, in which the narrator says *in propria persona* what one of the characters means'. Hernadi, *Beyond Genre*, p. 192.

59 Cavendish, *Natures Pictures*, p. 1. The women's avowals of poetic inadequacy, almost immediately refuted by the competence of their subsequent contributions, mirror Cavendish's own prefatory humilities.

60 One such couplet reads: 'For gallant Sword-men that do fight in War, / Do never use their Tongues to make a jar'. *Ibid.*, p. 10.

61 Sandra Sherman regards such univocality as a result 'of [Cavendish's] ... particular project: the creation of an absolute, unassailable self'. See Sandra Sherman, 'Trembling Texts: Margaret Cavendish and the Dialectic of Authorship', *English Literary Renaissance*, 24 (1994), 184–210 (p. 199). Sherman regards the 'self' Cavendish projects as predominantly discursive or textual, exploring how: 'The inescapable irony is that this creator of an absolute self ultimately desires to be known as a text'. *Ibid.*, p. 206.

62 This is not to suggest that the first book of *Natures Pictures* has not previously been read as political or autobiographical. James Fitzmaurice offers, for example, an analysis of the frontispiece to the Huntington Library copy of the 1656 edition of *Natures Pictures*, in which he interprets as political the assembly round the fire, and identifies in the ambiguity of the act of the figure opening or closing the window, a comment on the Royalist experience of retreat during the Interregnum. James Fitzmaurice, 'Frontispieces, Prefaces, and Commendatory Verses in Books by Margaret Cavendish' (unpublished paper presented to the Margaret Cavendish Reading Group, Gonville and Caius College, Cambridge University, spring 1996).

63 Cavendish, *Natures Pictures*, p. 88. There are two subsequent poems, but they are both clearly attributed to William Cavendish. At the end of Plato's *Symposium* it is perhaps significant that Socrates' discourse has also changed to a new theme. Suggestively, he is addressing issues of literary genre as day breaks. Plato, *The Symposium*, p. 113.

64 Cavendish, *Natures Pictures*, p. 88.

65 *Ibid.*, p. 89.

66 *Ibid.*

67 *Ibid.*, pp. 91–2. 'The Loyall Sacrifice' was an anonymous royalist pamphlet, attributed to 'Philocrates', and circulated in 1648. Tom Hodgson of Colchester Museum, Essex, believes it may be by Sir John Berkenhead. An original copy is held in the Thomason Tracts at the British Library. The pamphlet's cover engraving depicts Sir Charles Lucas prostrate, with Sir George Lisle facing the firing squad, declaring 'Shoot Rebells. Your Shott, your shame / Our fall, our fame.' 'The Loyall Sacrifice', cover. Cavendish's poem echoes this in the lines: 'His Light of Honour out, but pow'rfull Fame / Did throw their spight back on their heads with shame'. Cavendish, *Natures Pictures*, p. 91. For the attribution to 'Philocrates' see Roger Hudson, ed., *The Grand Quarrel: From the Civil War Memoirs of Mrs Lucy Hutchinson ... [and] Margaret, Duchess of Newcastle* (London: The Folio Society, 1993), p. viii.

68 Cavendish, *Natures Pictures*, p. 92.

69 *Ibid.*, p. 93.

70 *Ibid.*

71 *Ibid.*, p. 287.

72 These remarks come from Cavendish's opening epistles to her readers. *Ibid.*, sigs c3v-r. In his '*To the Lady Marchioness of* NEWCASTLE, *on her Book of Tales*', William Cavendish too makes the claim that, because of the virtuous content of the work, 'A Vestal Nun may reade this, and avow it, / And a *Carthusian* Confessor allow it'. *Ibid.*, sig. br.

73 It is in these same avowals that Cavendish clearly states her mimetic intent. As has been demonstrated, however, mimesis operates as a thin veil for polemic in much of *Natures Pictures*. Further, the idea that the text is 'DRAWN ... TO THE LIFE', must be reinterpreted in the light of texts, such as *Assaulted and Pursued Chastity*, set in fantastic lands, or in mythical times.

74 *Ibid.*, p. 289.

75 Ten years later, in her *Blazing World*, Cavendish reverses this situation: the Empress does not dispense advice, but experts from the societies of virtuosi come to her to answer her queries.

76 Cavendish, *Natures Pictures*, p. 290.

77 *Ibid.*, p. 293.

78 MacCarthy, p. 131.

79 Denise Riley, '*Am I that name?*' *Feminism and the Category of 'Women' in History* (Basingstoke: Macmillan, 1988), p. 26.

80 Cavendish, *Natures Pictures*, p. 393.

81 *Ibid.*, p. 393. The work to which Cavendish refers is *Philosophical and Physical Opinions*.

82 Cavendish, *Heavens Library*, p. 358. Socrates' critique of the weaknesses of mimesis is clear. In Book X of *The Republic* he declares that 'representative art is an inferior child born of inferior parents'. Plato, *The Republic*, p. 371.

83 This desire for input continues even once the book has been printed; in the copy of the 1656 edition I studied there were frequent hand written emendations, probably by Cavendish herself. An additional, presumably unintentional, irony occurs at the end of the volume in Cavendish's complaint about the carelessness of printers, '*A Complaint and Request to the Noble and Learned Readers of my several Works*'. Those pages of the complaint which should fall on '403' and '404' are mistakenly printed as being on '387' and '390'. Sherman examines the mundanity of the process of printing necessitated by Cavendish's 'messy penmanship', and the relation of this to a 'pressure toward textuality' which also has the non-physical motivation of a desire for fame. Sherman, 'Trembling Texts', p. 198.

84 Cavendish, *Poems, and Fancies*, p. 148.

85 *Ibid.*, p. 196.

4

Travellia's travails:
Homeric motifs in
Assaulted and Pursued Chastity

History, if it be simuliseing, and distinguishing, it is pure poetry, if it be a lie made from truth it is Romancy. (Margaret Cavendish, 'What Romancy is', *The Worlds Olio* (1655), p. 9)

Ye now fare all like exiles, not a mirth
Flasht in amongst ye but is quencht againe.[1]

So Circe, exemplar of the tension between terror and desire, addresses Ulysses and his men. Goddess and sorceress, she wields a terrifying power, rendering men powerless by denying them their very humanity. A paradigmatically opposite but no less complex Homeric woman, Penelope, is a key focus in this chapter. What did George Chapman's translation of Homer (1614–15) suggest to Margaret Cavendish? How did she rework his ideas about exile, leaving on them her idiosyncratic and culturally daring mark?

To begin to answer such questions one might first turn to a sixteenth-century Dutch broadsheet which depicts in a series of woodcuts the preposterous consequences for a society where cultural norms have been inverted; where the world has been turned upside down.[2] It is a world where monarchs go by foot, and children beat their parents; where the sighted are led by the blind, and fish nest in the high branches of trees. Cavendish's own familiarity with this inversion trope is apparent in her poem, '*The* Ruine *of the* Island':

To *Parents Children* unnat'rally grow,
And *former Friend-ship* now's turn'd cruell *Foe.*

For *Innocency* no *Protection* had,
Religious Men were thought to be *stark mad*.[3]

Amongst the broadsheet's tableaux of the unthinkable is a scene inscribed 'Het wyf trect na de krych', or, 'The woman marches to war'.[4] A woman is standing, laden with weapons. She faces her seated husband, from between whose legs rises a distaff. Her stance is active, even aggressive; his is passive and domesticated, as he has been emasculated by the symbol of culturally inscribed femininity, the distaff. That this scenario is to be read as inherently grotesque and unnatural is made apparent by its presence in a world where ships go by land, and oxen drive their masters.

By the sixteenth century the association of needlecraft with a passive femininity was thus deeply ingrained into the popular consciousness. The interconnection had connotations for women's sexuality because of the metonymic relationship irrevocably forged by the Classical exemplar of the famously chaste weaver, Penelope. In Cavendish's exilic work, through an adroit manipulation of domestic images connected with varieties of needlework, she negotiated her position as a writing woman. Central to these passages and arguably to much of her overall project is this motif of the virtuous Homeric Penelope. A reading of Cavendish's evocations of Penelope divulges how the author skilfully and pragmatically redefined notions of gender and femininity so that her act of publication should seem acceptable, even socially *desirable*, rather than monstrous and transgressive. Cavendish's publications extirpate the 'silently' from Gilbert and Gubar's declaration that 'like Ariadne, Penelope, and Philomela, women have used their looms, thread, and needles both to defend themselves and silently to speak of themselves'.[5]

In *Assaulted and Pursued Chastity* Cavendish creates a dynamic fusion of epic and romance with the specific intention of taking from the former genre attributes for her heroine, Travellia, which are associated with masculinity, public action and oratory. Her simultaneous maintenance of a romance discourse, however, allows the same heroine to retain characteristics which are conventionally regarded as desirably feminine (such as chastity), whilst aspiring towards an epic heroism and morality. Crucially, it is in her manipulation of genre that Cavendish pragmatically and imaginatively reworks the cultural concept of feminine virtue. This process is exemplified by the character of Travellia, and by Cavendish's writerly self-characterisation too.

That it was the epic genre's emphasis on this virtue and moral worth which was important to Cavendish is made clear in the intensely didactic prologue to *Assaulted and Pursued Chastity*. 'In this following tale', Cavendish writes, 'my endeavour was to show young women the danger of travelling without their parents ... to guard them'.[6] The universe she proposes is one wherein 'Heaven' takes care of those whose chastity is threatened through events over which they have no control, leaving those who find themselves in danger because of their own 'ignorance, indiscretion, or curiosity' to their own fate.[7] Cavendish's final assertion in the prologue, that 'those are in particular favoured with Heaven, that are protected from violence and scandal, in a wandering life, or a travelling condition', may be read as an audacious piece of self-aggrandisement, since, given the evidence provided in her autobiography in the same volume, this is how she typifies her own, exilic existence.[8] In some sense she understood herself to be an epic hero, a construction which, as will be shown, was doomed to ultimate failure.[9]

On a personal level, then, the epic genre presents Cavendish with a medium for the expression of a longing for the empowerment of the dispossessed, recalling in its narrative structure something of the contingent *fatum* which characterised her own life. Her heroine, part Penelope, part Ulysses, stands to justify Cavendish's self-characterisation as writer whose repeated emphasis, in her story, on natural leadership may be read as signalling her support for monarchical rule. Homeric epic, specifically as delineated in *The Odyssey*, provides for Cavendish not so much a literary form (she is writing in prose, not verse) as a set of identifiable literary characteristics which she plunders and reinvents. This is the case with *Assaulted and Pursued Chastity*, wherein Cavendish evokes Homeric topoi in the creation of a female protagonist who both encompasses and subverts the heroic discourses of *The Odyssey*.[10] The topoi which facilitate this literary manoeuvre are, in ways which will be shown later in this chapter, gendered, and the protagonist Travellia's complex interactions with them register her oscillation between the two polarities of masculine and feminine activity. This oscillation, however, functions expressly to protect a specifically female notion of sexual chastity exemplified by Penelope. There is, further, a twist in Cavendish's tale. Travellia's climactic failure to conform to the Homeric topos of the homecoming, an event which traditionally reasserts gendered roles, functions to dissociate chastity from domesticity (that is, Penelope from the loom), in a way which has repercussions for Cavendish as author. Through her generic manipulations of the nebulous boundary between epic and romance, Cavendish portrays a character, Travellia, who is chaste *without* being confined to the loom.

The cultural elision of needlework with the ostensibly passive, virtuous femininity which finds its ideal in Penelope is etymologically reinforced; is 'inculcated not innate'.[11] Cavendish effects and exploits the possibilities of a discursive shift which, in the broadest terms, may be characterised as a move from needle to pen. As late as the nineteenth century the word *work* used in the context of women's lives refers almost invariably to 'needlework'. Further, that potent symbol, the *distaff*, being a staff on to which flax or wool was wound, by extension also came to refer to the female sex.[12] The Latin verb *texere* means 'to weave', and from this derive both *textile* and *text*; it is here that Cavendish identifies and seizes upon an opportunity to execute a literary transition from the occupation of needlework, or the creation of textiles, to the occupation of writing, that is, the creation of a text. She negotiates the reductively dichotomous anti-thetical relationship of the 'masculine' pen and the 'conventional' needle. It is predominantly in her subversive use of the figure of Penelope that she makes this negotiation appear natural and justifiable.[13] The symbolism with which I shall argue Cavendish invests Penelope contradicts Cecilia Macheski's insistence that textual representation of the activity of needlework should not be read as 'a classical allusion, with little or no concern with realism'.[14] Cavendish's treatment of Penelope refutes Macheski's assertion that such symbolism is the preserve of 'male writers', who 'almost always' use it 'as an allusion, or a symbol'.[15]

There is in *Assaulted and Pursued Chastity*, then, a radical interpretation of Penelope and her relationship with Ulysses, which may be read as a further step in a process of self-characterisation which Cavendish began in *Poems, and Fancies*.[16] A brief exploration of her attitude to Penelope in that work may explain in part the importance for Cavendish of resisting a straightforward identification of Travellia with Penelope in *Assaulted and Pursued Chastity*. In her epistle 'To Poets' in *Poems, and Fancies*, Cavendish expresses apparently conventional anxieties about her first incursion into print, and attempts to stave off adverse criticism, or the parody of 'Poets Satyrs, *and their* Faiery Wits'.[17] The discourse she employs in her defence is expressly domestic. '*I hope you will spare me*', she writes, '*for the* harth *is swept cleane, and a* Bason *of* water *with a* cleane Towell *set by, and the* Ashes *rake'd up*'.[18] Within, and precisely because of the existence of, this spruce homely setting, the author's desire is that her 'harmlesse Bookes rest' may be undisturbed.[19] Significantly, the discursive realm into which the author would be forced by unfavourable comments about her publication is masculine. She constructs her eloquence as being restricted to domestic discourses, so, in an imagined courtroom scenario, she would be rendered inarticulate and defenceless. '*I have*', she complains, '*no* Eloquent Orator *to plead for me, as to perswade a* Severe Judge', explicitly equating oratory with public agency.[20] Desirous of appearing non-threatening, the woman writer's assurance is that, should she transgress cultural delimitations of the feminine, she would be impotent.

However, Cavendish's self-identification, later in the same epistle, with Penelope, arguably attenuates this eloquent self-abasement. '*'Tis true*', she writes:

> *my* Verses *came not out of* Jupiters Head, *therefore they cannot prove a* Pallas: *yet they are like* Chast Penelope's Work, *for I wrote them in my* Husbands absence, *to delude* Melancholy Thoughts, *and avoid* Idle Time.[21]

Cavendish's construction of Penelope is neither as conventional nor as anodyne as it may, upon a first reading, appear. The explicit point of comparison being established between Cavendish and Penelope in this epistle is that each maintained her chastity whilst apart from her husband, her main means of doing so being writing in Cavendish's case, weaving in Penelope's. By ostensibly aligning her writing with Penelope's weaving, Cavendish is assuring her audience that her sexual chastity will not be threatened by her publication of her work (one might recall at this point Stansby's 'illustrious whore'). Penelope, however, as this quotation suggests, is not an entirely unproblematic exemplar of female passivity and chastity, and underlying Cavendish's construction of her is a trace of pragmatic deceit. This is implicit in her use of the ambiguous words 'Work', and '*delude*', and the evocation of Pallas, the goddess who, in Homer's *Odyssey*, was responsible for Ulysses' disguise upon his return to Ithaca. Penelope, then, functions not simply as a paragon of passive female domesticity but as a motif of ingenuity and initiative.[22] Like Penelope, Cavendish recognises the potential of the loom as metaphor for self-expression, self-preservation and the singularity of a woman with imagination and the artistic ability to exploit it.[23]

An examination of the edition of *The Odyssey* available to Cavendish, George Chapman's translation of 1614–15, suggests how she formed this individual and ultimately eminently serviceable interpretation of the figure of Penelope.[24] That Chapman's Penelope possesses a strength which resides in her intellect rather than in her body is repeatedly emphasised, perhaps most clearly in Book Four. The unruly suitors who have taken over Ulysses' house in his absence, led by Antinous, determine to set sail from Ithaca in pursuit of Telemachus, Penelope's son, who has gone in search of his father. Their departure is detailed in a dispassionate, technical way, symptomatic of Homeric delimitations of masculine activity and decisiveness:

> All hasted, reacht the ship, lancht, raisd the mast,
> Put sailes in, and with leather loopes made fast
> The oares, Sailes hoisted.[25]

This account is intercalary, appearing between two passages which centre on Penelope. In the first she shrieks and offers up a prayer to Pallas to protect Telemachus. The second passage describes her retreat to her chamber and refusal to eat or drink because her 'strong thoughts wrought so on her blamelesse sonne'.[26] Penelope's heightened emotions, her bodily debility and her confinement, stand in stark contrast to the very physical, out-of-doors activity of Antinous and his men.

This is not the first episode in *The Odyssey* where Penelope has had to have recourse to emotional, rather than bodily powers. In the second book Antinous denies that the unruliness of the suitors is their fault, instead blaming Penelope, and calling her 'first in craft', an ambiguous epithet pertaining both to her needlecraft and to her cunning, and one which perhaps recalls Cavendish's use of the word 'Work'.[27] He reports how Penelope pleaded that she must finish weaving Laertes' shroud before choosing a new husband, and of her attendant three-year-long deceit in unravelling each night that day's weaving. Even the duped Antinous cannot fully conceal his admiration for Penelope's ingenuity. No other woman, he states, compares '(For solide braine) with wise Penelope'.[28] Her actions for three years appeared as those of a dutiful daughter-in-law, but the consequence of her subterfuge was that, by not completing the shroud, she was actually preserving her chastity. Her deceit, then, operated not as a transgressive force but rather as one which reaffirmed patriarchal demands on a woman's sexuality.

In her presentation of herself as writer Cavendish too plays off appearance against actuality. Whilst she compares herself expressly with 'chast Penelope' in the epistle 'To Poets' in *Poems, and Fancies* and adopts an explicitly domestic discourse, by contrast, in the dedicatory epistle to Charles Cavendish, she continues that discourse whilst intentionally characterising herself as unable to perform domestic activities. Charles's 'Bounty *hath been the* Distaffe' for the threads of *Poems, and Fancies*, a project which, through a sustained conceit, the author characterises as akin to a spinster's respectable, domestic endeavours.[29] Dressed in Charles's patronal mantle, Cavendish may go about the production of her own 'Garment *of* Memory', the manufacture of which is represented as being implicitly similar to the '*more proper*' feminine activity of 'Spinning *with the* Fingers'. This spinning is carefully differentiated from, and yet importantly comparable with '*studying or writing* Poetry, *which is the* Spinning *with the* braine: *but* I', she continues:

> *having no skill in the* Art *of the* first (*and if* I *had*, I *had no hopes of gaining so much as to make me a* Garment *to keep me from the* cold) *made me delight in the* latter; *since all* braines *work naturally, and incessantly, in some kinde or other; which made me endeavour to Spin a* Garment *of* Memory, *to lapp up my* Name, *that it might grow to after* Ages: I *cannot say the* Web *is* strong, fine, *or evenly Spun, for it is a* Course *peice; yet* I *had rather my* Name *should go* meanly clad, *then* dye *with* cold.[30]

Cavendish's writing is characterised as the natural, almost inevitable, consequence, of having an active imagination which might turn to less proper thoughts and activities if not occupied. Her rhetoric has transformed writing into a respectable pursuit for a woman, and the implication is that it operates with the same force, and to the same ends, as weaving did for Penelope.

Cavendish, fully aware of Penelope's articulate and paradigmatic possession of both wile and virtue, has adopted Homer's figure and rewritten her to function in defence of her writing, not ordinarily conceived of as a domestic activity in the same way as needle-craft.[31] This redefinition of chastity (exemplified by Penelope) and domesticity (here extended to include writing) is central to Cavendish's construction of the character of Travellia in *Assaulted and Pursued Chastity*, a work which is ostensibly a romance but which exploits epic generic characteristics. Travellia rejects domesticity in favour of epic-heroic activities but simultaneously maintains her chastity like a romance heroine.

One might accord with W. T. H. Jackson's assertion that 'epics spring from violent social disturbance, when patterns of civilization of long standing are being challenged or overturned', and so regard it as logical that, for her fifth published volume, and in her twelfth year of exile, Cavendish should turn to epic as a genre suited to her contingent life.[32] Furthermore, Cavendish's literary model was 'the exile work of all exile works', Homer's *Odyssey*.[33] Having, in her first published work, *Poems, and Fancies*, used Lucretian modes of presentation, and having produced a suggestive interpretation of the figure of Penelope, Cavendish returned to classical paradigms in *Assaulted and Pursued Chastity*.[34] What, then, was the literary tradition with which Cavendish engaged?

The text which arguably defined the concerns of English epic in the late sixteenth and early seventeenth centuries was Spenser's *Faerie Queene*, itself influenced by Ariosto's *Orlando Furioso*.[35] Spenser's apparent redirection of heroic energies from personal, romantic love to a quest for civic revivification opened the way for epic to become a useful vehicle for the expression of political sympathies of all persuasions, and Tasso, in his *Discorsi ... del poema eroica*, recognised the didactic propagandist power an exemplary epic might possess, as he characterised readers 'seek[ing] to shape their own spirit after that example'.[36] In *Gerusalemme liberata* he produced a text which placed an emphasis on historical fact but permitted an admixture of fiction. The mongrel *genera mista* thus began to be legitimised as the seriousness of historical narrative and the imagination of poetry combined into epic romance. Jacques Amyot's Renaissance Heliodoran romance *L'Histoire aethiopique* has been identified as central to seventeenth-century conceptions of the genre.[37] It is this Heliodoran model which seems to have offered much to Cavendish, with, as Annabel Patterson expresses it, its emphasis on: 'the survival of chaste and faithful love in the face of all odds; wild adventure and coincidence in an uncivilized environment, where piracy and shipwreck symbolized human and natural anarchy'.[38]

By the mid-seventeenth century Edmund Waller, author of the *Panegyrick to my Lord Protector*, had recognised the political expediency of the epic genre, and Thomas May's allegiances had shifted to republicanism following his translation of Lucan's *Pharsalia*.[39] In Cavendish's immediate circle Lucan's text was interpreted rather differently by Cowley, whose *Civil War* and *Davideis* placed contemporary characters within an epic idiom, and Davenant's *Gondibert*, itself virtually a *roman à clef*, exploited still further the malleability of the genre in its examination of the tensions between love and civic duty.[40] Indeed, Cowley, in his comparison of the death in 1643 of the young Charles Cavendish with that of Virgil's Pallas, brought partisan rewriting of epic right into Cavendish's family circle.[41] Margaret Cavendish's adoption of the genre of Greek epic is as eclectic and idiosyncratic as her experimental forays into other forms, such as Platonic dialogue or Lucretian verse, have been shown to be, and so her use of earlier genres is not as accurate or as complete as, for example, Virgil's use of Homer, where the later writer constrains his material into boundaries set by the original.[42] Her *Assaulted and Pursued Chastity*, whilst ultimately showing a woman in a position of considerable civic power, does simultaneously favour a victory of romantic love over aspirational, occupying a generic position between epic and romance.

The full title of *Natures Pictures* (the text where *Assaulted and Pursued Chastity* is located), where generic styles as apparently diverse as '*Tragi-Comical, Poetical, Romancical, Philosophical, and Historical*' are advertised, is overtly inclusive, but 'epic' is not included. Such descriptive subgenres as these may, in Cavendish's mind, all be concatenated under an umbrella concept of 'epic'. Certainly, Homer's poems contain tragi-comic, poetic, philosophical and historical elements, as well as incorporating fundamentals of romance. As with her smooth conjunction of poetry and science in *Poems, and Fancies*, Cavendish may, as she wrote *Natures Pictures*, have been intimating that she did not believe clear distinctions to exist between, for example, historical and epic narrative.[43] One implication of this generic fluidity is that for a narrative to contain identifiably 'romancical' elements was a quite different thing from a text being categorically 'a romance'. This is evinced by the presence of romance elements in *Assaulted and Pursued Chastity*, which, paradoxically, frame Cavendish's protagonist's distinctly articulated disdain for romances. 'Will you have some romances[?]' one character asks of the heroine, who 'answered no, for they extoll virtue so much as begets an envy, in those that have it not'.[44]

The romance form was extremely fluid in the mid-seventeenth century. Works such as Barclay's *Argenis*, in their historical emphasis, moved the genre of romance away from the fantastic worlds of its chivalric and pastoral antecedents. Patterson goes so far as to describe the discourse which emerged as being 'the Protectorate genre'.[45] The new emphasis on probability and seriousness meant that the genre could, for the exiled royalists, share the positive political role of epic. Cotterell's 1652 version of De la Calprenède's *Cassandre*, for example, encouraged the reader to make direct links with 'the afflicted estate of his Royal Family in exile and Captivity', and the 1653 anonymous royal romance *Cloria and Narcissus* appears to have been written by a royalist exile.[46] *Assaulted and Pursued Chastity* may be read as a text perched on the threshold between epic and romance, for in the combination of Travellia's engagement with Classical topoi, and her romance characteristics, a quite deliberate composite of the genres emerges. How, then, did this composite redefine feminine virtue?

Three epic topoi feature most prominently in *Assaulted and Pursued Chastity*. The first is the topos of the storm and consequent shipwreck. *The Odyssey* is punctuated repeatedly by episodes of this nature which function largely to define a particularly masculine heroism and sphere of activity. Ulysses' resistance of the sirens' song, recounted in the twelfth book, is facilitated by his being tied to 'th'erected Mast' of his vessel, as though the very body of the ship were intrinsically bound up with his honour and virtue.[47] By contrast, mortal women are figured within the confines of dry land where their physical passivity is underscored by their engagement in altogether less life-threatening activities. Mastery of the waves is metonymy for successful rule, and the ability to build strong ships functions as a barometer of a civilisation's accomplishments. The second central topos is that of story-telling, or, put more brutally, mendacity.[48] *The Odyssey* is a thoroughly palimpsestic text, where much of the action is either interrupted by digressions or is reported in narrative flash-backs. Ulysses himself frequently lies about his identity which, in turn, is often defined in terms of his responses to others' tales. His tears in the Phaeacian court as 'the divine Expressor', Demodocus, sings of the Trojan wars indicate the emotive possibilities of reported speech.[49] Unlike seafaring, story-telling is an exercise which is not restricted to male characters, and it is its implications for, and uses by, female characters, particularly Penelope, which are central to this discussion. Female guile and eloquence function in *The Odyssey* as coterminous with circumscriptively feminine activities such as weaving. In turn, these activities metonymically represent female sexual chastity.

The third topos which is under consideration here is that of the homecoming. The drive of *The Odyssey* is towards Ulysses' return to Ithaca in the thirteenth book, but narrative resolution cannot come about until he is recognised by Penelope in the twenty-third. Disguised by Pallas, Ulysses' self-revelation is protracted further by his deliberate misinformation.[50] Whilst Penelope's slowness in recognising him as her husband is attributable to this, it could also be read as a response to the implications for her of his return home. For Penelope the homecoming necessitates a relinquishment of the power and self-rule she has commanded during his absence.[51] The loom she returns to is once again the site of a specifically feminine activity, its instrumental role in her discursively cunning preservation of her chastity having paid off, but also having come to an end.

Read, then, in the context of the topoi of the ship in the storm, story-telling and the homecoming, the audacity of Cavendish's heroine, Travellia, may be better understood.[52] A text which is ostensibly about a woman as victim of assault and pursuit, becomes a text about a woman with agency who preserves her chastity through her own initiative. Travellia is at once Ulysses and Penelope, active and chaste. Cavendish's failure to stage a homecoming (in a traditional sense) for her heroine signifies her reluctance to have her subsumed back into an orthodox domestic setting where her considerable powers would have to be given up.

By not returning to her native Kingdom of Riches, Travellia does not have to yield the Ulysses part of herself and become all Penelope. Cavendish instead stages a bold compromise, settling her heroine in a new land. She writes:

114

> Then there was a declaration read to the army of the agreement of
> peace: and when it was read that the Prince should be Viceroy in the
> Kingdom of Amity, all the soldiers, as if they had been one voice, cried
> out, Travellia shall be Viceregency; which was granted to pacify them.
> Whereupon there were great acclamations of joy.
> But the Prince told his mistress, she should also govern him.
> She answered, that he should govern her, and she would govern the
> kingdom.[53]

The brazenness here of Travellia's answer is significant, and the set
of circumstances she has been instrumental in bringing about point
to her as the only natural choice of ruler. This is a romantic attach-
ment underpinned by Travellia's awareness that her husband's
government of her is purely nominal, since she possesses the real
power, which resides in the support she enjoys from the populace
and militia.[54] In effect, her statement that 'he should govern her'
signifies less an assumption of a position of submission than a kindly,
and ultimately insignificant, concession. As did Penelope, so Travellia
employs her intellectual resources in order to preserve her chastity,
but significantly unlike Penelope, marriage does not mean powerlessness, as Travellia resists coming home to the loom. Exposed to
the suitors by her maids, the Homeric Penelope's intellectual scam
is brought to an end, and her autonomy is further circumscribed by
her husband's return to rule. Travellia's defence of her chastity in
Assaulted and Pursued Chastity, however, entails a more permanent
self-determination. The writer's adoption of classical topoi functions
to signal that Travellia is to be understood as a hero in Homeric
terms, choosing romantic love whilst simultaneously demonstrating
the capacity to rule.[55] In her manipulation and metamorphosing of
her characters' identities, Cavendish functions like Homer's Pallas,
and the character hitherto referred to as Travellia in fact began
Assaulted and Pursued Chastity under the name of Miseria, 'a Lady . . .
enriched by nature with virtue, wit and beauty'.[56]

The hapless victim of civil wars in her native Kingdom of Riches,
Miseria has been in exile. Her return home, however, is frustrated
by a storm, her ship landing instead on the shores of the Kingdom
of Sensuality where she is sold 'to a bawd, which used to merchan-
dise, and trafficked to the land of youth, for the riches of beauty'.[57]
The narrative rhythm being established is already a familiarly
Homeric one. The tale opens, as does *The Odyssey*, *in media res*, past

wars having already taken place and having changed the protagonists' lives, setting them on the long journey home by sea, a journey which functions metaphorically as one towards maturation and social reintegration.[58] Both Ulysses and Miseria take with them on their travels something which must at all costs be protected, being rightful rule in Ulysses' case, chastity in Miseria's. The rhythm of the epic, which from the outset is established by the topos of the ship in the storm, is one of a movement from danger, to escape, to danger, to stasis, and back again.[59] The protagonists' encounters along the way are what define them or what, for Miseria, radically redefine her in terms of gender and identity.

The bawd prepares Miseria for the sexual attentions of 'a subject Prince of that country, which was a grand monopolizer of young virgins'.[60] The threat to Miseria's chastity is, significantly, figured in terms of the nautical motif. Loss of chastity would be 'a shipwreck' for Miseria, and the concomitant fear 'drove her from one end of the room to the other, like a ship at sea, that is not anchored nor ballasted, or with storm tossed from point to point, so was she'.[61] The figuring of Miseria's thoughts using language from this masculine sphere of activity prepares the way for Miseria's first proactive, phallic action, the obtaining of a pistol and the shooting of her assailant, which in turn marks another step towards her becoming the predominantly Ulyssean Travellia. Miseria is imprisoned at the house of the wounded prince's aunt, where her masculine erudition is displayed through the two women's discussions. 'I learn', declares Miseria, 'all arts useful and pleasant for the life of man, as music, architecture, navigation, fortification, water-works, fire-works, all engines, instruments, wheels and many such like, which are useful'.[62] Significantly absent from Miseria's list of accomplishments are archetypally feminine activities such as needlework. She tells her convivial gaoler the story of the circumstances which led to her present predicament. This lengthy passage of reported speech does not add to the reader's previous knowledge of Miseria's background but serves as Ulysses' digressive accounts do throughout *The Odyssey*, rather to remind, and to reinforce already articulated ideas. The retrospective narrative facilitates the movement forward of the present one, and the epic generic model for this vindicates what might otherwise have been perceived as bad, repetitious writing.[63]

The character of Miseria oscillates between being able to be identified with Penelope as the victim of repeated attempts at seduction, and with Ulysses. Both Penelope and Ulysses use story-telling to aid them in their respective predicaments. Unlike Penelope, however, Miseria does not have the loom to protect her, and it is from the empathy which her recital evoked in the prince's aunt that her opportunity for escape comes. Miseria poisons herself, and, once recovered, is helped by the aunt to disguise herself as a page boy, and thus gain entry into the masculine realm of a ship, which departs the Kingdom of Sensuality. Like Ulysses, Miseria's eloquence has helped her receive *philoxenia*, friendliness shown to strangers, and it is this which sets her on her way to her next adventure, and to her reinvention as Travellia.[64]

On board the ship Miseria once more recounts her adventures, 'only she fained she was a youth, and had served her lady as her page'.[65] This narrative deceit moves the ship's captain, too, to a demonstration of *philoxenia*, and she is permitted to stay, eventually becoming his adoptive son.[66] The reader is first acquainted with the heroine's new name, Travellia, as the ship is wrecked in a storm. Cavendish writes:

> Fortune playing her usual tricks, to set men up on high hopes, and then to cast them down to ruin, irritated the gods against them ... which caused them to raise a great storm, making the clouds and seas to meet ... the anchor was lost, the rudder was broke, the masts were split, the sails all torn, the ship did leak, their hopes were gone ... Travellia (for so now she called herself) followed close her old new father.[67]

The scene, and the four-line verse which follows it, are distinctly Homeric, recalling Ulysses' encounter with Scylla and Charybdis.[68] In Chapman's version the terrified crew are powerless, 'strugling they lay beneath [Scylla's ...] violent rape', but those who survive find themselves in 'the Ile Triangulare', apparently a place of rest and plenty.[69] However, Circe had warned them not to kill the 'Oxen of the Sunne' which live there.[70] This warning ignored, the period of stasis is abruptly ended, Jove's wrath leading to another shipwreck of which Ulysses is the sole survivor.[71] This same narrative rhythm characterises Travellia's adventures, where she and the ship's captain are the only survivors of the wreck.[72]

Cavendish's accent on the topos of the shipwreck may be understood as having a specifically political edge to it, which is intrinsically linked to the image of the island upon which the shipwrecked land. This island may be a haven or a place of grave danger, and is a locus for the exploration of alien systems of rule. The island mentality of Homer's *Odyssey* has been identified as the chief reason behind the text's immense influence over British culture:

> An island-civilization, sea-drenched and guarded by stormy waters at every crucial season in its history, will find in Homer's *Odyssey* not only a book of common prayer – 'may I endure this storm, may I reach the harbour' – but of shared adventure and global promise.[73]

When a ship is portrayed as failing to reach its intended port because of storms, its crew landing instead in a strange land, the representation may take on an expressly political allegorical significance. For Cavendish, writing *Assaulted and Pursued Chastity* whilst in exile, Travellia's sea-borne and sporadically insular attempts to preserve her chastity perhaps represent the bodily integrity of the *virgo intacta* of the British Isles being severely assaulted. This notion of an intact England echoes the opening lines of Cowley's *Civil War*, as the narrator asks, 'What rage does *England* from it selfe divide / More then Seas doe from all the world beside?'[74] The image of the ship in the storm was, however, non-partisan, used by republicans within the island's confines, as well as by royalists in exile across the Channel. By placing her protagonist in a position where she has to endure interrupted sea journeys, which lead her to redefine her role in alien environments, Cavendish is, therefore, making use of an already established set of image systems and tropes. Shakespeare's *Tempest*, a play which arguably shares many elements with *Assaulted and Pursued Chastity*, is another text which adapts the Homeric topos of storm, shipwreck and alien isle, and which appears, in its paradigmatic pattern of wreck preceding rightful restitution, to have held a particular fascination for Interregnum and Restoration royalists.

The natives of the island where Travellia and the captain land recall, in their monstrous hybridity, the strange beings Ulysses meets on his travels, such as the lotophagi, or the cyclops. Washed up on the shore, the shipwrecked are transported to the splendours of the chief city. Cavendish writes that:

The King's palace stood in the midst of the city, higher than all the other houses; the outward wall was crystal ... [there was] a walk, where on each side were beasts cut artificially to the life out of several coloured stones ... This walk leads to another court which was ... railed with white and red cornelians ... From the rails went only a plain walk paved with gold.[75]

In rhetorically similar terms, Chapman's Homer at length describes Ulysses' first impressions of the wondrous luxuries of Alcinous's palace in the seventh book of *The Odyssey*:

> Ulysses to the loftie-builded Court
> Of King Alcinous made bold retort ...
> On every side stood firme a wall of brasse ...
> Which bore a roofe up that all Saphire was;
> The brazen thresholds both sides did enfold
> Silver Pilasters hung with gates of gold,
> Whose Portall was of silver ...
> On each side, Dogs, of gold and silver fram'd,
> The house's Guard stood.[76]

There are further similarities between the two civilisations in which the shipwrecked find themselves. In the Kingdom of Phancy, where Travellia has landed, daily activities are clearly allotted according to the sex of the participant. Thus (despite its apparent room for error), 'their exercise was hunting, where the women hunted the females, the men the males'.[77] The great success of Phaeacia as a civilisation is because of its organisation along similar lines, where certain activities are gendered according to typically Homeric codes. The Phaeacian men, then, surpass 'All other countrimen in Art to build / A swift-saild ship', and the women 'For worke of webs past other women were'.[78] The significant difference between the two societies is that, unlike at the court of the benevolent Alcinous, in the Kingdom of Phancy the absence of *philoxenia* is life-threatening, and it is only through her recourse to her intellect, whilst still disguised as a boy, that Travellia avoids becoming a victim of ritual sacrifice. She learns the language of her captors and addresses them in a lengthy speech which, in its narrative self-containment, again recalls the story-telling in which Ulysses engages in Phaeacia.[79] Like Penelope, Travellia escapes imminent danger because of her intellect and, as is often so with Ulysses, her disguise is physical. In common with both, she averts crisis through narrative duplicity.

In her new, usurpatory role, Travellia shoots dead the chief priest and assumes the part of demigod.[80] To signify the very public repercussions of Travellia's oratory, wherein she plays on the superstitious fears of her audience, constructing herself as semi-divine, Cavendish replaces the feminine personal pronoun with the masculine. She writes, 'Travellia advanced *him*self so much higher than the rest, as they might hear *him* round'.[81] Such audacious narrative manoeuvres are to some extent normalised by their appearance within an epic-romance construction, which, in its easy conjunction of the human and the divine, the mundane and the fantastic, provides a suitable protean literary model. In this instance the paradigm may be Pallas, who appears to Ulysses as a woman, returning later in the guise of a man.[82]

It is at this point in the narrative of *Assaulted and Pursued Chastity* that the perspective shifts, and returns to the Kingdom of Sensuality, where the story is told of the prince's discovery of Travellia's deceit and his subsequent pursuit of her. His journey follows the outlines of the familiar seafaring topos of Greek epic, being at once metaphorical, with 'love sailing in the ship of imagination'; actual, 'his body sailed in the ship on the ocean of the sea'; and interrupted, this time not by a storm but by pirates who take him prisoner, recognise his 'noble disposition' and make him their leader.[83] The narratives are united at sea, as Travellia and her adoptive father leave the Kingdom of Phancy, shortly afterwards being captured by the prince's pirates. The movement to the next period of stasis in the story is hastened by yet another shipwreck which leaves the crew of the pirate ship on an island, where, fearing that the prince might recognise her, Travellia and her adoptive father put out to sea, are captured by merchants and taken to the Kingdom of Amity. It is here that Travellia eventually finds true self-determination and stasis, the cyclical narrative of movement, crisis, rest and movement having finally ceased.

The prince, too, is an heroic figure, whose adventures follow the same Homeric narrative pattern, but he is one in need of moral re-education. His pursuit of Travellia functions to further his journey towards the moral rehabilitation which he must achieve in order for the narrator to condone his eventual partnership with the heroine. His humility and self-characterisation of himself and his crew as '*we poor watery pilgrims*', before the King of the Kingdom of Amour, are further steps in his growth.[84] The King of Amour is the prince's own Alcinous, for, as Ulysses was integrated into the Phaeacian court because of his story-telling abilities, so the prince gains acceptance through his recounting of his adventures. This act of acceptance serves to delineate the King of Amour as sympathetic too, for in terms of Greek epic, just as story-telling reveals the character of the teller, so too the ability to listen and respond stands as an indication of maturity of character.[85] For the ending of *Assaulted and Pursued Chastity* to be satisfactory, it is important that, despite their warring, the King of Amour and the Queen of Amity may be understood as having potentially as natural and stable a marriage as that of the prince and Travellia. As the sojourn at Alcinous's court marked for Ulysses the prelude to the final episode before his homecoming, and Travellia's stay at the Court of the Queen of Amity operates eventually to establish her in her final identity, so too with the prince the Kingdom of Amour functions to provide the final period of stasis before the calamity which leads to resolution and social reintegration at the conclusion of *Assaulted and Pursued Chastity*.

Travellia's promotion within the Queen of Amity's court follows the hero-intruder paradigm of Greek epic, whereby the exiled protagonist seeks to assert himself in a new culture, since, ruling the kingdom in the Queen's absence, Travellia wins over the populace who initially resent her lowly origins as 'a shipmaster's son'.[86] However, her first military victories mark her out as a natural leader. The Queen of Amity captured, the prince at the Court of Amour, unaware of Travellia's involvement in the conflict, rejects reports that his forces have been conquered. He asks: 'How can that be, ... most of the nobles being here, and none but peasants left behind, who have no skill in wars, only to fight like beasts[?]'[87] Travellia's motivation has been an admiration for the Queen's 'heroic virtues', here described as being compatible with conventional constructions of heterosexual femininity; this is emphasised by Cavendish, who writes that Travellia 'could not have those affections in her for the Queen as a man'.[88] The lengthy passages which follow are located within the specifically masculine sphere of the battlefield, a discursive site within which it is acceptable and natural, given her successful combination of feminine chastity and masculine heroism, for Travellia to be articulate. Ultimately, however, Travellia has 'no skill in the art and use of the sword', and is wounded in a duel with the prince, who none the less allows himself to be taken prisoner by her armies.[89] This episode signifies another step in the reform of the prince, who has made the transition from pursuer to captured. Once news reaches him that his first wife has died, the way is open for his relationship with Travellia to be legitimated.[90]

Travellia's public revelation of her true identity is a less bloody version of Ulysses' reassertion of his might in Ithaca, and is literally spectacular. She first appears to her troops in her masculine clothes, and explains her deceit. *'Necessity did compel me to conceal my sex'*, she announces, *'to protect my honour ... and a sword becomes a woman when it is used against the enemies of her honour'*.[91] She is simultaneously chaste Penelope and heroic Ulysses. At the core of her speech is her chastity, a feminine concern, but her public oratory, her apparel and the battlefield location all indicate her continued involvement in a conventionally masculine sphere of activity. Going effectively off-stage, into her tent, she next emerges in 'her effeminate robes'.[92] She declares that *'with ... [her] masculine clothes ... [she] has laid by ... [her] masculine spirit'*, a declaration which is materially challenged by the crowd's establishment of her as their ruler.[93]

Travellia has not come home to her native land, but she has come home in a sense of finishing a journey towards self-determination and maturity, in guarding her chastity, and in reaching a point where her public role may co-exist with her own sexuality. Her chastity is intrinsically linked with her oratorial success. Although assaulted and pursued, it has ultimately become the site of her active production, and maintenance, of her own autonomy. Like Ulysses, Travellia seizes power; like Penelope, she remains chaste. However, she is significantly unlike Penelope, in that her version of the homecoming does not necessitate a relinquishment of autonomy.[94] In Travellia, then, Cavendish has powerfully reinterpreted the Greek topos of the homecoming. It has come to signify a disruption of gendered cultural stereotypes which does not have to culminate in a subsumptive return to a domestic setting. It is a coming home to a new realm of self. By extension Cavendish has defended and dignified her own continued presence in the masculine realms of print and publication. That is, she does not sew, but writes; enters the public realm of the printed word, but constructs it so as to maintain a sense of modesty. Ultimately it is her rescripting of the gendered aspects of the epic and romance genres which has facilitated this.

The Dutch woodcuts with which this chapter opened spun a fantastical tale of illogicality and transgression. In order to tell her own stories, and to deflect precisely such charges of monstrosity, Cavendish spins a complex web of self-representation and justification.[95] Having similarly shunned the distaff, she is in one sense analogous to the aggressive warrior woman of the broadsheet, armed, however, not with masculine weapons of war but with the desire to spin stories. It is a desire which she first realises in *Poems, and Fancies*, owing to her inventive appropriation of the symbol of Penelope in order to deflect criticism. It was essential for Cavendish's self-construction and presentation for her to appear to surpass the paradigmatic Penelope, that is, that she did not relinquish her autonomy over her publications in a way analogous to Penelope's relinquishment of Ithaca to Ulysses upon his return home. She forcibly emphasised such self-identification, as has been seen, in the prefatory material of *Poems, and Fancies*, and, some three years later, in her imaginative negotiation of the romance genre and her refiguring of the epic topos of the homecoming in her *Assaulted and Pursued Chastity*. Travellia epitomises and transcends the figure of the Homeric Penelope as a symbol replete with significance for the woman writer, whose very chastity could be called into doubt by the audacious and necessarily self-promoting act of publication.

The totality of Travellia's autonomy, however, must remain a dream for Cavendish. The material cultural circumstances under which she is producing her text serve to highlight the central irony in her construction of her protagonist. That is, whereas Travellia is empowered precisely because she resists taking the final step in a process of homecoming, Cavendish's political powerlessness is attributable to her inability to return home out of exile. Her actual desire to go home remains resolutely poised in counterpoint to her metaphorical decisiveness, expressed not only through the character of Travellia but also through the very fact of her publication of her writing, that she will not return home to a patriarchally circumscribed domestic life. Homeric epic has provided Cavendish with both masculine and feminine possibilities for Travellia. At the same time she subverts the genre, creating a heroine whose chastity cannot be called into doubt, but whose experience of the phenomenon of the homecoming differs significantly from that of her chaste counterpart, Penelope. Ultimately, Cavendish herself is more Penelope than she is

Travellia, for when the story of *Assaulted and Pursued Chastity* ends, she is, politically at least, no less impotent than she was at its start. In the next chapter I show how she participated in contemporary scientific debate in an attempt to redress precisely such political powerlessness.

Notes

1 Circe to Ulysses and his men. See Allardyce Nicoll, ed., *Chapman's Homer: The Iliad, The Odyssey and the Lesser Homerica*, 2 vols (London: Routledge and Kegan Paul, 1957), II, 183. All further quotations from Homer will be drawn from this edition.

2 Such broadsheets were common throughout Renaissance Europe. Their popularity is discussed by David Kunzle, 'World Upside Down: The Iconography of a European Broadsheet Type', in Barbara A. Babcock, ed., *The Reversible World: Symbolic Inversion in Art and Society* (Ithaca: Cornell University Press, 1978), pp. 39–94. The particular woodcut to which I refer, published in Amsterdam by Ewout Muller, is reproduced in Babcock, pp. 46–7.

3 Cavendish, *Poems, and Fancies*, p. 120.

4 The original Dutch inscription makes no mention of the man's similarly reversed occupation, focusing instead solely on the woman's incongruous employment. Recent interpreters have, however, seen it as necessary to provide a gloss which emphasises the man's role in the tableau. See, for example, Kunzle: 'wife goes to war and husband spins'. Kunzle, p. 45. My thanks to Richard E. Wilson for providing translations from the Dutch.

5 Sandra Gilbert and Susan Gubar, *The Madwoman in the Attic: The Woman Writer and the Nineteenth-century Literary Imagination* (New Haven: Yale University Press, 1980), p. 642.

6 Cavendish, *Assaulted and Pursued Chastity*, in *Natures Pictures*, p. 47.

7 *Ibid.*

8 *Ibid.* Cavendish constructs herself similarly in her autobiography. Of going into France with Henrietta Maria she writes: 'I was like one that had no Foundation to stand, or Guide to direct me, which made me afraid, lest I should wander with Ignorance out of the waies of Honour'. See *Natures Pictures*, p. 374.

9 Cavendish's attempts at presenting herself as heroic are remarked on by, among other critics, Gallagher and Sidonie Smith. Smith discusses her autobiographical 'dilemma – how to maintain the virtuous woman's silence and simultaneously pursue public power', and how 'her recourse to the combat trope betrays the confusion at the heart of her project'. See Sidonie Smith, ' "The Ragged Rout of Self": Margaret Cavendish's *True Relation* and the Heroics of Self-Disclosure', in Anita Pacheco, ed., *Early Women Writers: 1600–1720* (London: Longman, 1998), pp. 111–32 (pp. 123, 126).

10 For a definition of *topos* as a 'traditional theme or complex of themes' see

John Kevin Newman, *The Classical Epic Tradition* (Madison: The University of Wisconsin Press, 1986), p. 531. In my assessment of *Assaulted and Pursued Chastity* as working with heroic discourse thus, I problematise B. G. Mac-Carthy's proposition that 'The Duchess of Newcastle kept clear of the entire school of the Heroic Romance'. MacCarthy, p. 128.

11 Rozsika Parker, *The Subversive Stitch: Embroidery and the Making of the Feminine* (London: The Women's Press, 1984), p. 104. By *needlework* I intend to suggest the gamut of activities which involve threads, from spinning to weaving, knotting to embroidery. The emphasis is perhaps rather more on the 'work' than the 'needle'.

12 Hence, in genealogical terms, the 'distaff side' is the female branch of a family.

13 Needlework and female ingenuity are often paired in Greek myths, such as that of mute Philomela, who tells in a tapestry the story of her rape. For further etymology see Linda Woodbridge, 'Patchwork: Piecing the Early Modern Mind in England's First Century of Print Culture', *ELR*, 23 (1993), 5–45 (pp. 34–7); for the etymology of *text* see J. Hillis Miller, *Ariadne's Thread: Story Lines* (New Haven: Yale University Press, 1992), p. 7; on the gendered significance of *work* see Laurie Yager Lieb, '"The Works of Women are Symbolical": Needlework in the Eighteenth Century', *Eighteenth-century Life*, 10 (1986), 28–44.

14 Cecilia Macheski, 'Penelope's Daughters: Images of Needlework in Eighteenth-Century Literature', in Mary Anne Schofield and Cecilia Macheski, eds, *Fetter'd or Free? British Women Novelists, 1670–1815* (Athens: Ohio University Press, 1986), pp. 85–100 (p. 88).

15 *Ibid.*, p. 89.

16 Significantly, it is in this work that Cavendish declares: 'there will be many Heroick Women in some Ages'. See Cavendish, epistle 'To all Writing Ladies', *Poems, and Fancies*, unnumbered page.

17 *Ibid.*, pp. 121–3. The 'Faiery Wits' are characterised as at once ethereal and, in keeping with the Lucretian tenor of her volume, as minuscule, atomised structures which '*passe through every* small Crevise, *and Cranie of* Errours, *and* Mistakes'. *Ibid.*, p. 121.

18 *Ibid.* This discourse recalls that of early conduct books such as William Gouge's *Of Domesticall Duties: Eight Treatises* (London: for William Bladen, 1622). The Puritan emphases of such works would have alienated Cavendish even had their stress on the importance of female domestic accomplishments not done so. See N. H. Keeble, ed., *The Cultural Identity of Seventeenth-Century Woman: A Reader* (London: Routledge, 1994) on Gouge's demonstration of 'the essential idealism of the Puritan position'. Keeble, p. 145.

19 Cavendish, *Poems, and Fancies*, p. 121.

20 *Ibid.* This was a theme to which Cavendish was more explicitly to return in her *Orations of Divers Sorts* (London, 1662). Her careful negotiation of issues of female oratory and modesty in itself rewrites a Classical generic model. In his *Institutio oratoria*, Quintilian equates oratory with a specifically male

agency and citizenship. 'The man who can really play his part as a citizen', Quintilian declares, 'and is capable of meeting the demands both of public and private business ... is assuredly no other than the orator of our quest'. See Quintilian, *Institutio oratoria*, trans. H. E. Butler, 4 vols (Loeb Classical Library) (London: Heinemann, 1969), I, 11. On early modern conceptions of how 'the speech of a woman cannot be launched into public circulation like a man's' see Sylvia Brown, 'Margaret Cavendish: Strategies Rhetorical and Philosophical Against the Charge of Wantonness, Or Her Excuses for Writing So Much', *Critical Matrix*, 6 (1991), 20–45 (p. 22).

21 Cavendish, *Poems, and Fancies*, p. 122. In Greek mythology Pallas sprang fully grown and armed from the head of her father, Zeus (here, 'Jupiter').

22 This is a characterisation which Ovid's Penelope applies to herself in the first letter of *Heroides*. She complains that, were Ulysses with her, her bed would not be 'deserted', and 'nor would the hanging web be wearying now my widowed hands as I seek to beguile the hours of spacious night'. See Ovid, *Heroides and Amores*, in *Works*, trans. Grant Showerman, 6 vols (Loeb Classical Library) (London: Heinemann, 1986), I, p. 11.

23 On this 'self-preservation' as necessary because 'by not merely speaking, but speaking in the learned and literary context of the published book, Cavendish risked diminishing her virtue beyond recuperation', see Brown, p. 24.

24 Cavendish was not entirely complimentary about Chapman's translation, presumably the one to which she is referring in *The Worlds Olio*, when she writes that: '*Homer* is not yet matched in our Language; for though the worke was indeavoured to be translated, yet it is not like him'. Given her inability to read Homer in the original, this opinion could only have been adopted from those who could. Cavendish, *The Worlds Olio* (London, 1655), p. 12.

25 *The Odyssey*, p. 84.

26 *Ibid.*, p. 85.

27 *Ibid.*, p. 31; Cavendish, *Poems, and Fancies*, p. 122.

28 *The Odyssey*, p. 32. The second account of the same plot and its subsequent exposure is told in Book 19, following Ulysses' return. Here, however, Penelope speaks for herself, telling her own story of how she spun the suitors a yarn. See *ibid.*, p. 332.

29 Cavendish, *Poems, and Fancies*, sig. A3v. The potency of the distaff as domestic emblem with repercussions for the female writer is apparent twice more in *Poems, and Fancies*. In '*The Elysium*', poets 'The *World* as *Flax* unto their *Distaffe* bring / This Distaffe spins fine canvas of conceit, / Wherein the *Sense* is woven even, and strait', and in '*Of the* Spider', the spider's '*Body* is the *Wheele* that goeth round. / A *Wall* her *Distaff*, where she sticks *Thread* on, / The *Fingers* are the *Feet* that pull it long', pp. 142, 151.

30 Cavendish, *Poems, and Fancies*, sigs A2r–A3v.

31 In *The Worlds Olio*, Cavendish questions Penelope's chastity which, she avers, was flawed because she allowed the suitors too much licence: 'she was Chast, but she gave her self leave to be Courted, which is a degree to

Unchastity'. Cavendish, *The Worlds Olio*, p. 133. With two published volumes to her name, Cavendish may criticise even established exemplars from a position of superiority, as expressed in her conclusion that, 'there is nothing dearer to a Man than his Fame, so a Wife should have a care to keep it'. *Ibid.*, p. 133. It is a theme which is also in evidence in her 1664 work, *CCXI Sociable Letters*. In letter CL, Cavendish once more stresses that, because she writes rather than weaves, she does not lack Penelope's virtue. The 'Idle Time' trope of *Poems, and Fancies* is again invoked, as the writer claims that her virtue actually surpasses Penelope's, since writing engrosses all of her senses. 'Had *Penelope*'s Ears been so Barr'd', she writes, 'her Lovers Petitions ... would have been kept without doors ... then it was likely her Amorous Lovers would have gone away, and not stay'd to Feed upon her Cost and Charge, as they did'. Cavendish, *Sociable Letters*, p. 315. Ariadne, another innovative needleworker, is also mentioned in this volume. Cavendish, *Sociable Letters*, p. 24. It was a trope to which Cavendish continued to have recourse. In 1666 she defended her writing thus: 'if all Women that have no imployment in worldly affairs, should but spend their time as harmlessly as I do, they would not commit such faults as many are accused of'. See Cavendish, *Observations*, n.p.

32 W. T. H. Jackson, *The Hero and the King: An Epic Theme* (New York: Columbia University Press, 1982), p. 2. On how Cavendish's exilic years may be described as 'contingent' see my introduction.

33 Jackson, p. 92. Whilst *The Odyssey* is the model on which I focus here, there are Virgilian echoes too. For the differences between Hellenistic and Latin epic poetic discourse, see Brooks Otis, *Virgil: A Study in Civilised Poetry* (Oxford: Clarendon Press, 1964).

34 This story appears in the eighth book of *Natures Pictures*, pp. 218–72. For ease of reference, however, I have used Kate Lilley's 1992 edition. See Margaret Cavendish, *Assaulted and Pursued Chastity*, in *Blazing World*, ed. Lilley, pp. 45–118. All further quotations from *Assaulted and Pursued Chastity* will be drawn from this edition.

35 This background material is derived largely from Burrow's impressive study *Epic Romance: Homer to Milton* (Oxford: Clarendon Press, 1993).

36 For this reading of Spenser see Burrow, pp. 102–46. The quotation is from Tasso, quoted in Burrow, p. 174, n. 91. This argument is not to suggest that epic was apolitical before the seventeenth century.

37 See Patterson, p. 163.

38 *Ibid.*

39 In 1643 Waller had been banished for his royalist activities. Upon his return from exile in 1651 he wrote an epic panegyric for Cromwell. For a discussion of Waller's 'panegyrical deployment' of epic, that is, how the epic form aided him to celebrate Cromwell's political legitimacy through an emphasis on the qualities of inherent princeliness, see Burrow, p. 179. On May's translation of Lucan see Burrow, pp. 197–8.

40 Cowley's royalist sympathies are unmistakable: 'Three thowsand hot-brained Calvinists there came; / Wild men, that blot their great Reformers

Name. / Gods Image stampt on Monarchs they deface; / And 'bove the Throne their thundring Pulpits place'. See Abraham Cowley, *The Civil War*, ed. by Allan Pritchard (Toronto: University of Toronto Press, 1973), p. 108. On *Davideis* as offering a specifically royalist, yet pragmatically conciliatory, interpretation of David see Mary Ann Radzinowicz, 'Forced Allusions: Avatars of King David in the Seventeenth Century', in Diana Treviño Benet and Michael Lieb, eds, *Literary Milton: Text, Pretext, Context* (Pittsburgh: Duquesne University Press, 1994), pp. 45–66. For Hobbes's influence on *Gondibert's* 'scrupulously analytic treatment of heroic passion' see Burrow, pp. 240–1.

41 Charles Cavendish, born in 1620, was the second grandson of William's cousin, the third Earl of Devonshire. A royalist commander-in-chief in Nottinghamshire and Lincolnshire, he was godson to Charles I, and was killed at Gainsborough on 28 July 1643. See Pritchard, pp. 93–4, 152.

42 On the conflicting demands which inhere in adopting and adapting an Homeric literary paradigm see Burrow: 'The process of imitating a narrative is not a simple linear movement towards accuracy or fidelity: it is an oscillation between indulging a new interpretation and deliberately restraining that interpretation in the interest of returning to the overall shape of an earlier story'. Burrow, p. 34.

43 This generic elision has been identified in seventeenth-century French epic, where 'narration oscillated between the two genres, so that we can never firmly fix on the boundaries between epic and history'. See David Maskell, *The Historical Epic in France, 1500–1700* (Oxford: Oxford University Press, 1973), p. 47.

44 Cavendish, *Assaulted and Pursued Chastity*, p. 54. On the significance of the romance form in royalist terms see Chapter 1, above.

45 Patterson, p. 180.

46 Cotterell, quoted in *ibid.*, pp. 189–90. On *Cloria and Narcissus* see *ibid.*, p. 191. I demonstrated in Chapter 1 how Charles I and Henrietta Maria exploited and appropriated versions of romance.

47 *The Odyssey*, p. 214.

48 Ulysses 'has presented himself as a liar throughout the narrative' according to one critic. See Elizabeth Gregory, 'Unravelling Penelope: The Construction of the Faithful Wife in Homer's Heroines', *Helios*, 23 (1996), 3–20 (p. 11). Gregory fails, however, to give full import to Penelope's weaving as a form of discursive eloquence. She notes that, like Ulysses, 'Penelope too is a skilled fabricator, though of duplicitous textiles rather than duplicitous texts'. *Ibid.*, p. 13, n. 20.

49 Of the Trojan wars Homer tells that Demodocus, 'the divine Expressor did so give / Both act and passion that he made it live, / And to Ulysses' facts did breathe a fire / So deadly quickning that it did inspire / Old death with life'. *The Odyssey*, p. 146.

50 In the nineteenth book, for example, Ulysses tells his wife that he is from Crete, and Euryclea's recognition of his scar marks another step towards reassimilation in the court.

51 Gregory also comments on this possibility: 'In insisting up to the point of Odysseus' return that she need not remarry, Penelope has stood on the threshold of a repudiation of patriarchy'. Gregory, p. 16. The reunion of Penelope and Ulysses is characterised by Chapman in nautical terms. They cling to each other with as much joy as 'sad men at Sea [who,] their ship quite lost …, craule up to Land'. *The Odyssey*, p. 399.

52 As Maskell explains in his study of seventeenth-century epic, these topoi are not exclusive to epic narratives, but, crucially, 'what we have looked for is the repetition of certain combinations of these elements, which suggest that the poet had a definite structure in mind'. Maskell, p. 207. He goes on to argue how, whilst some epic topoi operate for structural effect, others function to demonstrate rhetorical skill. He identifies the storm topos as able to operate as either. *Ibid.*, pp. 208–12, 214–32.

53 Cavendish, *Assaulted and Pursued Chastity*, p. 116.

54 The idea that in order to be a successful ruler an individual had to have the militia on his or her side, may be traced back to Machiavelli, who wrote that, 'princes control their own destiny when they command enough money or men to assemble an adequate army and make a stand against anyone who attacks them'. See Machiavelli, *The Prince*, ed. Robert M. Adams (London: Norton, 1992), p. 30. It was an idea which William Cavendish echoed in the 1650s in his *Advice* to Charles II: 'without an Army in your owne hands, you are but a king upon a Curtesey of others'. See Slaughter, p. 5.

55 Peter Toohey identifies the epic hero as being socially superior, even aristocratic, demonstrating courage through battle, and being outstandingly intelligent. Working on these guidelines, Travellia's linguistic abilities, her natural aptitude for rule and her military successes stand as testament to her heroic nature. See Peter Toohey, *Reading Epic: An Introduction to the Ancient Narratives* (London: Routledge, 1992), p. 9.

56 Cavendish, *Assaulted and Pursued Chastity*, p. 48. In *The Odyssey* it is Pallas who is responsible for disguising Ulysses as a beggar upon his return to Ithaca, and who, in her representation of both home and battlefield, perhaps stands as another useful paradigm in understanding the construction of Cavendish's protagonist. The letters which Miseria leaves for the bawd and the prince upon her escape later in the narrative are signed 'Affectionata'. Cavendish, *Assaulted and Pursued Chastity*, pp. 76–7.

57 *Ibid.*, pp. 48–9. There are obvious parallels between Miseria's story and that of Marina in Shakespeare's *Pericles*. For a comparison of Marina with Apollonius of Tyre's daughter, Tarsia, see Elizabeth Archibald, ' "Deep clerks she dumbs": The Learned Heroine in *Apollonius of Tyre* and *Pericles*', *Comparative Drama*, 22 (1988–89), 289–303.

58 For an exploration of the epic journey as 'a metaphor of growing up' to 'a more *integrated* existence' see Thomas Van Nortwick, *Somewhere I Have Never Travelled: The Second Self and the Hero's Journey in Ancient Epic* (Oxford: Oxford University Press, 1992), p. x. Nortwick identifies an epic pattern of 'confrontation, denial, journey into darkness, and (potential) reintegration', which, arguably, may also be seen in Cavendish's text. *Ibid.*, p. 183. As both Ulysses

and Aeneas must visit the underworld before going home, so for Travellia the dark possibilities of her sexuality, and the perceived threats to her chastity, mean she has to confront a personal, metaphorical hell on her journey. On the epic reader and the journey to 'the *telos* of tranquillity', being 'the Epicurean who has attained *ataraxia* [and] has ... both metaphorically and literally escaped from these storms' see Gale, *Myth*, pp. 126, 120–1. For the significance of an epic narrative beginning *in media res*, see A. D. Nuttall, *Openings: Narrative Beginnings from the Epic to the Novel* (Oxford: Clarendon Press, 1992), p. 30.

59 This movement is more succinctly expressed by Radzinowicz as the 'epic rest-and-Recreation pattern of activity'. Radzinowicz, p. 53.

60 Cavendish, *Assaulted and Pursued Chastity*, p. 50.

61 *Ibid.*, p. 51.

62 *Ibid.*, p. 55.

63 Cavendish's use of classical models leads her to experiment occasionally with *hypotaxis*, being the oral, or written, construction of sentences using conjunctions rather than subordinate clauses. This perhaps explains her occasional extraordinarily long built-up sentences, such as that depicting Travellia's confrontation with the prince, beginning 'Wherefore most noble sir', and concluding, no fewer than sixteen lines later, with 'I will kill or die for security'. Cavendish, *Assaulted and Pursued Chastity*, p. 52. On such classical narrative modes see Toohey, pp. 14–16.

64 The concept of *philoxenia* may have had a specific resonance for the Cavendishes. In her *Life* of her husband Cavendish lists his '*Blessings*', fourth among which was 'The Kindness and Civilty which my Lord received from Strangers, and the Inhabitants of those places, where he lived during the time of his Banishment'. Cavendish, *Life*, p. 136.

65 Cavendish, *Assaulted and Pursued Chastity*, p. 61.

66 That *philoxenia* is a universally understood and desirable quality in *The Odyssey* is emphasised in Ulysses' conversations with his herdsman, Eumaeus, who is addressed as 'Friend to humane Hospitality!' *The Odyssey*, p. 243. Eumaeus's reply is that 'it were a curse / To my poore meanes to let a Stranger tast / Contempt for fit food'. *Ibid.*, p. 243. The connections between *philoxenia* and eloquence, even mendacity, are forged in this exchange too, as Ulysses presents himself to his herdsman as coming from Crete, and supports this assertion with lengthy stories which, whilst they do share with his real story the themes of exile, war and shipwreck, none the less are fabrications. If the hero finds it expedient (as was the case with Miseria and the sea-captain), it is permissible within the generic codes of epic narrative to receive *philoxenia* without a concomitant revelation of true identity.

67 Cavendish, *Assaulted and Pursued Chastity*, p. 62.

68 This encounter is one of many which are reported by Ulysses to Alcinous's court. Ulysses recalls how 'all the Rocke did rore / With troubl'd waters: round about the tops / Of all the steepe crags flew the fomy drops'. *The Odyssey*, p. 217.

69 *Ibid.*, pp. 217, 213.

70 *Ibid.*, p. 213.

71 The point in the tale Ulysses has reached is that where he lands on Ogygia, Calypso's island, where he was to spend more than seven years. His departure from there is what begins the tale of *The Odyssey*, and his recounting of the tale up to that point marks the end of his stay in the court of Alcinous.

72 On this narrative rhythm as 'staircase structure' see Newman, p. 530.

73 See George Steiner, ed., *Homer in English* (Harmondsworth: Penguin, 1996), p. xx. Thomas Grantham's joyful 1660 translation of the first and third books of *The Iliad* demonstrates how political significance may be attached to the island of Britain. His dedicatory poem to the third book reads: 'Go meet King CHARLES, my Book, at Dover Clifs / For now his Foes are put unto their shifts'. See *Ibid.*, p. 56.

74 See Cowley, ed. Pritchard, p. 73. Pritchard's conclusion is that 'Cowley was too much at the mercy of unfolding forces of history and too much committed to the needs of propaganda to allow *The Civil War* to be in any full sense an epic'. *Ibid.*, p. 36.

75 Cavendish, *Assaulted and Pursued Chastity*, pp. 66–7. The 'perfect orange colour' of the Kingdom of Phancy's royalty is perhaps intended, along with their idyllic existence, to recall Hesiod's 'race of men that the immortals who dwell on Olympus made first of all [which] was of gold'. See Cavendish, p. 68; Hesiod, *'Theogony' and 'Works and Days'*, ed. M. L. West (Oxford: Oxford University Press, 1988), p. 40.

76 *The Odyssey*, p. 121. Burrow claims that 'the garden of Alcinous and the continual festivities that go on in the land make it the first earthly paradise in the Western epic'. Burrow, p. 223.

77 Cavendish, *Assaulted and Pursued Chastity*, p. 65. Burrow has characterised as an 'acute limitation' in pre-Miltonic English epic the way in which journeys serve as metaphors for self-discovery rather than as descriptions of alien encounters. He writes that 'there are few Odysseys into strange and magical realms in English sixteenth-century romances, and this limits the whole tradition'. Burrow, p. 220. Cavendish's acute interest in societies different from her own, and her fantastic descriptions of their inhabitants, balances the allegorical import which can, rightly, be attached to the heroic journey, and so perhaps exempts her from Burrow's generalisation.

78 *The Odyssey*, pp. 121–2.

79 The Russian-doll narrative structure of *The Odyssey* has been remarked upon by Gregory, who writes that 'The series of tales which Odysseus tells across the poem and the emphasis on how his story-telling abilities shape what happens to him make this story a meta-story – a story about story-telling and its role in the construction of reality'. Gregory, p. 13. The same is true of Travellia.

80 This act of brutality is not questioned within the text. Like Miseria's near-fatal wounding of the prince at the start of the narrative, it is perhaps best understood as a necessary and therefore correct act, given the circumstances and the centrality of the preservation of chastity. Read in these terms, it

would certainly elicit a plea of self-defence or justifiable homicide. The priest has to die as part of Travellia's staging of herself as divine and able to strike down with '*small thunderbolts*' any would-be assailants. Cavendish, *Assaulted and Pursued Chastity*, p. 71. Ulysses' execution of the suitors and the serving-women towards the conclusion of *The Odyssey* may be similarly understood, for 'to question the violence of book 22 … is not so much to commit anachronism as it is to ignore plain signals given by Homer'. See Toohey, p. 64.

81 Cavendish, *Assaulted and Pursued Chastity*, p. 72. My emphases.

82 See *The Odyssey*, where Pallas 'like a yong wench showd', and appeared 'like a Shepheard, yong and quaint, / As King's sonnes are'. *Ibid.*, pp. 119, 233.

83 Cavendish, *Assaulted and Pursued Chastity*, p. 78.

84 *Ibid.*, p. 88.

85 For the argument that Homer's work 'insinuates that the ability to respond to stories is what it means to have an identity', see Burrow, p. 32.

86 Cavendish, *Assaulted and Pursued Chastity*, p. 92. Comparisons may be drawn with Homer's *Iliad*. In effect, the Queen of Amity is an Agamemnon figure, bending to the pressures of Travellia–Achilles, the intruder. Like Achilles, Travellia has no actual obligations to the Kingdom she finds herself in, but leads and fights because of her innate heroic characteristics. This hero/ruler dichotomy arguably 'produces, almost enforces, an 'inside-outside' structure, a central passive court structure surrounded by a moving and not very predictable hero'. See Jackson, p. 132. Jackson argues that a work is not properly an epic without this dynamic, and that 'there is no major epic in which the hero is not in some sense an exile'. Jackson, p. 5. Towards *The Odyssey's* conclusion Ulysses, disguised as a beggar, is in effect a hero-in-intruder upon his return from exile, since he wrests power from the suitors, who have effectively taken control of his court. See Jackson, p. 101.

87 Cavendish, *Assaulted and Pursued Chastity*, p. 94.

88 *Ibid.*, p. 95.

89 *Ibid.*, p. 100.

90 Cavendish has gone to some lengths to demonstrate that the prince's elation upon hearing of his wife's death is not as callous as it might at first appear. She establishes that the prince's was not a companionate marriage, and that the woman was already a widow, and infertile. The young prince had found himself 'wedded more to interest than love'. *Ibid.*, p. 54. Travellia's emotions are mixed upon hearing the news: 'when … [she] heard he was a widower, her heart did beat like to a feverish pulse, being moved with several passions, fearing that it was not so, hoping it was so, joying if it were so, grieving that she ought not to wish it so'. *Ibid.*, p. 113.

91 *Ibid.*, p. 115.

92 *Ibid.*

93 *Ibid.*, p. 116. These revelatory scenes on the battlefield recall, in their representation of gender ambiguities reconciled through an overarching emphasis on female chastity, the speeches of Queen Elizabeth I to her troops

at Tilbury Docks. Further, it was on this occasion that Sharp, the military chaplain, compared Elizabeth with Pallas. In a letter Elizabeth wrote to King Edward in 1553, she used nautical imagery thus: 'Like as a shipman in stormy weather plucks down the sails tarrying for better wind, so did I, most noble King ... pluck down the high sails of my joy'. See Maria Perry, *Elizabeth I: The Word of a Prince. A Life from Contemporary Documents* (London: Folio Society, 1990), pp. 285–6, 77.

94 Cavendish clearly characterises such a seizure of power as acceptable because of Travellia's inherent qualities. Travellia 'should rule; who was so beloved of the people, as if she had not only been a native born, but as if she had been born from royal stock'. Cavendish, *Assaulted and Pursued Chastity*, p. 114. Jackson discusses how, for Ulysses, Penelope is to some extent depersonalised and desexualised, becoming encrypted as 'a symbol of hearth and home', and an emblem of 'the stability and continuity of civilized life'. Jackson, pp. 96, 106.

95 The centrality of the image of the web to Cavendish's imaginative processes is explored in Bowerbank.

5

Figures of speech:
The Animall Parliament

In a Monarchical Government, to be for the King, is to be for the Commonwealth; for when Head and Body are divided, the Life of Happiness
dies, and the Soul of Peace is departed. (Margaret Cavendish, *Life of
William Cavendishe* (1667), p. 173)

In the last chapter I showed how Travellia's triumphant and climactic
coming to power was spectacularly realised through her dramatic
self-revelation of her figure in women's clothes, and her oratory. In
The Animall Parliament, from *Poems, and Fancies,* Cavendish utilises
the ancient trope of the body as kingdom to facilitate a seditious
commentary on Puritan parliamentary procedure, and to adduce
monarchical rule as natural and right. The ungendered body which
houses the Animal Parliament is Cavendish's figure of polemical
speech, a figure, as has been shown, which was to be concretised
some three years later in the character of Travellia. In its successful
exploration and sustaining of an elaborate allegorical conceit *The
Animall Parliament* marks the author's engagement with an established literary genre of using the human body to figure as a political
structure. Cavendish's text, whilst constituting her interpretation of
a tradition dating back to Livy, reflects and adapts the responses to
that tradition of close contemporaries, predominantly William Harvey and Thomas Hobbes. As Lucretian poetic techniques softened the
author's polemic earlier in her volume, here, at its conclusion, *Poems,
and Fancies* may be characterised by a royalist edge which is presented
through the skilful allegory which is *The Animall Parliament.* Before
we look in detail at Cavendish's text, however, its generic antecedents
need to be considered, starting with Shakespeare's *Coriolanus*:

I receive the general food at first
Which you do live upon, and fit it is,
Because I am the storehouse and the shop
Of the whole body. But, if you do remember,
I send it through the rivers of your blood
Even to the court, the heart, to th' seat o'th' brain;
And through the cranks and offices of man
The strongest nerves and small inferior veins
From me receive that natural competency
Whereby they live.

(*The Tragedy of Coriolanus*, I.i.128 [1])

There is a powerful ambiguity in this, the Belly's tale, as recounted by Menenius Agrippa at the beginning of *Coriolanus*. The scene has opened with a horde of angry citizens resolved to murder the patrician Caius Martius, later Coriolanus, whom they blame not only for their hunger but for supporting the practice of usury in Rome. 'Worthy Menenius Agrippa, one that hath always loved the people' has been sent in to placate them (I.i.48). The ambiguity is that the moral of Menenius's fable means different things to different listeners. To Menenius himself, what is being analogised is the senate's natural hierarchy over the people, and the varying degrees of benefit which derive from that relationship. By contrast, however, the First Citizen hears in the fable a lesson about the mutual interdependence of state and people, missing the irony that the 'belly' of the Roman senate has not, in fact, been supplying the members of its commonwealth with sufficient nourishment. Menenius's fable is a generic construct with a long history, told, for example, by Livy in the second book of his *Roman History*, translated into English by Philemon Holland in 1600.[2] Livy records how, in 494 BC, the dictator Valerius had pleaded with the senate to review its treatment of debtors. Anticipating civil war following the senate's rejection of his proposals, he stepped down, winning the people's support. Unnerved, the senators failed to disband the armies, which decamped to the Sacred Mount, where Menenius addressed them and the assembled plebeians with his fable of the Belly.

He describes a human body wherein the limbs and organs articulate their resentment with the Belly, for which they daily provide, but which, in Holland's translation, 'lying still in the mids of them, did nothing else but enjoy the delightsome pleasures brought unto her'.[3] It is decided that the Belly should be starved as the result of a process whereby each organ ceases to fulfil its allotted biological task. Thus 'neither the hands should reach and convey food into the mouth, nor the mouth receive it as it came'.[4] The unanticipated result of this mutiny, however, is that the entire body 'pined, wasted, & fell into an extreme consumption', and so the Belly's vital role in distributing 'by the veins into all parts, that fresh and perfect blood whereby we live', is forcibly emphasised.[5] Menenius's locutionary, and, it is implied, concomitant moral, superiority is signalled by the commoners' enthusiastic response to his rhetoric:

> Comparing herewith, and making his application to wit, how like this intestine and inward sedition of the body, was to the fell stomack of the commons, which they had taken and born against the [S]enators, he turned quite the peoples hearts.[6]

Through his speech, Holland's Menenius causes the commoners figuratively to look both within their own bodies, their 'fell stomack[s]', and to understand themselves as part of a greater civic macrocosm. His recourse to bodily images, in an appropriate figure of speech, was successful, since it 'turned quite the peoples hearts', an expression which serves to remind how parts of the body have culturally diverse meanings, operating both discursively and existing materially.[7] The result is that a political compromise is reached, with adequate representation for the plebeians being promised.

Whilst her concern would not have been for the plebeians, Cavendish's *Poems, and Fancies* does contain a series of poems which shows her exploring such textual possibilities of representing the body allegorically. These, however, are sketchy foreshadowings of that technique's fullest exposition: *The Animall Parliament*.[8] 'Who knowes', asks the poet in '*Of small* Creatures, *such as we call* Fairies', 'but in the *Braine* may dwel / Little small *Fairies*; who can tell?'.[9] She continues in the same speculative tone, characterising the human eye as a fairy ocean, and also as a sun or a moon, and attributing toothache to fairy excavations in the quarries of the mouth. The conceit continues in '*The* City *of the* Fairies', where the skull is figured as the location of the royal court, and where, in language directly foreshadowing that of *The Animall Parliament*, Oberon dwells in 'a *Royall Head*', in 'the *kernell* of the *Braine*'.[10]

These communities of fairies exist in a reciprocal relationship with their host body, which figures not as an abstract entity but as a physical presence, the very human actions of which have immense repercussions within the microcosm, where a shipwreck can result from a tear being wiped from an eye.[11] The relationship in terms of emotions rather than physicality, however, is less reciprocal. Apparently motiveless depressions may be attributable to fairies in the brain dying, causing 'some *place* in the *Head*' to be 'hung with *blacke*'.[12] The relationship here between the macrocosmic body and its minute inhabitants is tellingly non-reciprocal, since the thoughts and feelings of the host have their inception in the fairies' activities but the host's thoughts apparently may not sway the fairy world in a way comparable with its considerable physical influence. In this way, the fairies stop operating as it were as a charmingly separate community making do within a dangerously inhospitable host body, and become instead more straightforwardly analogical or psychomachic representations of those mental processes for which Cavendish had no other explanation.

When Cavendish offers fairy-tale models for physical and psychical processes, the similitude chimes with contemporary theories about physiology. In her comparison of 'Those *Spirits* which we *Animal* doe call' with '*Men*, and *Women* ... and *Creatures* small', she demonstrates an awareness of basic anatomy, and, especially important in terms of her *Animall Parliament*, of the fundamentals of the theory of the circulation of the blood.[13] She describes how:

> The *Heart* the *West*, where *heat* the *bloud* refines,
> Which *bloud* is *gold*, and *silver heart* the *mines*.
> *Those* from the *head* in *ships* their *Spice* they fetch,
> And from the *heart* the *gold* and *silver* rich.[14]

The human body here is the site of many contemporary discourses – mercantile, New World, anatomical – which Cavendish synthesises into a poetic whole.[15] This image of the heart as a warehouse for the valuable gold blood recalls the politico-anatomical role of Livy's Belly. The heart is at the centre of a far-reaching mercantile system of exchange, of import and export of precious commodities, but it is only the '*West Indies*', to the '*East Indies*' of the '*Head*', where '*spicy Fancie growes*'.[16] Without the co-operation of head and heart, the equilibrium of the entire system of exchange is shattered; the blood of commerce cannot flow, and, as in Livy's fable, the body dies.[17] This interdependence of head and heart is especially important in the context of William Harvey's politico-anatomical terms, as shall be seen. This group of poems seems to reach a conclusion in 'Similizing the Body to many Countries'.[18] In the poems preceding this one the body has been epitomised as a compact, orderly system, having either a reciprocal and interdependent relationship between head and heart or a relationship within which one element has a dominant, monarchical status. Further, this symbiotic relationship finds an analogous counterpart in that which exists between the macrocosmic host, and the interior, miniature communities of Cavendish's ontology. In 'Similizing the Body' the scope of the world contained within the body is considerably enlarged, with the animal spirits inhabiting a world where 'The *Nerves* are *France*, and *Italy*, and *Spaine*', and the lungs 'are *Rocks*, and *Cavernes*, whence rise *winds*', and where the humours characterise geographical features, the spleen being '*Æthiopia*, which breeds in / *A* People that are black, and tawny skin'.[19]

The Animall Parliament may be read as a consolidation of this poetic treatment of the body as found in the earlier poems. It differs in its complexity, and sustained nature, where the central conceit is explored over some thirteen pages. Given its length, the absence of any form of prefatory material or introduction to it is deeply uncharacteristic, as Cavendish launches straight into the narrative with the declamatory statement that 'The *Soul* called a *Parliament* in his *Animal Kingdom*'.[20] Diverse discourses converge in the ensuing text, a convergence facilitated by the flexibility of her generic model, which functions to incorporate political critique, advice for rulers, anatomical treatise and satirical allegory, in a witty and dynamic whole.[21] Of this generic model Leonard Barkan writes in *Nature's Work of Art* that the simultaneously 'unified and diverse' structure of the human form makes it 'the perfect vehicle for allegory', since allegory functions through the representation of 'single abstractions' as 'concrete multiples'.[22] The systems of body and parliament are rendered accurately in their own right in Cavendish's text, and operate harmoniously together. This sophisticated use of the trope marks, in Barkan's terms, a movement away from static analogous relationships between body and cosmos or kingdom, to genuine, mutually informative correspondences. The figure's 'corporeal nature, ... self and ... destiny, are made analogous to the idealized body which is itself analogous to the State'.[23]

Cavendish's Animal Parliament is a tripartite structure wherein the soul, in its act of summoning the Parliament, asserts the predominance of rational over sensitive matter in this quasi-mechanist ontology, where soul, body and thoughts are placed in a specific hierarchy. The upper house of the parliament is where the King is surrounded by his nobility. It is located in the head, where the soul is the King; the Judges are the fives senses; Black Rod is ignorance; the Speaker is understanding, and the Clerk is memory. This structure recalls that explicated earlier in *Poems, and Fancies*, in '*Similizing the Head of Man to a Hive of Bees*', where 'The *Soule* doth governe all, as doth their *King*'.[24] The lower house is found in the heart, where the knights and burgesses, being the passions and affections, are found along with the Speaker, love, and the Clerk, fear. Information passes between these two houses via the arteries, which connect brain and heart, and the nerves, which connect the heart with the rest of the body, being the muscles which work on the extremities. Cavendish is very specific in her detailing of parliamentary process:

> The severall *Writs* that are sent out by this *Parliament*, are sent out by the *Nerves* into every part of this *Animall Kingdom*, and the *Muscles* execute the power and *Authority* of those *Writs* upon the *Members* of the *Common-wealth*. The *lower House* presents their *Grievances*, or their *desires*, to the *upper House* the *Braine*, by the *Arteries*.[25]

The model is prima facie democratic, with the system accommodating differences of opinion between the two houses. Further, the entirety of the kingdom can be reached through an efficient administrative network. The hierarchy ensures, however that any 'Grievances' which are given consideration come not from the vaguely defined populace, on whom the parliament's will may be imposed, but instead from a carefully controlled lower house, wherein dissent is not entertained as a possibility. The two houses assembled, the King details his reasons for calling parliament, conveying a picture of a land torn apart by faction and deceit. His aim is to 'quench the rebellion of superfluous words', in order to 'make and enact strict Lawes to a good Life'.[26] Subsidies of justice, prudence, fortitude and temperance need to be raised, and here once more the monarch's voice is apparently conciliatory, yet actually imperious. He may appear to be a constitutional monarch, but in fact issues of agency, duress and consent are complicated throughout the text.[27]

The Lord Keeper confirms that, because the King is most concerned with the subjects' interests, any move to refuse subsidies would have to be regarded as seditious, and the opponent would be expelled from the kingdom. It is arguable that Cavendish is here writing from a nostalgic perspective. The King has desired to act 'before the fire growes too violent for your help to quench [it] out', and the Keeper stresses how unwilling the monarch was to impose heavy taxation on his subjects.[28] The allegorical setting of the text appears momentarily forgotten, and Cavendish's desire to reinterpret history is pronounced, as the keeper declares that 'it is as *imprudent* to disturbe a peaceable *Common-wealth* with *doubts* of what may come, as to be so negligent to let a *threatning ruine* run without opposition'.[29] Indeed, Cavendish's textual creation of a tripartite parliamentary system is of itself a nostalgic act which runs counter to dominant ideologies, for the early months of 1649 had seen the Puritans effectively dismantle existing monarchical governmental structures.[30] The High Court's sessions had started on 8 January; Charles was tried on the 27th, and executed some three days later. The House of Lords was abolished before the end of the first week of February; as was the institution of monarchy. The republic's Council of State was created on 14 February.[31] Debates had long been taking place about whether abolition of the House of Lords would be regarded as too radical an alteration of the constitution. Cromwell had initially opposed the abrogation on the grounds that it might provoke a rebellion, and, as David Underdown expresses it, 'until after the King's execution the matter was left in abeyance, a pathetic handful of peers continuing their desultory sessions, able only to "sit and tell tales by the fireside", as a contemptuous observer described their meetings'.[32] The abolition came about, according to Underdown, after the Lords' messengers were refused entry to the Commons – the 'blood' no longer flowed between the vital organs of the body politic.[33]

By contrast, Cavendish's Upper House is dynamic and puissant, with the peers and episcopacy involved in torrid, yet punctilious, exchanges over the raising of subsidies. The language remains equanimous, as in this reply to the Lord of Objection's recommendation that 'a *Subsidy of Faith*' be raised:

After he had spoke, rose up the *Bishop* of *Resentment*, and said ...
My Lord:

It may be easily perceived, that this *Lords* desire is, that the *King* should lay the heaviest *Subsidy* upon the *Church*: not but that I dare say so much for the *Ecclesiasticall Body*, as they would be as willing to assist the *King* in his Warres, as any of his *Lay Subjects*; yet what the *Clergy* have, belongs to the *Gods*; and what they take from us, they take from them.[34]

The contemporary political critique is clear as the role of the Church in the raising of subsidies is discussed by the Lords and Bishops. The Bishop of Adoration speaks in support of offering prayers, 'which are the *effects* of *Faith*', the offer being delivered by a judge along 'the *Arteries* to the *lower House*'.[35] Once the writ has been accepted, the decision is taken back to the Upper House.[36] Also implicit is a critique, not uncommon in Cavendish's work, of the clergy, the ecclesiastical body, a body within the body politic, yet which is characterised as not serving it in a meaningful or productive sense.[37] This critique finds voice in the character of a Gentleman who describes the Church as factious and parasitical. Monastic seclusion is characterised as the establishment of 'great *Colledges* of *Factions* ... [which] doe not only disturbe the *Common-wealth*, but impoverish it very much'.[38] Further, the Church's system of raising tithes is portrayed as severely damaging to the parishioners. The critique of the clergy expressed by the members of the Animal Parliament is traditional, and has at its base, among other sources, that explicated by Hobbes in *Leviathan*, the text which earned for its author the title of 'the Beast of Malmesbury' on account of what was perceived of as its heretical content.[39]

The central, and in many respects the most interesting, of the various speeches Cavendish includes in her parliament is that of the '*Rationall Lord*', whose plea for the replacement of superstitious and false moral ideas with 'true' scientific ones taps into diverse contemporary intellectual movements.[40] The speech begins as a catalogue of the carnivalesque social inversion which came about because of the passing of Acts, or '*Opinions* ... when the *Parliament* of *Errours* sate, in the yeare of *Ignorance one thousand eight hundred and two*'.[41] A world-turned-upside-down scenario, wherein values are inverted and integrity is ridiculed, is evoked as the Rational Lord describes the opinions of this '*Parliament* of *Errours*' which had decreed that:

> those which have new and strange *Fantasmes*, must be thought the only men
> of knowledge. That none must be thought Wits, but *Buffoones*. That none

must be thought learned, but Sophisterian Disputants ... That none must be thought valiant, but those that kill, or be killed. That none must be thought bountifull, but those that are prodigall ... That all duty and submission belongs to power, not to vertue ... That all those that marry on Tuesdayes and Thursdayes, shal be happy ... That the falling of Salt portends misfortune. Those that begin journies upon a Wednesday, shall run through much danger.[42]

As the Rational Lord's diatribe against the old regime continues, it becomes apparent that many aspects of Puritanism, for example an emphasis on sobriety of apparel, are objects of the satire. Logic is stretched to extremes, descending into anarchic absurdity.

In Chapter 1 of this book it was seen how, in the mid-seventeenth century, certain recreational activities, from organised theatre to country customs such as the Maypole, carried a political significance. The corollary to this was that identification with certain activities became an inherently political choice. On 24 May 1618 James I had published *The Kings Maiesties Declaration to his Subjects, concerning lawful Sports to be used*, known as *The Book of Sports*, which Charles I had reissued in 1633, with the support of Archbishop Laud, and which William Prynne, in *Canterburies Doom*, criticised for making 'not only lawfull, but convenient and necessary' activities such as 'May-games, Wakes, Revells, Dancing [and] Interludes'.[43] Designed to be read from the pulpits, *The Book of Sports* demonstrated, in its tone, a happy conjunction of the divine and the recreational:

> after the end of Divine Service, Our good people be not disturbed, letted, or discouraged from any lawful recreation, such as dauncing, either men or women, Archery for men, leaping, vaulting, or any such harm-lesse Recreation, nor from having of May-Games, Whitson Ales, and Morris-dances, and the setting up of Maypoles & other sports therewith used.[44]

When the Puritan Long Parliament convened in 1640, Laud was imprisoned, the Commons resolving a year later to keep the Sabbath and forbid dancing. On 5 May 1643 *The Book of Sports* was publicly burned. A year later, Parliament's bill for the Sabbath, 'An Ordinance of the Lords and Commons assembled in Parliament, for the better observation of the Lords-Day' was passed, forbidding, among other activities, 'Wrestlings, Shooting, Bowling, Ringing of Bells for plea-sure or pastime, Masque, Wake ... Church-Ale, Dancing, Games,

Sport or Pastime whatsoever'.[45] The wording and objectives of the Rational Lord's speech to Cavendish's Animal Parliament directly recall Puritan control of public recreation, which pervaded legislation of the 1640s. On 8 June 1647 'Festival dayes' such as Christmas, Easter and Whitsuntide were abolished and it was decreed, with a precision evocative of that which Cavendish's Rational Lord attributes to the legislation of 'Parliament of Errours', that every Tuesday workers were to be afforded 'convenient reasonable Recreation and Relaxation from their constant and ordinary Labours'.[46]

Other contemporaries of Cavendish were of course imaginatively inspired by the potential of the body as analogy for the cosmos. Thomas Browne wrote in the 1630s that 'the world that I regard is my selfe, it is the Microcosme of mine owne frame, that I cast my eye on', and the target of Charles Cotton's later, polemical, usage of the analogy is audaciously specific:

> Alas! my reason's overcast,
> That sovereign guide is quite displac't,
> Clearly dismounted from his throne,
> Banished his empire, fled and gone,
> And in his room
> An infamous usurper's come,
> Whose name is sounding in mine ear
> Like that, methinks of Oliver.[47]

Cotton's equivalence of reason and sovereignty is that which is found in The Animall Parliament, where 'The Head is the upper House of Parliament, where at the upper end of the said House sits the Soul King'.[48] Cavendish's decision to depict the head as the source of authority, rather than the belly, or the heart, as was the case with the ancient paradigms, is in itself a political statement, and a response to what various critics have seen as the dethronement of the heart which took place in the late 1640s in the anatomical writings of William Harvey.[49] The brain, as conceived of by Cavendish, is the power-house of creativity and imagination. Like a political kingdom, it is open to invasion, here in the form of 'Rhyming Pirates'.[50] The new Acts which the Rational Lord proposes to replace the old are an amalgamation of contemporary scientific theories and advances. At times this amalgamation conceals potential paradoxes. The Rational Lord's declaration that 'the Soul is a Kernel in the Braine', for example, is apparently contradicted by his statement some few lines later that *'the Soule is a thing, and nothing'.*[51] The Cartesian doctrine of primary and secondary qualities is recalled in the declaration that *'all light is in the Eye, not in the Sun'*, but Hobbesian discourse has been evoked – *'all those that have got the power, though unjustly, ought to be obeyed, without reluctancy'* – and is promulgated, as when the Rational Lord declares that *'Motion is the Creator of all things, at least of all formes. That Death is only a privation of Motion'.*[52] On the subject of motion, and explicitly Harveian, is the Rational Lord's declaration that *'the bloud goeth in a Circulation'.*[53] The popularity of the Rational Lord's proposals is evinced by its reception: 'This motion which this *Noble Lord* made, was *enacted* by the whole *Parliament* with much applause'.[54]

When John Donne wrote that 'the Heart alone is in Principalitie, and in the Throne, as King, the rest as Subjects', he was, according to Charles Webster, epitomising Jacobean medical thought.[55] His heart is 'a metonym of micro- and macrocosmic monarchy'.[56] This was the anti-Galenic intellectual strain which William Harvey also espoused when, in 1628, he published his mechanist work on the circulation of the blood, *De motu cordis*. The dedication 'To the most Serene and most Puissant Charles' explicitly constructs an analogous parity between heart and sovereign.[57] Its language is hyperbolic and unequivocal:

Most Serene King!
  The animal's heart is the basis of its life, its chief member, the sun of its microcosm; on the heart all its activity depends, from the heart all its liveliness and strength arise. Equally is the king the basis of his kingdoms, the sun of his microcosm, the heart of the state.[58]

Harvey goes on to argue that understanding the physiological workings of the heart is a royalist act, because, as he elaborates in a complex rhetorical twist, just as the structures of the state might provide an analogy for the workings intrinsic to the human body, so too might the biological operations mean that it is possible to model 'several of our concepts of royalty on our knowledge of the heart'.[59] In some of his earliest lectures whilst Lumleian lecturer at the Royal College of Physicians in 1615, Harvey's royalism and its capacity for being expressed through his anatomical discoveries was clear, as he wrote of a belch rising from the stomach as being a *'motion from the lower Hous'.*[60] In Harvey's empirical discourse, the result of 'the use of my own eyes instead of through books and the writings of others', anatomy and analogy become implicitly coterminous.[61] This discursive reciprocity had been in evidence to him in 1615, too, when he had declared of anatomists that 'politicians [can acquire] many examples from our art'.[62] This self-elevation functions as part of the European metamorphosis, begun by Vesalius in the 1540s, of the anatomist from superior observer to active participant, 'a new, autonomous role for the anatomist who wishes to be understood as a heroic figure'.[63]

The generic status of Harvey's own text is complicated by his language which, in its use of figures of speech, and its rhetorical tropes, veers between the scientific and the literary.[64] Writing of the ejaculation of semen, for example, he has recourse to personification as he writes that 'the prolific spirit leaves the body with a throb like some animal itself departing'.[65] Other sources of elucidative imagery include the world of machines. The systaltic motion of the heart 'recalls that mechanical device fitted to firearms in which, on pressure to a trigger, a flint falls and strikes and advances the steel, a spark is evoked ... all these movements, because of their rapidity, seeming to happen at once'.[66] Harvey's mechanistic conception of the human body was remarked upon by Martin Llewellyn, a poet-physician who described how Harvey's '*Observing* Eye' first identified 'all the *Wheels* and *Clock-work* of the *Heart* ... What Pullies *Close* its *Cells*'.[67] On the circular motion of the blood, Harvey has imagistic recourse to the natural world where moisture drawn from the earth falls back down as rain. As the blood comes to the heart, it is 'perfected, activated, and protected', since 'the heart is the tutelary deity of the body, the basis of life, the source of all things, carrying out its function of nourishing, warming, and activating the body as a whole'.[68] Further, the motion of the blood is detailed in language similar to that which Cavendish uses in her description of parliamentary process within the Animal Parliament. 'The artery, is a vessel', writes Harvey, 'which carries blood from the heart to the component parts of the body', and, just as Cavendish's Houses of Parliament exchange writs, 'the other is a vessel which carries blood from those component parts back to the heart'.[69] There can be little doubt, then, that the heart, 'site and source of warmth, a sort of hea[r]th and home ... the beginning of life', is the figure dominating Harvey's 1628 text.[70] Its pre-eminence is categorically averred:

the heart is the first part to exist ... it was the seat of blood, life, sensation and movement before either the brain or the liver had been created ... the heart, like some inner animal, was in place earlier ... Just as the king has the first and highest authority in the state, so the heart governs the whole body. It is, one might say, the source and root from which in the animal all power derives, and on which all power depends.[71]

Cavendish's *Animall Parliament*, in its scope and imagery, and the specificity of its parliamentary procedure, not only suggests a familiarity with the worlds of masculine activities of politics and science but combines the two using an established generic trope. Her privileging of the head over the heart, this latter organ being reserved for her Lower House, is her own political decision. It is a decision arguably motivated in response to Harvey's later shift from a mechanist to a vitalist construction of the circulation of the blood, that is, by his dethroning of the heart.[72]

By 1649, the year of the regicide, Harvey's correspondence with the anatomist Jean Riolan suggested that the heart was no longer 'the central organ of man's body ... the likeness of [Charles's] ... own royal power'.[73] It had been dethroned by the blood, now characterised as passing 'solely through the lungs (and not through the septum of the heart)'.[74] The primacy of the heart is dismissed as an Aristotelian error and in his answer to those who declare 'that the heart is the prime cause of pulsation and life', Harvey is unambiguous: 'If I may speak openly, I do not think that these things are so'.[75] The heart, veins, arteries, and blood are now, within Harvey's configuration, of equivalent status within the physiological hierarchy. As John Rogers expresses it, 'in a republic, it is more prudent to demote the proud heart to a simpler functionary of the more powerful blood'.[76] This 'powerful blood' is self-moving, with a vitalist agency quite independent of the heart, and the responsibility for distributing heat throughout the body. The heart has become (in language which Cavendish recalls with her 'they fetch, / ... from the *heart* the *gold* and *silver*'), 'the warehouse, source, and permanent fireplace ... like a hot kettle'.[77] The vitiation of Harvey's imagery, from the grandiloquent cosmological language of 1628 to the domestic terminology of 1649, is marked. The blood has become 'the primary efficient cause of the pulse', since, after the regicide, the figurative 'sun' of Harvey's 1628 writings had set.[78]

Harvey's pragmatic espousal of vitalism and its concomitant anti-hierarchical implications co-exists uncomfortably with his royalist politics. The theory of the revolution of the blood within the human body has been transformed following the revolution within the polity. By contrast, in *The Animall Parliament*, Cavendish, whilst similarly shifting the centre of power from heart to head, none the less maintains a mechanist ontology to complement her staunchly royalist politics.[79] Whereas Harvey was, by 1649, figuring the blood as self-moving and independent, it has been seen how, in Cavendish's Parliament, writs are sent between the Houses, that is, there is an element of compulsion. Cavendish's text is up-to-date in its physiological detail, but, wishing to avoid the liberal (because non-hierarchical) implications of a vitalist ontology, she maintains a mechanist hierarchy.[80] The structure of *The Animall Parliament* is therefore a specifically political pro-monarchical choice, constituting a direct avoidance of the self-determining, anti-authoritarian implications of vitalism. The concession Cavendish does make to Harvey's reconfigured philosophy is to shift the centre of power from the heart to the head of the body politic, but ultimately hers is still an obstinately mechanist model which recognises, and operates because of, monarchical superiority.[81] She has not dethroned the king, but has relocated the throne-room.[82]

John Rogers suggests that the increasing popularity of and familiarity with the corpuscular atomism of Democritus and Epicurus, with which Cavendish has been seen to engage in the scientific poems which constitute the first part of *Poems, and Fancies*, provided not only a model but also the impetus for a new doctrine of individualism. 'The lifeless and inert atoms of matter', he argues, 'provided for many in this period, most notably Hobbes, tempting analogues for individual human beings'.[83] Cavendish's imagined parliamentary structure is distinctively Hobbesian, in that, whilst privileging monarch over parliament, there is enough of a reciprocity between the institutions for divine right not to be the particular sort of monarchy being espoused.[84] The fairy kingdom poems in *Poems, and Fancies*, in their attribution of the causes of human psychology to materialist sources, that is to the motions of the body, also follow the paradigm established by Hobbes.[85]

Hobbes differentiates the long-term goals of reason from the immediate gratification desired by the passions, and this is a model which can be seen in *The Animall Parliament*, where the passions are 'the *Knights* and *Burgesses*' in the heart, reason, personified as Lord Reason, and the Rational Lord, being given preeminence by being located in the Upper House.[86] Further, the systems of choice and agency at work in Cavendish's Parliament – exemplified by the King's ambiguous, and slightly ominous statement, 'I make no question, but every one which are in my *Parliament* will be willing to consent' – are Hobbesian in that the Sovereign by virtue of his position expects the obedience of his people, not in a contractual sense, but rather more voluntarily than that.[87] Implicit in the Hobbesian gift of obedience which the people owe to their sovereign is an agreement that they will not disobey the sovereign's laws because this would lead to that which it is in the interests of every human being to avoid, namely, the state of nature.[88] As one critic expresses it, 'expediency, not morality, is for Hobbes the motive for political obedience'.[89] In turn, the sovereign must not give the people cause to regret giving him the 'gift' of this obedience: 'This is not Contract, but Gift, Free-Gift, Grace'.[90]

The very frontispiece to the first edition of *Leviathan* shows the giant figure of the crowned monarch composed of many smaller figures, looming over the landscape. It is the visual representation of Hobbes's recommendation that members of a commonwealth should 'conferre all their power and strength upon one Man, or upon one Assembly of men, that may reduce all their Wills, by plurality of voices, unto one Will: which is as much as to say, to appoint one man, or Assembly of men, to beare their Person'.[91] In Hobbes's philosophy the human individual is simultaneously creator and constituent of a greater whole which, in turn, is the sum of many individuals. The non-organic use of the analogy in *Leviathan* is made explicit from its start, and the language, images and structures found in the introduction are distinctly like Cavendish's in *The Animall Parliament*. If life is essentially mechanical, goes Hobbes's reasoning, why might not a mechanical construct, the State, also have a life of sorts? 'Nature (the Art whereby God hath made and governes the World)', he begins:

> is by the *Art* of man, as in many other things, so in this also imitated, that it can make an Artificial Animal ... For by Art is created that great Leviathan called a Common-wealth, or State, (in latine Civitas) which

is but an Artificiall Man ... and in which, the *Soveraignty* is an Artificiall *Soul*, as giving life and motion to the whole body; The *Magistrates*, and other *Officers* of Judicature and Execution, artificiall *Joynts*; *Reward* and *Punishment* (by which fastned to the seate of the Soveraignty, every joynt and member is moved to performe his duty) are the *Nerves*, that do the same in the Body Naturall.[92]

It can be seen how similar to Hobbes's mechanist model is Cavendish's. She not only has recourse to the same generic paradigm in order to express her political opinions but creates the same correspondences as Hobbes does: her sovereign, like his, is a soul; her body politic has lesser officers such as magistrates, and the machine that is both state and body is mobilised through the nerves or, more specifically in *The Animall Parliament*, and in contemporary, Harveian terminology, the veins and arteries.[93] The sensory faculties of Cavendish's construct, that is, reason, taste, sight and others, may appear vitalist in as much as they have a degree of self-determination, but decisions made in one House must be actively conveyed to the other; they cannot move themselves. The model then is predominantly mechanical. It is the monarch where parliamentary processes begin and end, and is the monarch that has directional power over the rest of the body.[94]

To return to *The Animall Parliament*, then, the Upper House assents to a motion to defeat the '*Rhyming Pirates*' with '*Armes of Rhethoricke*', and the narrative attention switches to the Lower House where the debate centres on the '*Naturalizing*' of a foreign man, whose loyalties have been called into doubt.[95] The narrative shift is signalled by Cavendish's use of the expression 'In the meane time', suggestive as it is of an unceasing, continual process which applies both to the autonomic systems of the human body and to the processes of parliamentary procedure which must continue ceaselessly for the maintenance of a peaceful life within the body politic.[96] The relentless functioning recalls once more the Harveian paradigm of the 'unceasing, circular sort of movement' of the blood.[97] The foreign man is granted citizenship 'for he had been so industrious in Petitioning every *particular Member*'.[98] The text here functions as a kind of wish-fulfilment, a testament to Cavendish's recurring fantasy, expressed in various guises in her work, of public oratory or successful petitioning (so unlike her own experiences at Goldsmith's Hall in 1651) leading to naturalisation, that is, to the granting of the status of citizen. It is a trope in evidence here, and, as has been seen, in the figure of Travellia, and it is one which permeates the judicial structure of *Heavens Library* too.

The locus of the parliament within a human body is occasionally forgotten, as in the exchange between the Lord Reason and one of the judges about '*false Coyne*', a conceit which operates on the level of mercantile metaphor: '*false Coyne, as dissembling tears, and hollow sighs*'.[99] Here the idea that the kingdom is inside a body is largely irrelevant, and the collecting together of all the coinage 'in the *Kingdome*, to make a triall of the currantnesse', is a purely political notion which, beyond the tears metaphor, neither furthers nor benefits from the bodily conceit.[100] However, the Lord Reason's next speech moves the discourse back into the realms of the body, and, what is more, into contemporary debates over blood consumption and conservation, here rendered in distinctly Livian terms. The kingdom of the body is threatened by the rich and indigestible food which has been consumed, and which does not allow for the stomach to 'breed new bloud'.[101] In reply, Judge Taste, with the logic of Menenius, avers that 'if the *stomack* should eate sparingly, and not such things as the *Appetite* doth desire, the *Body* of the *Kingdom* would grow weak and faint'.[102] By way of a remedy, he proposes moderation instead of the extremes of excess and 'perpetuall *abstinency*', so that the limbs, earlier identified as the members of the commonwealth, may continue to function.[103] On the whole, Cavendish's placing of the parliament within a human body, in its correspondence of biological part with logical function, differs from the Classical generic antecedents of Plato or Aristotle, whose largely idealistic counterpointing of body and state had no real analogue in the human body.[104] Her successful detailing of the processes of both body and state make her use of the analogy, as Barkan expresses it, 'plausible'.[105] The human body has moved from being the abstract entity of the earliest uses of the paradigm, to having recognisable physical characteristics and functions. Natural, political and ecclesiastical bodies exist in their diversity within the unifying frame of the analogy.[106] The real and the idealised co-exist in a mutually informative relationship.

At times the body is represented in Cavendish's text less as a body politic than as a physical, geographical kingdom. This representation also has a political bias, functioning in part as a critique of the Puritan sequestration of royalist estates. In this portrayal the digestive tracts become roads, the nose becomes a bridge and the full stomach becomes an impassable quagmire. Most pointedly, given the archetypal Cavalier appearance, 'the *Puritans*, and *Roman Priests* cut downe all the *stately* and *thick woods* of *Haire*, as there is almost none left grown to build *ships* of *ornament* with'.[107] The explicit, and uncharacteristic, mention of the Puritans, their actions pointedly described in the past tense, marks Cavendish's attempt figuratively to write them out of power. The text projects to a time when the Puritan regime's errors, as she perceives them, may be viewed retrospectively, that is, as something past. It has already been seen how the Parliament is represented as sitting in 1802 – their statutes running 'from this present of *January*, one *thousand eight hundred and two*' – a framework in the future within which current regimes are represented by looking back, a paradox which facilitates a directly contemporary critique.[108] As the body which is the Animal Parliament houses a multiplicity of other bodies – the ecclesiastical, the monarchical and the polity – so too does the text simultaneously operate within three chronologies: a present, an imagined past and an anticipated future.

The committee's report into the decrepit state of the kingdom is quickly drawn up, and hybrid discourses emerge, the suggested remedies being at times cosmetic, at times medical. Silver pins, for example, are to be used to prop up the bridges of noses ravaged by, presumably, venereal disease. Suggestively, given the analogous significance of the trees, 'the *Woods* of *Haire*' will grow only on young heads – the old must remain 'bare, and bald'.[109] The parliament may pass new Acts, but some of the damage of the old regime is irreparable. Restoration of the kingdom having been planned, 'an Act of prevention' is passed banning sweetmeats and '*Healths*'.[110] However, the power of the populace is suggested by the mutiny of the young people, demanding alteration to this Act. The legislation is accordingly altered. Cavendish's parliament is strongly hierarchical, but, on relatively minor matters such as this, able to present a placatory front.[111] Certain issues arise from this mutiny. Its ontology is unclear. That is, its nature and location are predominantly of the world of the kingdom, not of the body. The commonality does not seem to have a carefully delineated analogical counterpoint on an anatomical level and the mutiny marks a moment of the text exceeding

Cavendish's control, breaking out of the poetic boundaries which, in her choice of generic model, she established for it. The allegory has been momentarily forgotten. Similarly, whilst she appears to be in control of her text, political circumstance serves to remind her of her comparative disempowerment in the real world.

The anatomical framework is returned to, and new personifications which have their basis in the explicitly anatomical functions, not in allegorised representations thereof, emerge, in the form of the veins' petition. However, a paradox is in evidence here too, as the veins, previously mute carriers of decrees within a mechanist hierarchy, have a degree of vitalist autonomy, and the ability to represent their own grievances. Complaining about the quality of the blood they receive from the liver, the veins have recourse to mercantile images, since their 'Trading [is] utterly decayed'.[112] The liver, summoned by a specially established committee, blames the stomach for the poor quality of the blood, the result being that the House decides to purge the stomach twice a year. Not only does this description recall Livy's Belly but it also draws parallels between body and commonwealth in a way which recalls the Hobbesian paradigm once more. Like a human body, the commonwealth can be susceptible to sicknesses or diseases, as it is expressed in *Leviathan*, 'that proceed from the poyson of seditious doctrines'.[113]

The last speech of *The Animall Parliament* is that of the King, and a version of monarchical restoration is enacted. '*My good and loving Subjects*', he begins, '*I give you thankes for your care and industry, in rectifying the Errours of this Kingdome*'.[114] The speech takes place in a 'great *Hall*', being on one level the skull, on another, perhaps, a suggestion of Cavendish again slipping out of her analogy into a more straightforward, concretised representation of a parliament. Once more, issues of agency and consent are highlighted, as the King declares of his subjects: '*I make no question I shall finde them alwayes as ready to obey, as I to command*'.[115] The impression the King gives is that he wishes to rule with clemency rather than tyranny, and the whole piece ends in a highly affirmatory way, a Parliament united in its joyous, declamatory 'God save the King, God save the King'.[116] This happy dissolution of Parliament signals too Cavendish's dissolution of her allegorical conceit. The dispersal of the King's subjects, whilst recalling the exilic dispersal of the royalists, also constitutes the diffusion of many discourses within one text.

As a response to the atomised universe she perceived from exile, and in order to offer a critique of the regime which she blamed for turning her world and established systems upside down, Cavendish found in the genre of body as kingdom the perfect analogue for the expression of her royalism, and her engagement with, and deliberate adaptation of, new scientific discourses. Since Barkan's analysis of the history and permutations of the analogy has been so informative in this chapter, it is appropriate to conclude with his summary of its significance:

> In studying the cosmos, man comes to know himself; and in identifying the parallels of microcosm and macrocosm and understanding the relations of like to like in the two worlds, man grasps self and world at once. The existence of the parallels is a means for understanding each world in relation to the other, and at the same time an ever present proof that a harmonistic place of man in the cosmos can be found if only the parallels are successfully delineated.[117]

Harvey's fearful, and politically motivated, flight from the delineation of the parallels he at first understood between the natural body and the sovereign body, and Hobbes's mechanist conception of the analogy, provided for Cavendish the generic models which informed her *Animall Parliament*, in which, as in so much of her writing, she figuratively sought just such an 'harmonistic place' as Barkan indites. John Rogers has demonstrated how Cavendish's post-Restoration shift to vitalism marked a political, feminist agenda.[118] Similarly, then, it may be asserted that her mechanism was a direct response to the political demands of the 1640s and 1650s. In the generically anomalous status of *The Animall Parliament*, Cavendish does not present a text which is wholly political treatise or anatomical disquisition, but slips between divergent discourses – mercantile, medical, monarchical and religious – with an ease accorded by her responsiveness to a dominant generic model, and her attendant receptivity to contemporary political debate.

Notes

1 The edition used is William Shakespeare, *The Tragedy of Coriolanus*, ed. R. B. Parker (Oxford: Clarendon Press, 1994). Further references will be to this edition.
2 Livy, *The Romane Historie Written By T. Livius of Padua ... Tran[slat]ed out of*

Latin into English [Ab Urbe Condita], by PHILEMON HOLLAND, Doctor in Physick (London, 1659), p. 54 (Wing L2613). The first edition of Holland's work appeared in 1600, and so would have been available to Cavendish before she wrote *The Animall Parliament*. The long history of the Belly narrative is evinced, for example, by Sidney, who writes that 'the tale is notorious, and as notorious that it was a tale'. Sidney, p. 115. In *Coriolanus* the First Citizen's exasperating, yet astute, interruptions of Menenius's tale serve to emphasise his prior familiarity with it. He actually continues the analogy in his own words, talking of: 'The kingly, crownèd head, the vigilant eye, / The counsellor heart, the arm our soldier, / Our steed the leg, the tongue our trumpeter' (I.i.112).

3 Livy, p. 54.

4 *Ibid.*

5 *Ibid.* On the 'loose identification of heart and belly ... implied by the semantic vagueness of the seventeenth-century "belly"', see Rogers, p. 25, n. 56.

6 Livy, p. 54.

7 The use of 'hearts' seems to be Holland's own embellishment, since the original reads: 'flexisse mentes hominum', *mentes* being 'minds'. The Loeb Classical Library translation thus reads: 'Drawing a parallel from this to show how like was the internal dissension of the bodily members to the anger of the plebs against the Fathers, he prevailed upon the *minds* of his hearers' (my emphasis). See Livy, *Works*, trans. B. O. Foster, 14 vols (London: Heinemann, 1967), I, 325.

8 On these poems' formative if not substantive Lucretian characteristics see Chapter 2, above.

9 Cavendish, *Poems, and Fancies*, p. 162.

10 *Ibid.*, p. 163.

11 Cavendish writes that 'the *eye's* the *sea* they traffick in, / And their ship doth swim. / But if a *teare* doth breake, as it doth fall, / Or wip'd away, they may a *shipwrach* call'. *Ibid.*, p. 162.

12 *Ibid.*, p. 163.

13 *Ibid.*, p. 164.

14 *Ibid.*

15 I do not mean to suggest that Cavendish's unity within the human figure of a multiplicity of discourses is unique to her, but that in her writing it functions with a specific political agenda.

16 *Ibid.*, p. 164.

17 A similar mercantile/nutritive conceit is used by Hobbes, who writes of 'This Matter, commonly called Commodities', that 'The Nutrition of a Common-wealth consisteth, in the *Plenty*, and *Distribution* of *Materials* conducing to Life: In *Concoction*, or *Preparation*; and (when concocted) in the *Conveyance* of it, by convenient conduits, to the Publique use'. See Thomas Hobbes, *Leviathan*, ed. C. B. Macpherson (Harmondsworth: Penguin, 1985), pp. 294–5.

18 Cavendish, *Poems, and Fancies*, p. 165.

19 *Ibid.*

20 *Ibid.*, p. 199.

21 Walter Charleton, Cavendish's acquaintance in exile, made similar connections between anatomical and political discourses in *Oeconomia animalis* (London, 1669, Wing C3687). He argued that medicine was useful for the 'Viro *Politico* & *Militari*' because 'nullus est melior Aditus ad reconditam illam Resque Hominesque regendi Artem, quam cognoscendo Arcana Natura' (sig. *3v). My thanks to Stephen Clucas for drawing this reference to my attention.

22 Leonard Barkan, *Nature's Work of Art: The Human Body as Image of the World* (New Haven: Yale University Press, 1975), p. 5. Barkan identifies a three-stage circle of analogy whereby the cosmos, too great a concept to be grasped without reference to the familiar, is figured in terms of the human body which, in turn, supplies new models for the cosmos. See Barkan, pp. 62–3.

23 *Ibid.*, p. 81. Cavendish's representation is more sophisticated than some earlier paradigms, since, to quote Barkan, Livy, for example, 'in describing the mutiny ... offers some sense of a commonwealth of individuals, but none of the individuals is humanized. Consequently, neither the overall body nor the individuals comprising it seem particularly human'. *Ibid.*, p. 97. By contrast, whilst the human body is not 'humanized' in Cavendish's text, the members of the Parliament, to a greater or lesser degree, are.

24 Cavendish, *Poems, and Fancies*, p. 149. On the early modern knowledge of the organisation of the hive, and the assumption that the most important bee was a King rather than a Queen, and for the political uses to which the analogy of the hive could be put, see Timothy Raylor, 'Samuel Hartlib and the Commonwealth of Bees', in Michael Leslie and Timothy Raylor, eds, *Culture and Cultivation in Early Modern England: Writing and the Land* (Leicester: Leicester University Press, 1992), pp. 91–129.

25 Cavendish, *The Animall Parliament*, in *Poems, and Fancies*, p. 199. All further quotations from *The Animall Parliament* will be drawn from this edition.

26 *Ibid.*, p. 200.

27 For example, the Witch of Eloquence represented at the end of the text bewitches lovers, rendering them, paradoxically, '*voluntary slaves*'. *Ibid.*, p. 211.

28 *Ibid.*, p. 200.

29 *Ibid.*

30 The Long Parliament convened in 1640, and Pride's Purge took place in December 1648. The MPs who remained until April 1653 were called the Rump Parliament. This naming in itself suggests an analogy between political and bodily processes and structures, and has been examined by Blair Worden. He writes of the Parliament that it was 'described in 1649 by the purged MP Clement Walker as "this fag end, this veritable Rump of a parliament with corrupt maggots in it"'. See Blair Worden, *The Rump Parliament 1648–1653* (Cambridge: Cambridge University Press, 1974), p. 4.

31 This chronology is based on the account given by David Underdown in

155

Pride's Purge: Politics in the Puritan Revolution (London: Allen & Unwin, 1985), p. 172. The very wording of the Act to abolish monarchy is suggestive of Puritan unease with the singular structural integrity of the body politic: 'the office of a king in this nation, and to have the power thereof in any single person, is unnecessary, burdensome, and dangerous to the liberty, safety, and public interest of the people of this nation: and therefore ought to be abolished'. See Underdown, *Pride's Purge*, pp. 202–3.

32 *Ibid.*, p. 202.

33 *Ibid.*

34 Cavendish, *Poems, and Fancies*, p. 201.

35 *Ibid.*, pp. 201, 202.

36 Cavendish may not only, in her careful detailing of parliamentary procedure, be offering a critique of the Puritan abolition of the Upper House, but may also be pleading for a non-constitutional, absolutist monarchy, her specificity perhaps being able to be read as a parody of the necessarily dilatory and cumbersome nature of a democratic system.

37 This idea of bodies within bodies is one to which Cavendish was to return in *The Blazing World*, a text I briefly examine in Chapter 6.

38 Cavendish, *Poems, and Fancies*, p. 202.

39 On this epithet see Tuck, p. 141. Hobbes's dismissal of the papacy as being able to be 'compared not unfitly to the *Kingdome of Fairies*', contrasts with Cavendish's own representation of a fairy world. Hobbes, *Leviathan*, p. 712.

40 For the sake of simplicity, the '*Rationall Lord*' will be referred to as the 'Rational Lord' in my text.

41 Cavendish, *Poems, and Fancies*, pp. 202–3. Cavendish's peculiar choice of 1802 comes as something of a surprise given the intrinsically contemporary character of the text as a whole. It may be that setting the tale some one hundred and fifty years into the future acts, like its familiar generic structure, to deflect direct accusations of subversion. The date is discussed again later in this chapter.

42 *Ibid.*, p. 203.

43 Quoted in James T. Dennison, Jr, *The Market Day of the Soul: The Puritan Doctrine of the Sabbath in England, 1532–1700* (Lanham: University Press of America, 1983), p. 75.

44 Quoted in Hans-Peter Wagner, *Puritan Attitudes Towards Recreation in Early Seventeenth-century New England: With Particular Consideration of Physical Recreation* (Frankfurt: Verlag Peter Lang, 1982), p. 71.

45 Dennison, p. 93. On Laud's anti-Sabbatarianism, and for a detailed study of the controversy surrounding *The Book of Sports*, see *ibid.*, pp. 71, 92–3, and Wagner, p. 71. The chronology in this paragraph is based on Dennison's text.

46 Wagner, p. 72.

47 Thomas Browne, *Religio Medici* (1643; repr. Menston: Scolar, 1970), p. 171. *Religio Medici* was written in 1634, but not officially published until 1643. Charles Cotton, 'Melancholy. Pindaric Ode', in *Poems of Charles Cotton 1630–1687*, ed. John Beresford (London: Cobden-Sanderson, 1923),

pp. 207–8. Writers who engaged with the analogy after the publication of *Poems, and Fancies* include Walter Charleton, who wrote in 1659 that 'the most perfect Model or Form of Government ... is the Body of Man', and James Harrington, in his *The Commonwealth of Oceana* (1656), who declared that 'a Model of Government ... is no less than political Anatomy'. See Rogers, pp. 19, 23. Use of the analogy was not restricted to royalist sympathisers. William Prynne and others warned that 'the physical anarchy of the body is the first step towards anarchy in the body politic'. See Alan Shepherd, ' "O seditious Citizen of the Physicall Common-Wealth!": Harvey's Royalism and His Autopsy of Old Parr', *University of Toronto Quarterly*, 65 (1996), 482–505 (p. 497). Shepherd suggests of Harvey, much as I suggest of Cavendish, but from the reverse political perspective, that he used literary strategies to 'stave off misreadings or treasonous extrapolations' of what Shepherd identifies as, in Harvey's case, 'the republican implications of his cardiac research', present even in 1628. Shepherd, p. 483.

48 Cavendish, *Poems, and Fancies*, p. 199.

49 Such critics include Christopher Hill, who argues that 'Harvey dethroned the heart in the same year as the English Republic was proclaimed'. Christopher Hill, 'William Harvey and the Idea of Monarchy', in Charles Webster, ed., *The Intellectual Revolution of the Seventeenth Century* (London: Routledge, 1974), pp. 160–81 (p. 163). For the opposing view, that 'Harvey did not dethrone the heart in favour of the blood after 1649', see Gweneth Whitteridge, 'William Harvey: a Royalist and No Parliamentarian', in *Intellectual Revolution*, pp. 182–8 (p. 183). Whitteridge also, perhaps with reason, warns that 'a grain of evidence is worth a ton of conjecture on Harvey's political views'. Whitteridge, p. 187. For a summary of the debate between Hill and Whitteridge, see Christopher Hill, 'William Harvey (No Parliamentarian, No Heretic) and the Idea of Monarchy', in *Intellectual Revolution*, pp. 189–96.

50 Cavendish, *Poems, and Fancies*, p. 205. My argument is that Cavendish's choice of the head to represent the king is generically conventional on one level, but that on another it operates as a quite deliberate political choice made after Harvey's 1649 dethronement of the heart in his theory of the circulation of the blood. The twelfth-century writer John of Salisbury constructed in *Policraticus* a hierarchy similar to Cavendish's. 'The place of the head', he wrote, 'in the body of the commonwealth is filled by the prince, who is subject only to God ... even as in the human body the head is quickened and governed by the soul. The place of the heart is filled by the Senate'. Quoted in Barkan, p. 72.

51 Cavendish, *Poems, and Fancies*, p. 204.

52 *Ibid.*, p. 204. Hobbes held, in contrast to some of the Rational Lord's proposals, that 'All which qualities called *Sensible*, are in the object that causeth them'. Hobbes, *Leviathan*, p. 86.

53 Cavendish, *Poems, and Fancies*, p. 204.

54 *Ibid.*

55 John Donne, *Devotions upon Emergent Occasions*, quoted in Charles Webster, 'William Harvey and the Crisis of Medicine in Jacobean England', in Jerome

J. Bylebyl, ed., *William Harvey and His Age: The Professional and Social Context of the Discovery of the Circulation* (Baltimore: Johns Hopkins University Press, 1979), pp. 1–27 (p. 17).

56 Shepherd, p. 485.

57 William Harvey, *The Circulation of the Blood, and Other Writings*, trans. Kenneth J. Franklin, and intro. by Andrew Wear (London: Everyman, 1990), p. 3. Further quotations from *De motu cordis* and the correspondence with Riolan will be drawn from this edition. Shepherd argues, quite on the contrary to my argument, that 'the familiar doxology' of this dedication permits Harvey to forestall 'the impulse of readers to extrapolate from the research of an anatomist to the macrocosmic body politic'. Shepherd, pp. 488, 487. This is to regard his theories as purely discursive rather than as grounded in empirical research.

58 Harvey, *The Circulation of the Blood*, p. 3.

59 *Ibid.*

60 William Harvey, *Lectures on the Whole of Anatomy: An Annotated Translation of 'Prelectiones Anatomiae Universalis'*, ed. C. D. O'Malley, F. N. L. Poynter and K. F. Russell (Berkeley: University of California Press, 1961), p. 60.

61 Harvey, *The Circulation of the Blood*, p. 17. This trope of natural genius, unhampered by the views of others, is common in the period. Hobbes, for example, 'prided himself, like many dogmatists, on avoiding stuffing his mind with other people's opinions. Sir William Petty reported that he never saw more than half a dozen books in Hobbes' chamber and Aubrey recorded "He was wont to say that if he had read as much as other men, he should have knowne no more than other men"'. See Richard Peters, *Hobbes* (Harmondsworth: Penguin, 1967), p. 18. The empty library shelves of the study in which Cavendish appears in the frontispiece to *Philosophical and Physical Opinions*, and the verse which accompanies the engraving, have been taken as being similarly indicative of her independence of thought, or 'absolute privacy, void of other bodies and empty even of other minds'. See Gallagher, p. 30.

62 Harvey, *Lectures*, p. 215. Another link between anatomy and politics is evinced by the connection forged by the royalist press suggesting that the doctrine of mortalism had 'been partly responsible for the Civil War'. See Hill, 'William Harvey and the Idea', pp. 171–2.

63 Jonathan Sawday, 'The Fate of Marsyas: Dissecting the Renaissance Body', in Nigel Gent and Lucy Llewellyn, eds, *Renaissance Bodies: The Human Figure in English Culture c. 1540–1600* (London: Reaktion, 1990), pp. 111–35 (p. 122). Sawday makes the interesting point that 'In many respects, a dissection was, quite literally, a theatrical performance, with music playing during the dissection and refreshment provided'. Sawday, p. 131. Aspects of the very discipline of anatomy, then, may be read, in their performative and spectacular character, as being royalist acts. Cavendish's vivisection of the body politic, as I argue here, has clear political implications.

64 In *De motu cordis*, for example, Harvey describes a ligature experiment, the role of which in explicating his theories 'is more illuminating than the light

of noon'. Harvey, *Circulation*, p. 54. Further, in his desire to illustrate, he intermittently resorts to the anecdotal. 'I once fell from my carriage', he states, 'and struck my forehead', continuing with a description of why he supposes the site of the injury immediately swelled. *Ibid.*, p. 60. As John Rogers expresses it: 'Throughout his career Harvey fashioned his explanation of the purpose of the circulation of the blood within the literary parameters of political philosophy. It is as an account of the ideal political body, a genre we recognize as utopia, that we must examine Harvey's most important contributions to medical science'. Rogers, p. 17.

65 Harvey, *The Circulation of the Blood*, p. 28.

66 *Ibid.*, p. 30.

67 Martin Llewellyn, quoted in Robert G. Frank, Jr, 'The Image of Harvey in Commonwealth and Restoration England', in Bylebyl, pp. 103–43 (p. 123). Frank identifies that 'On the most elementary level, Harvey's findings entered into literary works as facts that could be adduced to support one or another kind of argument, or as the foundation for rhetorical flights of fancy'. Frank, p. 117. Such possibilities were certainly not lost on Cavendish.

68 Harvey, *The Circulation of the Blood*, pp. 46–7.

69 *Ibid.*, p. 47.

70 *Ibid.*, p. 69.

71 *Ibid.*, p. 84.

72 Harvey, using personification once more, tells how 'Nature wished the animal as a whole to be created, nourished, preserved and perfected by that organ, to be in effect its work and its dwelling-place'. *Ibid.*

73 *Ibid.*, p. 3. However, in the introduction to *De motu cordis*, in positioning his findings in relation to Galenic theory, Harvey declares in an expression powerfully suggestive of the vitalism he was later to espouse, that 'Indeed, no one denies that blood as blood, even that which flows in the veins, is imbued with spirits'. *Ibid.*, p. 9. The exchanges with Riolan were published in 1649 as *Exercitatio Anatomica de Circulatione Sanguinis, or, An Anatomical Essay concerning the Circulation of the Blood*. See Harvey, *Circulation*, p. xiv, In *De generatione*, published in 1651, Harvey 'warns us to situate his theoretical revolution at a moment eight years before the regicide'. See Rogers, p. 29.

74 Harvey, *The Circulation of the Blood*, p. 134.

75 *Ibid.*, p. 135.

76 Rogers, p. 21. Rogers's assertion here is at odds with his later declaration that 'Harvey's deployment of a liberal discourse of political organization ... has more to do with the history of compelling patterns of discursive explanation than with literary strategies cunningly deployed for political gain'. *Ibid.*, p. 24. Ironically, given that the object of Rogers's discussion is the issue of agency, he apparently retracts the very agency he had previously bestowed on Harvey, again glossing over the fundamental empiricism underlying Harvey's methodology in his wish to characterise it as primarily discursive.

77 Harvey, *The Circulation of the Blood*, p. 136. This discourse is reminiscent of Menenius's Belly in *Coriolanus*, 'the storehouse and the shop' (I.i.130).

78 Harvey, *The Circulation of the Blood*, p. 136.

79 I am aware of, and would take care to avoid falling into, the trap of attributing to Cavendish's work that which Rogers terms 'unreflective political intentionalism'. Rogers, p. 22. However, as Rogers also makes clear, the political moment does facilitate a specific mode of scientific thinking, itself productive of a particular ontological paradigm. As generic boundaries between scientific and political discourses were being blurred, so too might the physiological discourses of the time have been informed by dominant politico-economic theories. See Rogers for an analysis of the vitalist movement's 'curious engagement of the first and most influential model of decentralized organisation: the economic paradigm of the self-regulating market'. *Ibid.*, p. 22. I have already shown how Cavendish, whilst not a vitalist in 1653, none the less occasionally adopts mercantile images.

80 This hierarchised body recalls that characterised by Harvey in 1615, where the 'Upper [venter]' of the body is described thus: 'head, brain; domicile, shrine, citadel of the spirit where the animal senses, where the intellect and reason [reside]'. Harvey, *Lectures*, p. 35.

81 Cavendish's less than egalitarian political philosophy is also evinced through her outspoken passion for honorific titles. On the title-page to *Poems, and Fancies*, for example, she styles herself 'the Thrice Noble, Illustrious, and Excellent Princess the Lady Marchioness of Newcastle'. Harvey, by contrast, never knighted, regarded titles as 'wooden leggs'. Quoted in Hill, 'William Harvey', p. 178.

82 One critic has identified a contradictorily vitalist mechanism in *Poems, and Fancies*. See Stevenson, pp. 527–43. He argues that for Cavendish, order as expressed in her atomist poems 'is not absolute, or even rational in a Hobbesian sense, but contingent on the interplay of autonomous, independent forces'. *Ibid.*, p. 532. I cannot, however, concur with Stevenson's depiction of Cavendish as non-partisan in her writing, and in her creation of a material universe. 'Cavendish uses atoms to explain, rather than to criticize', argues Stevenson, 'such political problems as war and revolution without taking sides as she would had she incorporated moral values into her cosmology'. *Ibid.*, p. 535. It would appear that the success of Cavendish's politically motivated generic dissimulation persists.

83 Rogers, p. 36. Rogers's identification of Cavendish, in contrast to Hobbes, as having a commitment to an 'alternative vitalist genealogy of the individual by the strength with which [she] ... propound[s] the monistic infusion of body with spirit', refers to her later works. Rogers's 'Vitalist Moment' occurs in Cavendish's case later into her writing career. *Ibid.*, p. 1. I do not identify this vitalist ontology in *Poems, and Fancies*. Rogers goes on to demonstrate how the individualism of vitalist monism differed from a mechanist, Hobbesian version. *Ibid.*, p. 37. The hierarchy Cavendish establishes in *The Animall Parliament* is not monist, but, on some levels, Hobbesian. Her later 'monistic materialism', Rogers argues, supports her 'social agenda ... – the liberation of women from the constraints of patriarchy'. *Ibid.*, p. 181. This 'agenda' is identifiable, he avers, in the 'personal, informal' prefatory

material to Cavendish's work. *Ibid.*, p. 182. I believe that to characterise the introductory apparatus to her texts in this way is to miss its public intent and calculated tones. On monistic vitalism as a philosophy of 'protoliberalism', see *ibid.*, p. 12.

84 Rogers assesses the implications for writers in the mid-seventeenth century of the intellectual shift from vitalist to mechanist discourses by arguing that 'the individual arose, then, not as the self-moving body indivisibly aligned with the soul, but as a personification of the *individuus*, the atomic particle that served as the indivisible building block of the authoritative edifice of mechanism'. *Ibid.*, p. 226.

85 However, the Hobbesian notion of materialism is complicated since he attempts to render it compatible with voluntary human desires and activities. It has thus been argued that Hobbes in fact ignores potential conflicts in his philosophy between determinism and free-will, and between 'materialist metaphysics and an ordinary account of human psychology'. See Ted Honderich, ed., *The Oxford Companion to Philosophy* (Oxford: Oxford University Press, 1996), p. 368. On Cavendish's understanding and utilisation of Hobbesian 'motion' see Rogers, pp. 186–7.

86 Cavendish, *Poems, and Fancies*, p. 199.

87 *Ibid.*, p. 200. On Cavendish's understanding of Hobbesian formulations of volition and consent, and the connections of these with vitalism see Rogers, p. 192. 'Hobbes's genius', asserts Rogers, 'lay in part in his ability to refigure every act of obligation, or even of coercion, into a drama of tacit consent'. *Ibid.*, p. 206.

88 Cavendish's familiarity with the Hobbesian idea of a state of nature is suggested in a poem earlier in the volume, 'Of a *Funerall*', where the exiled's anguish at being separated from her family is emphasised. Her brother has been killed, and she asks of, or for, him: 'Alas, who shall condole my *Funerall*, / Since none is neere that doth my *life* concern?', going on to declare, in clearly Hobbesian language, that '*men* no *pitty*, nor *compassion* have, / But all in *savage wildernesse* doe delight'. Cavendish, *Poems, and Fancies*, p. 195.

89 Christopher Hill, *Puritanism and Revolution: Studies in Interpretation of the English Revolution of the Seventeenth Century* (London: Mercury Books, 1962), p. 277.

90 Hobbes, *Leviathan*, p. 193. On the people's obedience as a 'gift', and the sovereign's appropriate response to this, see Honderich, where it is argued that, in Hobbes's philosophy, 'What is moral and immoral is determined by what leads to lasting peace, what is just and unjust is determined by the laws of the state. On this account, it is immoral to hold that the sovereign can act unjustly, for to hold this is contrary to the stability of the state and hence to lasting peace'. Honderich, pp. 369–70.

91 Hobbes, *Leviathan*, p. 227. On the frontispiece to *Leviathan* see Tuck, p. 143, Barkan, pp. 113–15. Barkan neatly encapsulates the title-page's significance: 'There could be no more literally anthropomorphic representation'. Barkan, p. 113. As Hobbes expressed it: 'The King of any Countrey is the

Publique Person, or Representative of all his own Subjects'. Hobbes, *Leviathan*, p. 449.

92 *Ibid.*, p. 81. On Hobbes's mechanistic, non-organic conception of state and individual see Barkan, p. 114.

93 The parallels I draw here refute John Rogers's assertion that 'Cavendish is not, like Hobbes, explicit about the analogical connection between the worlds of material and social organization'. Rogers, p. 204.

94 I do not mean to suggest a rivalry between Hobbes and Harvey where none existed. Rather, in his will, Harvey left 'to my good ffreind Mr Thomas Hobbs to buy something to keepe in remembrance of mee Tenne pounds'. Harvey, *Circulation*, p. 173. The presence of Hobbes in Harvey's will is suggestive of the central place he occupied in the web of the intellectual society of which the Cavendishes, too, were members. Hobbes was at the heart of the circulation of ideas, and wrote in 1655 in *De Corpore* that Harvey must be truly great to be recognised in his own lifetime. See Frank, p. 120.

95 Cavendish, *Poems, and Fancies*, pp. 205–6.

96 *Ibid.*, p. 206.

97 Harvey, *Circulation*, p. 68. Motion is central to *Leviathan*, and for Harvey's influence on Hobbes in this respect see Tuck, p. 162.

98 Cavendish, *Poems, and Fancies*, p. 206.

99 *Ibid.*, p. 204.

100 *Ibid.*

101 *Ibid.*, p. 205.

102 *Ibid.*

103 *Ibid.*, p. 206.

104 Barkan identifies the Epistles of St Paul as 'by far the fullest treatment of the analogy between the human body and the body politic up to its time'. Barkan, p. 67. Paul declares that 'the body is not one member, but many', and goes on to elaborate. Quoted in *Ibid.*, p. 67. Jonathan Sawday examines the relevance for the early anatomists of Christ's symbolic self-dissection at the Last Supper. Sawday, p. 130.

105 Barkan, p. 85.

106 As Barkan expresses the phenomenon: 'Once a real human being is clothed in this analogous human body ... his self is multiplied and diversified by a juxtaposition of his own natural body with the multiplicity of society for which that body is an analogue'. *Ibid.*, p. 89.

107 Cavendish, *Poems, and Fancies*, p. 207. Men's long hair was perceived by Puritans, citing I Corinthians 11.14, as being shameful and effeminising. See Tamsyn Williams, 'Polemical Prints of the English Revolution' in Gent and Llewellyn, pp. 86–110 (p. 93). Williams, in her discussion of civil war pamphlets and woodcuts, elaborates on how the human body could be imaged in a specifically political and propagandist way: 'Prominent images of human bodies were invaluable weapons in the smear campaigns'. Williams, p. 96. In 1628 William Prynne had published *The Unlovelinesse of Love-Lockes* against long hair. See Freeman, 'Preface' to Prynne, *Histriomastix*, p. 5.

108 Cavendish, *Poems, and Fancies*, p. 208.

109 *Ibid.*

110 *Ibid.*, p. 209. 'Healths' refers to alcohol in the form of salutary toasts (*OED*). The specificity of the Act – 'no *Healths* to be dranke but upon *Festivall days*' – is, in its presumption of the existence of such festival days as were banned by the Puritans, political in itself. *Ibid.*, p. 209.

111 The characterisation of the people as being 'the *Humours* and *Appetites*', and their concomitant low position in the bodily hierarchy recalls once more Shakespeare's Menenius's addressing of the First Citizen as 'the great toe of this assembly ... / one o' th' lowest, basest, poorest / Of this most wise rebellion, thou goes foremost' (I.i.152).

112 Cavendish, *Poems, and Fancies*, p. 209.

113 *Leviathan*, p. 365.

114 Cavendish, *Poems, and Fancies*, p. 211.

115 *Ibid.*

116 *Ibid.*

117 Barkan, p. 46.

118 Rogers argues that the 'republican organizational logic' of Cavendish's vitalist works resulted from her 'interest in female emancipation becom[ing] transmogrified into a natural philosophy of rational matter'. Rogers, pp. 200, 202. The monistic vitalism Rogers identifies is egalitarian because the model operates without the hierarchy of male (rational) spirit acting on passive female (sensitive) matter.

6

Fictions of the mind

MATRON Lady, for this time let the Theam of your discourse be of
Discourse.

(Margaret Cavendish, *The Female Academy, Playes* (1662),
III.16, p. 666)

As I wrote in an earlier chapter, any attempt to try to imagine the
enormity of the emotional impact of going into exile is impossible –
only hindsight supplies the 20/20 vision necessary for understanding
events in some kind of structure, and attributing to them a logic or
meaning. When she set off for Paris in 1644 Cavendish did not know
when or if she would ever see her family or native land again. Only
the ardent optimism of one fuelled by a belief that she was on the
side of moral right could have suggested the possibility of a return.
As Hobbes expressed it, 'The *Present* onely has a being in Nature;
things *Past* have a being in the Memory onely, but things *to come*
have no being at all; the *Future* being but a fiction of the mind'.[1]
Cavendish herself expressed such ideas thus:

> foreknowledge was only a prudent and subtle observation made by a
> comparing of things or actions past, with those that are present, and that
> remembrance was nothing else but a repetition of things or actions past.[2]

In this chapter I am going to try to peer in two ways into the future,
Hobbes's 'fiction of the mind', a nebulous void paradoxically replete
with potentiality. Firstly, I offer a reading of the generic construction
of Cavendish's *Orations of Divers Sorts* (1662), and show how
the author's attitude to genre subtly changed once the anticipated
'future' of the Restoration of the monarchy had come about. At the
same time, I show how this is manifest in her other texts published
in the 1660s. Secondly, I want to suggest how this is not so much

a final chapter as a gateway into future ways of interpreting Cavendish's use of genre after the Interregnum. My focus is on the *Orations*, where use of genre may have a different emphasis from those texts which have been examined elsewhere in my book. This focus does not, however, preclude a brief discussion of other of Cavendish's post-Restoration publications, primarily *CCXI Sociable Letters*, *The Description of a New World Called the Blazing World* and her two volumes of plays.

The Restoration granted Cavendish an opportunity to experiment with less opaque and more conventional generic discourses than had hitherto been the case. However, the impulse to subvert expectations endured. This subversion did not operate as we have seen it doing during the Interregnum, in a partisan political way, but rather emphasised what she actively construed as her singularity.[3] She desired to construct herself as the well-established, if not establishment, writer which, by the time of her death, she had become. This self-aggrandising construction took the form of a manipulation not only of genre but also, and not unrelatedly, of gender. It was a project the origins of which have been seen in her subversive Interregnum representations and rewritings of Penelope and Travellia.

In Cavendish's case the truism, that, from her going into exile in 1644, 'the future' had indeed been 'but a fiction of the mind', is emphasised by her literary experimentation with different possible versions of it. Like many other exiles during the Interregnum, Cavendish, in her engagement with implicitly royalist activities, and her cunningly polemical writing, had been keeping the faith in the likelihood of a Restoration, the imminence of which was persistently uncertain. Paradoxically, this optimistic looking forward was, at its base, characterised by a nostalgic retrospection. Cavendish's own nostalgia took the form of her emphasis on performance and her engagement with generic paradigms to facilitate her own critique of contemporary events.

In her plays, her orations, *CCXI Sociable Letters* and *The Blazing World*, Cavendish was arguably to find the fullest and freest explication of the ideas and generic experimentation with which she had engaged in exile. The emphasis or object of it, however, shifted. The Cavendishes were back in England, and, as members of the ruling elite, were ostensibly participants in dominant social and political discourses once more. However, this participation was not as uncomplicated as it may at first appear. In her *Life* of William, Cavendish subtly expresses her disappointment with the perfunctory treatment he received from Charles II in return for his enduring fidelity.[4] As a result of this treatment, in a sense the Cavendishes voluntarily persisted in an exilic existence, secluded from courtly culture by their retreat into the Nottinghamshire countryside. In the light of this it may be argued that a Lucretian generic mollification is still needed, but that it is manifested in a different way.

Of the seven volumes Cavendish published after her return to England, one, the *Grounds of Natural Philosophy* of 1668, was a reworking of the 1655 *Philosophical and Physical Opinions*. Two were volumes of plays, one of which was probably written but, significantly, not published during the years in exile, as were *Orations of Divers Sorts* and *CCXI Sociable Letters*. The *Life* of William was published in 1667, followed a year later by Cavendish's last publication, *Plays, never before Printed*. Second and third editions of *Poems, and Fancies* appeared in 1664 and 1668; *The Worlds Olio* was reissued in 1671, as was *Natures Pictures*; a second edition of *Philosophical and Physical Opinions* appeared in 1663. In 1668, second editions of *Orations* and of *Observations upon Experimental Philosophy* were published. *The Description of a New World Called the Blazing World* was published as a separate volume in the same year.

Cavendish's volume *Orations of Divers Sorts* is an extended generic experiment. Her exercise in this characteristically masculine literary mode functions as an example of how a careful choice of genre can facilitate socio-political comment, and serves to illuminate how she saw herself as a writer with a deliberately constructed readership. Further, it would seem that in this text genre is more personally, not politically, deployed. In contrast to the public nature and tenor of the *Orations* is Cavendish's *CCXI Sociable Letters*, a volume which marks the writer's engagement with a genre with strongly private characteristics, and for which the implied readership is female. Further, her plays, whilst being the most public of all genres, are rendered generically anomalous by the author's protestations against their performability. Thus her post-Restoration publications do manifest a continuation of the by now familiar manipulation of genre.

Whilst not publishing her volumes of plays in exile, Cavendish in her Interregnum texts had none the less repeatedly engaged with more complicated and tangential issues of performance and oration.

This engagement, then, not least in the publication of the two volumes of plays, found a more vociferous expression after the Restoration. In her preface to *Orations of Divers Sorts*, Cavendish offers her own generic description of her text:

> But before I did put this my Book forth, Know, Noble Readers, I did Inquire, to find whether any Person had Composed and Put out a Whole Book of Pure and Perfect Orations ...'Tis true, I have heard of Single Orations, made by Single Persons, in Single Parts; Also I have seen Orations mixt with History, wherein the Substance of the History is the Ground of their Orations; Also I have seen two Translations call'd Orations, but they are rather Orations in Name than in Reality, for their Nature is History ... yet those are not Perfect or Right Orations, but Adulterated, or rather Hermaphrodites.[5]

This, Cavendish's generic branding of her project appears in an epistle dedicated not to a sole reader, but, more confidently, perhaps, 'To the Readers'.[6] Her apologia suggests a continuity of readership, as she suggests that past criticisms confirm her place as a valid writer. 'This Age is so Censorious' she declares, 'that the Best Poets are found Fault with, wherefore it is an Honour to my Writings, which are so much Inferiour to theirs'.[7] In other words, the effect of such criticisms is to vindicate the humility which she had previously displayed in her prefatory material, whilst simultaneously dignifying her as a member of a wider literary community. She establishes an intimacy with her imagined reader: 'first imagining my Self and You to be in a Metropolitan City', she writes, 'I invite you into the Chief Market-place, as the most Populous place, where usually Orations are Spoken'.[8] The nostalgia which typified her exilic texts is once more in evidence here, lending weight to the idea that the bulk of the composition of the *Orations* took place during those years. The community she imagines is suggestively intact, with a central focus, the 'Market-place', being located outside of time and geographical (or climatic) restriction. Her awareness of the performative nature of the oratorial genre is apparent not only in the orations themselves but also in this prefatory material, where her readers are constructed as an audience who, consequently, should not read, but are told, 'you shall *hear*'.[9] The setting associated with the genre has for Cavendish utopian, even emancipatory, possibilities, and the 'New-built City' where one of the market-places is located has been, significantly, analogously reconstructed after the 'great Disorders, caused by the Ruins Warrs have made'.[10]

Cavendish adopts the persona of a stage-director, telling her anticipated readers where they must go, even what they must wear – 'Adorn your Selves fit for the Court' – and promising to return them, after they have been transported to various locations by the power of words, to the market-place.[11] She assumes a degree of intimacy, reporting that:

> one short Oration concerning the Liberty of Women hath so Anger'd that Sex, as after the Mens Orations are ended, they Privately Assemble together, where three or four take the Place of an Orator, and Speak to the rest; the only Difficulty will be, to get Undiscovered amongst them, to hear their Private Conventicles.[12]

Generic manipulation is still functioning to present the writer with the opportunity to experiment with gender roles. This quotation is telling in its author's positioning of herself in tandem with the (presumably male) reader, rather than with the women who are not of '*my* Sex', but of '*that* Sex'.[13] She does not construct herself as being unobtrusive enough to listen to the women's orations, instead experimenting with the opportunities the oratorial genre grants her to occupy diverse rhetorical and gender positions. The main motivation behind her generic usage appears, in this instance, no longer to present a broad political perspective but rather to aid her own characterisation and self-representation as powerful, performative, and persuasive. These are all attributes which she implicitly constructs as masculine through her very provision of a separate subgenre of women's orations. The women's orations still take place in private, that is, without the public connotations of those of male characters for whom the genre of 'oratory' has a completely different significance.

During the exilic years Cavendish created female protagonists like Travellia who could, because of a reworking of generic expectations, orate in public. By contrast, her prefatory material in *Orations* is where her own rhetorical persuasions take place, persuasions which she evidently feels have been successful because of her confident and intimate – 'after which return, I shall Kiss your Hands and take my Leave' – relationship with her readership.[14] Such audacity as Travellia's spectacular, generically enabled, oratory had been rethought and appropriated by Cavendish herself after 1660. The writer's coquettish self-affiliation with a predominantly male readership leads her both to renounce and to display her female power. It is renounced in her relegation of women's orations to the status of 'Private Conventicles', but it is displayed in precisely the same act of relegation. That is, Cavendish is the author and may create or solve difficulties, like that of overhearing the women, as she pleases.

The women's orations, in addition to their non-public status, are presented within the text to a fictional audience which, whilst not being of one mind, does not contain men, who are the object of some of the orators' anger. The principal oratorial generic function of persuasion is consequently considerably demoted; each speaker is preaching to the converted. The writer deliberately makes it impossible for women other than herself to participate properly in this genre, which has to be redefined for them. This redefinition, however, is not like the one this book has identified repeatedly in Cavendish's exilic texts, that is, for a specific political end. Rather, it would seem that now that her social status has been largely restored, Cavendish's concern is with being perceived more as a 'Writer' than as a woman writer.

In prefacing her work and suggesting that the female orations be overheard, the narrator declares: 'if you regard not what Women say, you may ride to a Country Market-Town, and hear a Company of Gentlemen associate together their Discourse and pastime'.[15] The irony of this declaration finds its full force in its implicit challenge to the interactive readers. If they truly do not 'regard what Women say', they will be no more interested in the orations of the Company of Gentlemen', themselves the constructs of a female writer, than in the explicitly female orations. Cavendish's self-presentation means that she attempts to emancipate herself and delineate her own right to discourse. The female advancement her words afford is singular, not inclusive. For the women in the text, the motivation to orate is deliberately debased and presented as stemming not from the desire to persuade but from an impotent rage at misrepresentation. Words, be they spoken publicly, or written privately, remain for Cavendish the key to her own empowerment.

The audience of the *Orations* is constructed as 'travelling' from scene to scene in an effortlessly incorporeal way as Cavendish blurs the boundaries between them, and her characters and herself.[16] This blurring, the writer's shape-shifting experimentation with voice, identity and point of view, is possible because of careful use of genre. The oratorial genre creates the illusion of a space for reciprocity and equivalence between creator and audience. It is a public stage for Cavendish. Throughout the *Orations* she slips between constructing her audience as readers, and as listeners, emphasising a safely didactic motivation: '*it hath caused me to Write my Orations rather to benefit my Auditors, than to delight them*'.[17] The inconsistency of writing for someone to hear is allowed to pass because of the flexibility of the genre, which affords opportunities for more personal experimentations with voice and identity.

This is evinced by the second address to the reader, 'A Præfactory Oration' to 'Worthy Country-men'.[18] The declamatory nature of the prefaces is formally delineated by the explicit use here of the form of an 'Oration'. Further, that oration's address to 'Worthy Country-*men*' is suggestive of Cavendish's notional readership as male.[19] Within this generic framework Cavendish explicates what she perceives to be the subgenres of oratory:

> You know, that there is difference between Orations of fancy, and Orations of business, as also difference between Orations of publick imployments, and private divertisements; The one sort requires Rational perswasions, the other only Eloquent expressions.[20]

Just as she has constructed a private/public dichotomy in her promise of sequestered female orations, so Cavendish here suggests an equivalence between active persuasion, that is, orating for a measurable end, and poetry – '*Eloquent expressions*' – without a discernible external purpose. Public action and masculinity are conflated in her definition of her chosen genre: '*the Subjects of my Orations being of the most serious and most concernable actions and accidents amongst Mankind, and the Places most common and publick*'.[21] However, at almost the last moment of her prefatory oration, Cavendish asserts her femininity and a concomitant ill-preparedness for '*publick Affairs, Associations, or Negotiations*'.[22] Her express desire is, despite her being of that sex for whom '*it were more easie and more proper ... to speak or write wittily than wisely*', to impress her '*Auditors*', and to be '*profitable to* [... *their] Lives*'.[23] The overall effect of the prefatory material is that it functions as a plea for the readers' complicity in her generic experiment, a plea for them to participate in the discursive matrix or the word-world she creates. As she did with more humility and self-effacement in the texts which were published during the Interregnum, so here Cavendish establishes a quasi-contractual relationship with her readers, telling them how to read and leaving very little to chance.[24]

The oratorial genre, then, allows Cavendish imaginative space to be many other people, and to exhibit a familiarity with diverse discursive realms. These range from the military, to that of 'Courts of Judicature'; from political and monarchical to civic, religious, and to 'Scholastical Orations'.[25] Significantly, Part XI, that containing seven 'Femal[e] Orations', is completely self-contained; women speak only as (usually aggrieved) women, not as soldiers, kings, scholars or priests.[26] They speak because of their nature, not because of their civic status. Almost every other oration in the volume has a sub-heading indicative of the way in which the argument contained within it will proceed. The female orations, by contrast, do not – the women are speaking about being women in society, not about any professions or activities they may undertake there.

The confinement of the 'Femal[e] Orations' to one short section in the centre of the volume as a whole ironically befits the female speakers' social exclusion. The claustrophobic nature of domestic seclusion echoed by the orations' location, is made clear in their content. In the orations of this section anger and bitter irony are evident. The first four open with variations on the theme of the first: 'Ladies, Gentlewomen, and other Inferiours'.[27] Men, declares the first female orator, 'Bury us in their Houses or Beds, as in a Grave; the truth is, we Live like Bats or Owls, Labour like Beasts, and Dye like Worms'.[28] The second orator continues in this vein, implicitly making the connection between articulateness and political status in her remark that 'our Words to Men are as Empty Sounds'.[29] The third speaker, by contrast, defends men, whom she characterises as leading active, public lives for women's sakes, these latter being 'Witless, and Strengthless, and Unprofitable Creatures, did they not Bear Children'.[30] The fourth orator returns to the theme of the second, that is, the connection of political or civic life and public speech. She advocates women taking on traditionally masculine roles and activities:

> let us Converse in Camps, Courts, and Cities, in Schools, Colleges, and
> Courts of Judicature, in Taverns, Brothels, and Gaming Houses, all

which will make our Strength and Wit known, both to Men, and to our own Selves.[31]

The genre of the text containing this audacious and ambitious declaration has already given its writer, Cavendish, a taste of what it is for a woman to 'Converse' in precisely such situations. The fifth speaker refutes the fourth, and voices conventional ideas about gendered roles. She declares that 'to have Femal[e] Bodies, and yet to Act Masculine Parts, will be very Preposterous and Unnatural', but just as the genre allows Cavendish to experiment with masculine voices and social roles, so too, her Interregnum rewriting of other genres meant that she could create characters such as Travellia, whose oration, because of its presentation within an ostensible romance framework, was not threatening to her chastity.[32]

After the Restoration, however, Cavendish can publish those works in which she more intrepidly expresses herself, not through an albeit reworked romance format but in the well-established and traditionally masculine oratorial genre. The subterfuge lies not so much in what she does to the genre to make it work for her, as in what an already existent genre allows her to do. The ideal woman which the fifth orator constructs contradicts much of what Cavendish had ever set herself or her characters up to be, or to be capable of:

> we cannot Alter the Nature of our Persons ... which is to be Modest, Chast, Temperate, Humble, Patient and Pious; also to be Huswifely, Cleanly, and of few Words, all which will Gain us Praise from Men, and Blessing from Heaven.[33]

Cavendish's previous works, and the ironic presentation of this declaration itself in an oratory form, undermine the argument here presented. For the author the adjectives on each side of the semicolon could be mutually inclusive. That is, her person, her activities and her participation in this most public genre argue that the attributes on the one side of the semicolon – chastity and piety – could exist without the confining terms on the other side – domesticity and silence. In *Assaulted and Pursued Chastity*, for example, Cavendish showed how chastity, one of the attributes here constructed to be natural for women, could indeed be utterly compatible with public life and, by implication, publication. It was an association she was at pains to uphold.

The penultimate female orator agrees with the fourth in her

advocacy of emulation of men, and the last female orator argues that women's lives are in fact preferable to those of men: 'Women have no Reason to Complain against Nature, or the God of Nature, for though the Gifts are not the Same they have given to Men, yet those Gifts they have given to Women, are much Better'.[34] Further, she asks: 'what can we Desire more, than to be Men's Tyrants, Destinies, and Goddesses?'[35]

The third book of the *Orations* is entitled: 'Orations to Citizens in the Market Place'.[36] Nostalgia and political commentary once more play a part, since those addressed are '*a dejected People, ruined by Warr*'.[37] The semi-autobiographical elements which have repeatedly occurred in one form or another throughout Cavendish's Interregnum texts are evident once more. The need to express these under a generic cover is again necessary, but for new and different reasons. Cavendish wants the King's favour, and also wants to express how much she and her husband suffered throughout the civil wars. She wishes subtly to encourage the monarch to recognise the sacrifices and loyalty of her and her husband. 'Where are your Chargeable Buildings', asks an orator:

> your Stately Palaces, your Delightfull Theatres . . . Where are your Wise Laws? all Broken; your Sporting Recreations? all Ceas'd; your Ancestors Monuments? all Pull'd down, and your Fathers Bones and Ashes dispersed.[38]

'Theatres' and 'Sporting Recreations' are here given as much significance as grave desecration. The orator goes on to blame the people themselves for having begrudged the taxes which had been sought before the wars, and which, had the revenue been forthcoming from the populace, might have prevented conflict. In the space of one oration, then, Cavendish both vindicates Charles I's prewar economic strategies and also bemoans the devastation of the wars. She does this through the adoption of a rhetorical stance which, because of the many and contrary sentiments expressed throughout the text, might or might not be the author's own voice. The oratorial genre sanctions personae through which to express opinions, just as different treatments of genre throughout the Interregnum period allowed her the opportunity more covertly to express partisan views. Orations are intended to be controversial and argumentative, and they also allow an opportunity for the expression of radical views which can masquerade behind the generic mask of experimentation with personae. Other topical orations in the third section debate the recording of history, the election of magistrates and debates for and against liberty of conscience. These last are written not so much with nostalgia as with hindsight – warning against the likelihood of a civil war should religious disputes not be settled.

This section, so clearly about recent political events, ends with *'An Oration concerning Playes, and Players'*.[39] It has been seen how Cavendish stage-manages her readership, and here she is like an actress, again adopting different roles. The oration includes a list of the attributes which a good actor should possess. Coming as it does at the end of her oration in praise of the didactic potential of well-acted plays, the list could be of the attributes which she, as author, is attempting to adopt throughout the text of her *Orations*:

> they must make Love Soberly, Implore Favour Humbly, Complain Seriously, Lament Sadly, and not Affectedly, Fantastically, Constraintly, Ragingly, Furiously, and the like; all which in my Opinion they do Senselessly, Foolishly, and Madly; for all Feignings must be done as Naturally as may be, that they may seem as Real Truths.[40]

The author's ventriloquism, itself necessitated by the generic nature of orations, is akin to acting. It is thus implicitly royalist, the equation of the Stuarts and performance having been emphasised and debated throughout the Interregnum. This section of the *Orations* clearly points up the connections Cavendish made in the exilic years between public affairs, politics, writing, recreation, performance and citizenship. The implication is that a profitable postwar society may come about only through the right conjunction of these elements.

Some of the continuities and discontinuities in Cavendish's use of genre in her post-Restoration publication *Orations of Divers Sorts*, in relation to those texts which were published after her return to England in 1660, should by now be apparent. I should like to conclude by suggesting how such ideas might be applicable to other texts, chiefly her *CCXI Sociable Letters*, *The Blazing World* and her two volumes of plays. Because of the focus of my book on the 1650s, this investigation must necessarily be cursory. Nevertheless, it should serve to indicate how studies (which are at present but 'fictions of the mind', to echo Hobbes once again) might proceed.

In the *Orations*, then, Cavendish realised an ambition which she had harboured since her first audacious incursion into print. By contrast with these ostensibly public presentations of versions of an oratorial self, the writers and recipients of *CCXI Sociable Letters* are, in keeping with the epistolary genre's private connotations, female. The drama of the letter is acted out on the private stage of the writing paper, and conventionally has an audience of one.[41] Such generic expectations are reversed in the act of the letters' publication, and, in her prefatory material to them, Cavendish comments on the dramatic quality of the letters, and continues to hint at the palliatory potential of genre:

> *Noble Readers*, I do not intend to Present you here with Long Complements in Short Letters, but with Short Descriptions in Long Letters; the truth is, they are rather Scenes than Letters, for I have Endeavoured under the Cover of Letters to Express the Humors of Mankind.[42]

Politics and domestic events of the 1650s are commented upon but not, as was the case with the *Orations*, directly engaged with. In the letters, paradoxically private yet published, fictional yet presented as factual, and with characteristics of a *roman à clef*, the feminine is privileged in a quite different way from in the *Orations*.[43] Cavendish's self-conscious separation from other women is again in evidence, but is qualified by an apparent frustration:

> as for the matter of Governments, we Women understand them not; yet if we did, we are excluded from intermedling therewith, and almost from being subject thereto ... we are not made Citizens of the Commonwealth, we hold no Offices, nor bear we any Authority therein ... we are no Subjects, unless it be to our Husbands ... [Men] seem to govern the world, but we really govern the world, in that we govern men ... Mothers, Daughters, Sisters, Aunts, Cousins, nay, Maid-Servants have many times a perswasive power with their Masters.[44]

Whilst this outburst at first seems to be inclusive, its expression in epistolary form rather than oration underlines its exclusivism. In the world of politics women have no voice, no citizenship, no representation. Their 'perswasive power' is not effective in an open market-place but is confined to a strictly domestic hierarchy. Women are once again figured as sequestered, finding their voices only within 'Private Conventicles' or private writing. This construction, because articulated by a woman writer, is, however, at once subverted. The exilic setting of the letters means that it should come as no surprise to the reader when their generic appearance is complicated by their content.[45]

Cavendish's two volumes of plays were published in 1662 and 1668. Their collective length precludes a full discussion of them here. Significantly, Cavendish believed that the 1662 volume 'would have been ... [her] last work', had she not started to write her 'other intended piece' already.[46] Whilst drama is arguably the genre most closely intended for public consumption, Cavendish, in her dedicatory epistle to William, separates the plays' printed publication from their public performance.[47] Her plays are 'like dull dead statues' which she would protect from going 'weeping from the Stage'.[48] She thus creates a generic formative hierarchy between publication and performance. This hierarchy is constructed directly in response to Puritan dictates against theatre, a construction which places the plays' composition in the 1650s, a fact rendered remarkable by their uncompromising support for the dramatic form and public theatre.[49] Their anti-Aristotelian novelty – 'I have not made my Comedies of one dayes actions or passages' – and their avowed non-performability makes them of a peculiar generic status.[50] Accompanying this generic anomalousness is a play on gender. 'I know no reason', Cavendish declares of conventional gender dichotomies, 'but that I may as well make them Hee for my use, as others did Shees, or Shees as others did Hees'.[51] Such gender manoeuvres are embodied in the character of Lady Sanspareille, whose articulacy stands as evidence enough against the gendered assumptions about genre made by the '3. Gentlemen' of Cavendish's dramatised introduction to the 1662 plays. 'A woman write a Play!' exclaims one.[52] 'You may be converted from your erroneous opinion' answers his companion, 'by seeing this Play [Loves Adventures], and brought to confesse that a Lady may have wit'.[53]

Issues of a woman's 'wit', of gender roles, and of the notion of private genres are explored from the opening of the 1662 play Youths Glory, and Deaths Banquet. The parents of the Lady Sanspareille argue about her upbringing, Mother Love regarding a Classical education as confinement, and domesticity – 'I will have her bred, as to make a good houswife ... not to be mewed and moped up' – as freedom.[54] Father Love's attitude, to have women 'bred in learned Schools, to noble Arts and Sciences, as wise men are', is in stark contrast to his wife's. Lady Sanspareille herself, in her erudite articulacy, exemplifies much of the singular self-characterisation which Cavendish has been seen to promote.[55] She composes poetry and, herself a character in a stage play, praises 'Stages and publick Theaters' which:

> were first ordained and built, for the education of noble youth ... these Theaters were publick Schools, where noble principles were taught, so it was the dressing rooms of vertue, where the Actors, as her Servants did help to set her forth ... Thrones are but glorious Theaters, where Kings and Princes, and their Courtiers acts [sic] their parts.[56]

Sanspareille, so clearly a representation of the playwright herself, in making this speech conjoins ideas of female articulacy, virtue, monarchy and performance.[57] The connection is explicit, and, whilst quite in keeping with the dominant discursive and ideological tenor of the 1660s Stuart culture in which it was published, was audaciously subversive when it was written.[58] Similarly, a character in *The Female Academy* advocates the theatre not only as a respectable place but as a proper place for women's discourse.[59] Femininity and performance are directly allied in a way which would have outraged Prynne and his Puritan contemporaries. 'A Theatre is a publick place for publick Actions, Orations, Disputations, Presentations', begins Lady Speaker, continuing:

> there are only two Theatres, which are the chief, and the most frequented; the one is of War, the other of Peace ... the Theatre of Peace is the stage ... on the Poetical Theatre I will only insist, for this Theatre belongs more to our persons, and is a more fitter Subject for the discourse of our Sex, than Warr is; for we delight more in Scenes than in Battels.[60]

Cavendish paradoxically sanctions women's engagement with a public genre by emphasising its private characteristics, that is, through highlighting its insulated, representational aspect as being quite separate from actual martial involvement. Matronesse and Lady Speaker continue in a discussion of various dramatic genres, debating issues of influence and translation. Cavendish's own apparent desires and beliefs – 'singularity as well as merit, advances fame' – are overtly ventriloquised in *Youths Glory and Deaths Banquet*.[61] By 1666, and the publication of *The Blazing World*, even the ventriloquism could be modified, as Cavendish herself self-consciously entered her text.

Recent critics characterise *The Blazing World* as a relatively un-problematically utopian text.[62] However, the world it depicts is a utopia where only the nobility, and, chiefly, men, may find peace and self-determination, and even this is both qualified and disturbed.[63] Further, the words which empower are almost dystopic in their fixity and inability to offer a means of interpreting the natural world:

> this opinion was contradicted by others, who affirmed that thunder was a sudden and monstrous blas, stirred up in the air, and did not always require a cloud; but the Empress not knowing what they meant by blas (for even they themselves were not able to explain the sense of this word) liked the former better.[64]

Playful though this scene may at first appear, a universe where neologisms are not understood even by those who coin them is a deeply troubled and uncertain place. It may not be wholly the utopia in the generic sense in which many critics understand it to be, but it does represent for Cavendish a literary representation of a realisa-tion of ambitions and fantasies which, throughout the years in exile, had to be articulated from behind complex generic play and subter-fuge.[65] The figure who addresses large assemblies in *The Blazing World* is not a mythical Travellia, but Cavendish, Duchess of Newcastle, herself, speaking as 'the Duchess's soul'.[66] The camouflaged wishes of *Assaulted and Pursued Chastity* have to some extent been fulfilled.

In her preface to the reader of *The Blazing World*, Cavendish herself debates the text's generic status. The elements are separated out, and a clear tripartite categorisation is established. According to its author, the story is '*romancical*', '*philosophical*' and '*fantastical*' by turn.[67] The text itself, however, does not conform so readily to this subdivision, and the overall wider description of it as 'a work of fancy' is perhaps more appropriate.[68] In calling it a 'work of fancy', Cavendish is eager to justify its appearance joined 'to … [her] serious philosophical contemplations', that is, to *Observations Upon Experimental Philosophy*. In language curiously evocative of Hobbes's, she offers necessary reassurances that the philosophical work is not 'a fiction of the mind', but that its none the less heuristic empiricism has more '*Reason*' than '*fancy*' to it.[69] The moral superiority and didactic significance of the former is made clear – it is 'a more profitable and useful study than … [*The Blazing World*], so it is also more laborious and difficult', and, as a result, fancy is needed 'to recreate the mind, and withdraw it from its more serious contemplations'.[70] Cavendish is not so much creating a hierarchy of genres as arguing for their necessary interdependence. Indeed, many genres or discursive modes – the martial, judicial, scientific and religious – figure in the text.

The Blazing World, in its temporal and spatial transfigurations, and avant-garde, utopian themes, might perhaps of all Cavendish's texts most properly be termed 'a fiction of the mind'. This interiority ultimately renders the utopian world quite private.[71] The accompanying singularity of the self, that aggrandising, almost dictatorial self-representation which has been seen to colour most of her works, reaches its spectacular apotheosis in the figures of the Empress and the Duchess. One is explicitly Cavendish, the other her fantastical self-projection realised through the empowerment of words.[72] 'You may perceive', she declares in her 'Epilogue to the Reader':

> my ambition is not only to be Empress, but Authoress of a whole world ... I esteeming peace before war, wit before policy, honesty before beauty; instead of the figures of Alexander, Caesar, Hector, Achilles, Nestor, Ulysses, Helen, etc. chose rather the figure of honest Margaret Newcastle, which now I would not change for all this terrestrial world.[73]

The use of the word 'now' in this quotation seems to me to be most significant. It marks the fulfilment of 'honest Margaret Newcastle['s]' ambition to author her own universe; to find a sense of order and containment. The multigeneric *Blazing World*, part science fantasy, part science fact, part prodigious autobiography, in its overt configuration of an omnipotent female ruler represents a coalescence of the themes of this book. In it are united issues of politics, selfhood, exile, oratory and iconic Classical figures. The union of these issues operates through carefully worked out generic codes to culminate in a contentment and self-confidence which, for its author in the 1650s, had been but far-off and yearned-for 'fictions of the mind'.

Notes

1 Hobbes, *Leviathan*, p. 97.

2 Spirits to the Empress, Cavendish, *The Blazing World*, p. 167.

3 In considering Cavendish's 'singularity', I would not wish to ignore the contrastive strain of community evinced in her work, especially by her drama. Examples may be found in *The Female Academy* in the 1662 volume, *Playes*, and Lady Happy's convent in *The Convent of Pleasure*, in Cavendish,

Plays, Never Before Printed (London, 1668). The liberatory impulse running through *The Convent of Pleasure* is commented upon by C. Andrea O'Reilly Herrera. She sees Lady Happy's convent as 'a female religious community where women have unlimited freedom and indulge in their wildest fantasies'. See C. Andrea O'Reilly Herrera, 'Nuns and Lovers: Tracing the Development of Idyllic Conventual Writing' (unpublished doctoral dissertation, University of Delaware, 1993; abstract in *Dissertation Abstracts*, 54 (1994), p. 2588), p. 9.

4 The second book of the *Life* reads like an account ledger, as Cavendish itemises the 'accountable losses, which My Dear Lord and Husband has suffered by the late Civil Wars, and his Loyalty to his King and Country'. Cavendish, *Life*, p. 105. She works out William Cavendish's losses to be in the region of £941,303. *Ibid.*, p. 102. The reliability or otherwise of her calculations is questionable when it is remembered that Gregory King, drawing up statistics in the late seventeenth century, estimated the average annual *per capita* subsistence expenditure to be about £7 10s *per annum*. Civic bureaucrats could expect to earn about £100 annually. See Joan Thirsk and J. P. Cooper, *Seventeenth-century Economic Documents* (Oxford: Clarendon Press, 1972), pp. 780–1, 779. Cavendish also takes the opportunity to hint at her husband's devotion to his King in her prefatory material to *The Blazing World*. Of the gold which features in that tale, she declares, she 'should only desire so much as might suffice to repair my noble lord and husband's losses'. Cavendish, *The Blazing World*, p. 124. Given her calculations of the amount of these losses, the 'only' in this statement is decidedly relative.

5 Cavendish, *Orations*, n.p.

6 My emphasis.

7 Cavendish, *Orations*, sig. a2.

8 *Ibid.*, n.p.

9 *Ibid.*, n.p. My emphasis.

10 *Ibid.*, n.p.

11 *Ibid.*, n.p.

12 *Ibid.*, n.p.

13 My emphases. The gender play contrasts with Cavendish's prefatory disapproval of the concept of hermaphroditic *genera mista*, and also, perhaps, marks a move towards purer forms. This is also the case in *The Blazing World*, where the multigeneric character of the text is, in the 'Preface to the Reader', simplified into three consecutive genres. Cavendish, *The Blazing World*, p. 124. In the same preface Cavendish does refer to 'my sex', but then goes on to compare herself with male paradigms: 'I cannot be *Henry the Fifth*, or *Charles the Second*, yet I endeavour to be *Margaret the First*' by emulating '*Alexander* and *Caesar*'. *Ibid.* It is her sex which means that she cannot 'conquer the world' as they did, leaving her instead to create her own. *Ibid.*

14 Cavendish, *Orations*, sig. a4r.

15 *Ibid.*, n.p.

16 The possibilities of this trope of incorporeal travel were to be more fully explored in *The Blazing World*.

17 Cavendish, *Orations*, sig. Br.

18 *Ibid.*

19 My emphasis.

20 *Ibid.*, sig. Br.

21 *Ibid.*

22 *Ibid.*

23 *Ibid.*, sigs Br–B2v.

24 In *Palimpsestes*, Genette discusses the relationship between this notion of contract and genre. He argues that any textual contract is more binding on writer than on reader. In other words, 'genre or other indications *commit* the author'. See Genette, p. 11, n. 15.

25 Cavendish, *Orations*, pp. 78, 292.

26 *Ibid.*, p. 225.

27 *Ibid.*

28 *Ibid.*, p. 226. This imagery is reminiscent of that employed in *The Worlds Olio*, where, in her 'Preface to the Reader', Cavendish reports the belief that women '*are become so stupid, that Beasts are but a Degree below us, and Men use us but a Degree above Beasts*'. Cavendish, *The Worlds Olio*, n.p. Many of the concerns of this preface are reworked into the 'Femal[e] Orations' here.

29 Cavendish, *Orations*, p. 226. Women's speaking has been seen to be a preoccupation for Cavendish, not only as it relates to oratorial claims to citizenship, but also, antithetically, as it is regarded as trivial and irritating and, by extension, as being in opposition to chastity. In *The Worlds Olio* the author states in her prefatory material that '*Womens Tongues are like Stings of Bees*', and in *Orations*, the speaker of '*An Oration against the Liberty of Women*' fears being 'Tortured with their Railing Tongues … Silence amongst them … would Cause them to be Huswifely in their Families, Obedient to their Husbands'. Cavendish, *Olio*, n.p.; *Orations*, p. 222. In his dedication to his wife at the beginning of the *Orations*, William disparages the deceiving 'perfum'd and oily tongues' of the orators of antiquity, in contrast to the 'soft and gentle' words of his wife. Cavendish, *Orations*, n.p.

30 *Ibid.*, p. 228. This could be read as bitterly ironic when Cavendish's own apparent infertility is taken into account.

31 *Ibid.*

32 *Ibid.*, p. 229.

33 *Ibid.*

34 *Ibid.*, p. 232. This image of the weak and feeble female constructed by the last orator, where power is predicated not on intellect but on physicality – 'we Labour not in Building, nor Digging in Mines, Quarries, or Pits … we Burn not our Faces with Smiths Forges' – recalls the prefatory material to *The Worlds Olio*, where women are debarred from no fewer than nineteen professions because of their alleged physical weaknesses. *Ibid.*, p. 231; *The Worlds Olio*, 'The Preface to the Reader'.

35 Cavendish, *Orations*, p. 232.

36 *Ibid.*, p. 49.

37 *Ibid.*

38 *Ibid.*, p. 50.

39 *Ibid.*, p. 75.

40 *Ibid.*, p. 77. Jacob and Raylor comment on this oration, and the author's emphasis on the didactic power for good of drama which the orator espouses: 'It is possible that Davenant was the "excellent poet" she had in mind for the post: he had long been a client of her husband ... the Duchess's advice is not for educating the common people but the gentry – those with the affluence and leisure to employ dancing masters'. Jacob and Raylor, p. 222. This last expression refers to the orator's claim that 'the Actors will shew them to Behave themselves more Gracefully and Becomingly, than their Dancing-Masters'. Cavendish, *Orations*, p. 76. There is an irony in the passage from Cavendish's *Orations*, in its portrayal of an action or an attitude *seeming* to be 'as Real Truths'.

41 This privacy of performance recalls Cavendish's 'Dedication' to her *Playes* of 1662: 'all the time my Playes a making were, / My brain the Stage, my thoughts were acting there'. Cavendish, as reproduced in *'The Convent of Pleasure' and Other Plays*, ed. Anne Shaver (Baltimore and London: Johns Hopkins University Press, 1999, p. 253.

42 Cavendish, *Sociable Letters*, n.p.

43 On *CCXI Sociable Letters* as a *roman à clef*, see James Fitzmaurice, ed., *Margaret Cavendish: Sociable Letters* (New York: Garland, 1997).

44 Cavendish, *Sociable Letters*, 'Letter XVI', pp. 27–8.

45 The composition of the letters before the Restoration is suggested by what amounts to an advertisement for them in the Epilogue to Cavendish's 1662 book of *Plays*: 'in one Fortnight I wrote above threescore Letters', she declared. Cavendish, *Other Plays*, p. 271. It is a statement which also confirms the letters' fictional status, despite the many autobiographical elements they doubtlessly include.

46 Cavendish, *Other Plays*, p. 253. The singular 'piece' implies that by 1662 Cavendish felt that she had somehow reached the climax of her writing career. The work referred to is her *Life* of William.

47 This is not to suggest that 'public performance' could not be restricted to a 'private' gathering, as in the case of masques or closet dramas.

48 Cavendish, *Other Plays*, p. 253.

49 In her second epistle to the readers of her plays, Cavendish declares that 'The reason why I put out my Playes in print, before they are Acted, is, first, that I know not when they will be Acted, by reason they are in English, and *England* doth not permit I will not say of Wit, yet not of Plays'. Cavendish, *Other Plays*, p. 254. Further, she feels that the length of the plays would preclude their performance. She also appears to be of the belief that, once having published her plays, they could not be performed because of their lack of novelty. Further evidence as to the date of their composition is supplied in the epilogue, where Cavendish writes of sending them 'into *England* to be printed'. Cavendish, *Other Plays*, p. 271.

50 Cavendish, *Other Plays*, p. 255. In her third preface to the reader Cavendish discusses what she understands to be the differences between comedies and tragi-comedies, and positions her own text in relation to them. This generic debate is continued in her last prefatory address: 'Tragedies, or Tragick Scenes', she writes, 'must not be read in a pueling whining Voice, but a sad serious Voice'. Cavendish, *Other Plays*, p. 262. This suggests that she may have intended the plays, if not to be performed, then to be read out loud.

51 Cavendish, *Other Plays*, p. 259. The disruptive potential of such deliberately ambiguous language recalls that of the woman writer's attempt on masculine print culture. This attempt is encapsulated by Hélène Cixous thus: 'A feminine text cannot fail to be more than subversive. It is volcanic; as it is written it brings about an upheaval ... There's no room for her if she's not a he. If she's a her-she, it's in order to smash everything.' Hélène Cixous, 'The Laugh of the Medusa', in Elaine Marks and Isabelle de Courtivron, eds, *New French Feminisms: An Anthology* (Amherst: University of Massachusetts Press, 1980), pp. 245–64 (p. 258). One could perhaps argue that generic ploys render Cavendish's own subversions more palatable for a wider audience.

52 Cavendish, *Other Plays*, p. 270.

53 *Ibid.*

54 Cavendish, 'Youths Glory', *Playes* (1662), I.i, p. 123.

55 See Tomlinson for an examination of the recurrence of the trope of female articulacy in Cavendish's plays.

56 Cavendish, 'Youths Glory', *Playes*, I.iii, pp. 126–7.

57 Problematically, of course, Lady Sanspareille dies, an event which Payne calls 'the most disturbing manifestation of Cavendish's ambivalence'. Payne, p. 29.

58 Wiseman suggests of the date of the plays' composition that 'It is perhaps the very absence of an actual playhouse, a circumstance particular to the 1650s, which permits such an intimate link between all the world and the stage of the imagination', at once conflating publicness and interiority, representation and politics. See Wiseman, 'Gender and Statue', p. 169. I would agree that the very contingency of the exile years offered opportunities for fantasy which were to some degree restricted by the Restoration. It is an idea which Trubowitz also examines, concluding that 'the Duchess's feminist desire for self-government ... is finally undermined by her aristocratic investment in monarchy'. Trubowitz, p. 241. 'Singularity' in an absolutist sense is a two-edged sword for the royalist woman writer who seeks space for autonomous creativity. See also Gallagher.

59 In the prefatory material to the 1662 volume of plays, Cavendish once more has recourse to needlework imagery. She characterises herself as being 'like as a poor Taylor' who had to 'sow [sic] each several Scene together'. Cavendish, *Other Plays*, p. 262.

60 Cavendish, 'The Female Academy', *Playes*, IV. xxii, pp. 669–70.

61 Cavendish, 'Youths Glory', *ibid.*, II.v, p. 130.

62 For example, Cavendish has been called an 'orthodox ... utopian', in her

adaptation of 'literary precursors' and others' utopian models'. See Marina
Leslie, 'Gender, Genre and the Utopian Body in Margaret Cavendish's *Blazing
World*', *Utopian Studies*, 7 (1996), 6–24 (p. 7). Leslie later qualifies this by
identifying in *The Blazing World* a 'profound revision of generic expectation'
by a woman's movement from victim to ruler. *Ibid.*, p. 13. I attempted to
identify a similar revision in my analysis of *Assaulted and Pursued Chastity*,
above. For an analysis of the 'dialogue between utopian writing and genre
theory' see Lilley, 'Blazing Worlds', pp. 102–5 (p. 103). Lilley also separates
'utopian writing' from 'the notoriously unstable notion of a utopia proper'.
Ibid., pp. 104–5.

63 Rogers argues that an 'acknowledgment of the limitations besetting the
separate sphere of female sovereignty is nowhere voiced so clearly as in *The
Blazing World*'. Rogers, p. 207.

64 Cavendish, *The Blazing World*, p. 140.

65 On such realisation of fantasies, especially in relation to *The Blazing World*
and the plays, see Payne.

66 Cavendish, *The Blazing World*, p. 197. Wilputte argues that *The Blazing World*
is 'a Platonic visionary scheme stemming from Cavendish's frustration with
social and sexual politics and the political denial of voice'. Earla A. Wilputte,
'Margaret Cavendish's Imaginary Voyage to *The Blazing World*: Mapping a
Feminine Discourse', in Donald W. Nichol, ed., *Transatlantic Crossings:
Eighteenth-century Explorations* (St Johns, Nfld: St John's Memorial University
of Newfoundland, 1995), pp. 109–17 (p. 110). See *The Blazing World*,
pp. 197–8, for this speech. Lilley reads it as a reimagined version of Cavendish's 1651 appearance before the Committee for Compounding, wherein
'her fictional counterpart supplies the missing defence, but is also unsuc-
cessful'. Lilley, p. 230, n. 33. Other critics have remarked on how 'the point
at which genre and gender intersect in the representation of utopian desire
is in the locus of discursive authority'. See Leslie, p. 7.

67 Cavendish, *The Blazing World*, p. 124. On echoes of this tripartite configuration see Wilputte, p. 114.

68 Cavendish, *The Blazing World*, p. 123. The text also shares some of those
epic topoi – tempests, shipwrecks, absolutist rule – which I have discussed
in Chapter 4. Wilputte identifies that at the beginning of *The Blazing World*
'the imaginary voyage genre takes over from the romance'. Wilputte, p. 111.
Wilputte also suggests some provocative connections between Cavendish's
text and some of Descartes's works of the 1630s. See *ibid.*, p. 112.

69 Cavendish, *The Blazing World*, p. 123. Hintz compares the bear-men's pref-
erence for their telescopes, 'mere deluders', over their 'natural eyes', with
defences of poetry as a genre (*The Blazing World*, p. 142; Carrie Hintz, ' "But
One Opinion": Fear of Dissent in Cavendish's *New Blazing World*', *Utopian
Studies*, 7 (1996), 25–37 (pp. 29–30)). The separation seems to be one
predicated on the same opposition of 'reason' and 'fancy' identified here by
Cavendish.

70 Cavendish, *The Blazing World*, p. 124.

71 This 'privacy' is characterised by the Blazing World's lack of conformity to

collective organisational imperatives such as time. As Trubowitz expresses it: 'we enter a world outside of logocentric time and history, a fluid, uncanny, and uncharted territory'. Trubowitz, p. 232. Trubowitz goes on to view *The Blazing World* as a reworking of Cavendish's autobiography. *Ibid.*, p. 239.

72 It has been shown how 'singularity' is a concept which is called into question in *The Blazing World*; whilst the absolute autonomy and spectacular self-presentation of the Empress is evinced throughout the text, at times it is part of a multiplicity of components – the narrator, the fictional Duchess, the actual Duchess, the Empress, and William Cavendish – which converge, in the scene at Welbeck, in one place. See Cavendish, *The Blazing World*, pp. 193–6. See also the Duchess's soul's declaration that she 'had rather appear worse in singularity, than better in mode'. *Ibid.*, p. 218.

73 *Ibid.*, p. 224.

Conclusion: rehabilitations

The World, [f]or the most part, judge not according to truth and right, but condemn according to malice and spight: but when Time hath rotted the teeth of spight, and blunted the edges of malice, [my book] ... may gain an applause. (Margaret Cavendish, 'A Complaint and a Request', *Natures Pictures* (1656), p. 400)

> But say that Book should not in this Age take,
> Another Age of great esteem may make;
> If not the second, then a third may raise
> It from the Dust, and give it wondrous praise.[1]

This is how Cavendish concludes *Natures Pictures*, in an optimistic display of peritextual resistance. However, it is a resistance undercut with anxiety, and this is a mixture which has been seen to resonate in one form or another through all of her exilic works. This book has been an attempt to 'raise' Cavendish's work from 'the Dust, and give it wondrous praise', continuing that ongoing critical project which has been concerned with the rehabilitation of the writer and her work.[2]

I have shown how Cavendish was not an anomalous eccentric humoured by an over-indulgent spouse, prolifically publishing random thoughts which were symptomatic of 'the freakishness of an elf, the irresponsibility of some non-human creature' and the products of an 'erratic and lovable personality'.[3] Rather, I have demonstrated how, in the 1650s, she utilised genre in a deliberate and subversive way to articulate and ameliorate her exile. I identified this exile as 'triple'. Legislatively, Cavendish was exiled because her spouse was a political delinquent who could not return to his native land. In terms of her gender, she was analogously exiled, her voice, like those of other early modern women writers, portrayed as speaking contrary to dominant ideological and literary discourses. Again in artistic terms, Cavendish's promotion of the anti-Puritan theatrical aesthetic may be formulated as being the third aspect of this triply restrictive exile.

This particular emphasis is new to Cavendish studies. I have engaged with those critics whose approach seemed best to exemplify other strands of the same rehabilitative project with which I engage. Thus this book may be read in relation to Trubowitz's identification of 'generic transgressiveness' and to Lilley's formulation of 'a meta-discourse on the relations of gender and genre' in Cavendish's writings.[4] There are, by contrast, many other critics who appear implicitly to concur with detrimental assessments of Cavendish's work, and who apparently persist in the critical maintenance of some aspects of the triple exile.

My own rehabilitative project has at its core the elements of genre, gender and exile. In terms of genre, my model incorporates elements of Seelig's 'intersections of literary forms' and Patterson's 'functional ambiguity'.[5] I showed how Bakhtin, whilst presenting a seductive but ultimately restrictive reading of genre, none the less provides a conceptual vocabulary valuable in theorising Cavendish's use of genre in exile. It seems clear, then, that Cavendish's generic idiolect is characterised by her engagement with precisely that 'organic receptivity' which Bakhtin reserves for the novel.[6] The overarching concern of this book as a whole has been to demonstrate how Cavendish's generic peregrinations were politically motivated, not only arising from, but being intended as specific responses to her experiences of the 1650s.

The nature of these experiences formed the main body of my first chapter. Here I engaged with the paratextual theories of Genette to show how the triple exile was registered by Cavendish not only in intertextual generic play (the subject of Chapters 2, 3, 4, 5 and 6), but also in the concrete material arrangement and appearance of her publications. I examined the peritextual aspects of these publications as evidence for my claim that here, too, is the impact of the triple exile felt. Cavendish's voice echoes beyond her prefaces and dedications, and defiantly resists conventional peritextual confinement. I also investigated how this defiance constituted a part of a wider royalist engagement with all aspects of 'theatre' in the 1650s.

In the main body of the book I concentrated my examination on two of Cavendish's exilic texts, *Poems, and Fancies* and *Natures Pictures*. In Chapter 2 the suggestive relationship between Cavendish's first publication and Lucretian generic modes was explored. The relationship serves, I showed, as proof of Cavendish's generically facilitated incursion into male print culture. The key to similar generic manoeuvres present in Cavendish's *Natures Pictures*, I demonstrated, lies in the short prose piece *Heavens Library*, a close reading of which formed the substance of my third chapter. Here I showed that incisive political critique can masquerade behind what appear to be the most innocuous of generic façades.

The generic nuances inherent in the relationship between Homer's *Odyssey* and Cavendish's *Assaulted and Pursued Chastity* were the focus of the fourth chapter, 'Travellia's Travails'. Here, I argued that the figure of the Homeric Penelope, adapted and adopted elsewhere in Cavendish's exilic writings too, provided a model for Travellia, an autonomous and audacious female protagonist who emerges from the dynamic conjunction of the generic traditions of epic and romance in *Assaulted and Pursued Chastity*.

The Harveian and Hobbesian intellectual paradigms in circulation in the fifth chapter of the book were contemporary with Cavendish, but in her *Animall Parliament* she also looked back to Classical generic models, adapting the Livian fable of the Belly. I showed how, by juxtaposing this model with Harvey's politically motivated presentation of his account of the circulation of the blood, Cavendish made genre work for her and produced in *The Animall Parliament* a startlingly original defence of the exiled court. Once this court returned from exile, I argued in my sixth chapter, and the monarch was restored, the varieties of exile Cavendish experienced were not ended but modified. Her engagement with genre altered accordingly, and in post-Restoration texts such as *The Blazing World* and *Orations of Divers Sorts* the emphasis is on Cavendish's self-constructed 'singularity', and her open engagement with archetypally masculine literary modes.

I should like to conclude my book by ending, as it were, at the beginning. In the first chapter I used Gérard Genette's formulations to examine how, in material and spatial terms, Cavendish's writings of the 1650s registered her experience of exile. In a sense this conclusion must itself figure almost as a threshold, being a point of departure from the present project, whilst suggesting the possibility of a crossing over into a future one. Such a project might extend the final chapter of this one, 'Fictions of the mind', and explore in depth Cavendish's post-Restoration engagements with genre. The moment for subversion that was the Interregnum might, as I have previously suggested, have passed. However, to return to the triple exile, because she was a woman writer Cavendish's exile in some sense endured until her death in 1673. It was seen in my Introduction how her contemporaries ridiculed her long after the Restoration, as is epitomised by Stansby's criticism not, significantly of '*Antwerp's*', but of '*Welbeck's* illustrious whore'.[7] The locale had changed; the antipathy had not. If this book does indeed occupy a liminal position, and fulfils its overarching rehabilitative agenda, it is to be hoped that precisely such antipathy may at last be left on the outside of the critical threshold. It seems appropriate to conclude with Cavendish's own hopes, and to quote the last four lines of the verse with which this conclusion began:

> For who can tell but my poor Book may have
> Honour'd renown, when I am in the Grave.
> And when I dye, my Blessing I will give,
> And pray it may in after Ages live.[8]

Notes

1 Cavendish, *Natures Pictures*, p. '390' (mispaginated).
2 This notion of the 'rehabilitative' nature of recent criticism derives from Kate Lilley, 'Blazing Worlds', p. 120.
3 Virginia Woolf, 'The Duchess of Newcastle', in *The Common Reader* (London; The Hogarth Press, 1925; repr. *A Woman's Essays* (Harmondsworth: Penguin, 1992)), pp. 107–14 (113–14).
4 See Trubowitz, p. 230; Lilley, 'Blazing Worlds', p. 104.
5 Seelig, p. 12; Patterson, p. 18.
6 On the novel being 'organically receptive to new forms of ... reading' see Bakhtin, p. 3.
7 Stansby, quoted in Grant, *Margaret the First*, p. 199. My emphases.
8 For full reference see note 1, above.

Appendix

'A horrible precipice':
Lucy Hutchinson's
Lucretius

In the late 1640s Cavendish's political adversary, Lucy Hutchinson, completed a verse translation of Lucretius's *De rerum natura*, which she presented to Arthur, Earl of Anglesey, in 1675.[1] In her autobiographical fragment, her *Life*, Lucy Hutchinson portrays herself as a woman whose existence is utterly governed by the twin ideologies of Puritanism and patriotism.[2] Her *Life* has a political tenor, effectively constituting an articulate apologia for the Puritan cause, and the motivation to write her autobiography stems from a need to make public her piety. She regards the text as:

> a means to stirre up my thankfulnesse for things past, and to encourage my faith for the future ... I meete with so many speciall indulgences as require a distinct consideration, they being all of them to be regarded as talents intrusted to my improovement for God's glory.[3]

Hutchinson reflects on the time of her birth not with sentimental nostalgia but with a bitter hindsight. 'The land was then att peace', she writes, continuing: 'if that quiettnesse may be call'd a peace, which was rather like the calme and smooth surface of the sea, whose darke wombe is allready impregnated of a horrid tempest'.[4] The Britain she depicts is one which is the flagship of pure Christianity, where Henry VIII was the first to break 'the antichristian yoake of from his owne and his subiects necks', and where began 'the early dawne of gospell light, by Wickliffe ... whom God rays'd up after the black and horrid midnight of antichristianisme'.[5] The author defines Britain's past as being characteristically a history of the uprising of the populace, the 'free brethren', to fight unjust rulers who govern them 'rather as slaves then subjects'.[6] The autobiography itself, then, is generically complex, being part history, part conversion narrative, and part political treatise.

The text veers from the widely political to the deeply personal. Hutchinson describes her parents' meeting (her mother was sixteen years of age, her father forty-eight), and her father's erudition, which is figured using a trope of natural genius which has also been seen in Cavendish's writing.[7] Hutchinson writes of her father that he did not study 'dead writings, but ... the living bookes of men's conversations'.[8] At one point in the narrative Hutchinson tells of a dream her mother had when she was pregnant with her in which a star descended into her hand, signifying, according to Lucy's father, that she was to 'have a daughter of some extraordinary eminency'.[9] This episode in the autobiography (which would not appear out of the ordinary coming from Cavendish's pen) seems oddly bold, and this notion is reinforced as the author recounts how, at the age of four she could read English 'perfectly'.[10] The organization of her education differs entirely from Cavendish's, as she recalls being seven years old and having no fewer than eight tutors. Like Cavendish, however, she rejected 'musick, dancing, writing, and needlework' ('and for my needle I absolutely hated it') because her 'genius was quite averse from all but [her] ... booke'.[11] She read so much that her mother, fearing for her health, would lock her books away. The enterprising young Lucy, however, felt 'animated' by this, 'and every moment [she] ... could steale from [her] ... play [she] ... would employ in any booke [she] ... could find'.[12] Pervading all aspects of Hutchinson's education was a sense of piety, but also of wit:

> for I was not at that time convinc'd of the vanity of conversation which was not scandalously wicked, I thought it no sin to learne or heare wittie songs and amorous sonnets or poems, and twenty things of that kind, wherein I was so apt that I became the confident in all the loves that were managed among my mother's young weomen.[13]

This differs entirely from Cavendish's separation from and disapproval of her mother's servants. Hutchinson's intellect and the thorough education she received are evinced by her translation of Lucretius's *De rerum natura*.

In the epistle prefacing her translation Hutchinson explicates the profound alteration which her attitude to the work has undergone in the decades between its composition and its presentation to Anglesey. The conventional dedicatory humilities appear to serve as palliatory covers for an underlying sense of personal unease. 'Preserve', the author implores of Anglesey, 'wherever your Lordship shall dispose this booke, this record with it, that I abhorre all the Atheismes & impieties in it'.[14] I showed in my second chapter how, in the early 1650s, Cavendish also found inspiration in Lucretius's poetic mediation of Epicurean doctrine. As the 1650s progressed, however, and certainly following 1660, Hutchinson's parliamentarian sympathies and, more especially, her Puritan pieties, necessitated her recantation of 1675. This eventual divergence of attitudes between the two women serves to render more remarkable the influence exerted by Lucretius's text which, in the late 1640s and early 1650s, offered creative and imaginative possibilities dynamic enough to traverse partisan lines. I would argue that the key to this initial commonality of interest lies less in the complex intricacies of Lucretius's philosophical exposition than in the very mode of that exposition, that is, in his verse.

Hutchinson's prefatory renunciation of her translation, significantly cross-generic itself, may be understood as her endeavour to distance herself from precisely those elements which so attracted Cavendish. The prefatory epistle is part-Puritan conversion narrative, as Hutchinson likens herself to 'one, that, walking in the darke, had miraculously scapd a horrible precipice, by day light coming back & discovering his late danger, startles and reviews it wth affright', so she 'in the mirrour of opposed truth and holinesse and blessednes, saw the ugly deformitie' of Lucretius.[15] The epistle also acts as a warning to future readers, as something of an indemnity clause, characterised as 'an antidote against the poyson' of the translation, 'for any novice who by chance might prie into it'.[16] The trope of the darkness of ignorance was also employed by Cavendish in *Philosophical and Physical Opinions*. Addressing her reader, she had claimed that the work: '*was writ in the dawning of my knowledge, and experience, and not having a clear light I might chance to stumble in dark ignorance on molehills of errors*'.[17]

Hutchinson's rescissory epistle; the arguments which preface each book; all of Book VI, and various marginal interpolations, are in the author's hand, the remaining material being in a more accomplished scribal hand.[18] The marginalia, in particular, demonstrate the unambiguous nature of Hutchinson's denial of Lucretius, and suggest some reasons for it. His description of non-interventionist deities in Book II, for example, is characterised as 'Horribly impious'; the poet is a 'poore deluded bewitcht mad wretch'; when he characterises the torments of hell as allegorical, the translator suggests that 'Many a wicked soule who would ease it selfe wth thinking soe will find it otherwise', editing out the erotic content of the fourth book altogether: 'much here was left out for a midwife to translate whose obsceane art it would better become then a nicer pen'.[19] Hutchinson's construction of her disgust is double-edged, since Lucretius offends her Puritan sensibilities through his impieties, and her conventionally constructed feminine ones through his obscenities. The translator fears the taint of association with the poet, and her displeasure with what she perceives to be Lucretius's designation of religion as an 'invention to reduce the ignorant vulgar into order & Government', could be read as a criticism of the Erastian tendencies of her peers, like Cavendish, who upheld state Anglicanism.[20]

Lucretius's highly effective image of the cup smeared with honey evidently impressed itself upon Hutchinson, for whom the draught was to lose all such saccharine qualities, becoming 'poysonous' instead.[21] Indeed, Hutchinson's attitude to poetry is deeply ambivalent and, despite the contradictory suggestions in her *Life*, she is in her prefatory material solicitous that she be characterised as mother and seamstress before she be perceived as translator. 'I turnd it into English', she writes of *De rerum natura*, 'in a roome where my children practizd the severall quallities they were taught, with their Tutors, & I numbred the sillables of my translation by the threds of the canvas I wrought in'.[22]

Hutchinson may have wished to represent herself as finding impious in their rich sensuality the very types of image Lucretius draws on. Lucretius, for example, is delectably extravagant in his description of why the number of types of atoms is finite. 'Were it not so', he writes, 'the richest robes of the Orient, resplendent with the Meliboean purple of Thessalian murex, or the gilded breed of peacocks, gay with laughing lustre, would pale before some new colour in things'.[23] Interestingly Hutchinson does not expurgate some similar parts of *De rerum natura*, and in her translation of Book IV, she appears rather to delight in poetic potential: 'Lisping Trauliza holds

her tongue and sneakes, / Mallicious, hott Lampadian is a scold / ...
Big Brested Ceres, foggie with the wine / ... All with perfumes their
nastie savours hide'.[24] The translator's evident enjoyment of this, one
of Lucretius's most misogynist passages, perhaps undermines her
subsequent abjuration.

It has not been my intention in this appendix to argue that
Cavendish had access to Hutchinson's unpublished translation, although it is not inconceivable that she came across it during her
visit to England in 1651. Rather than attempt to forge such a causal
link in the face of scant evidence, I have tried to identify instead
what Lucretius offered to both women, particularly in terms of, and
predominantly because of, genre.[25] Paradoxically, the potency of *De
rerum natura* is such that it allows, even in the very act of rejection
and dissociation, the opportunity for a Puritan republican to assert
many of her own political and religious opinions in much the
same way as it provided similar opportunities for Cavendish. What
Cavendish understands as the irreducible sanity of science, however,
must figure for Hutchinson as a highly irreverent doctrine. Further,
that which alienates Hutchinson functions differently for Cavendish,
who finds in *De rerum natura*, as I have demonstrated, not only
justification for her self-presentation as writer, but also a paradigm
for the feminisation of Nature and Creation.

Hutchinson, presenting her translation in 1675, appears to associate it not with a sense of Epicurean possibility but with an attitude
of embarrassment and disappointed failure. By contrast, Cavendish's
text was ultimately optimistic. The ending of Hutchinson's text,
however, as conveyed in the Argument to the sixth book, suggests
a not unexpected impatience, as the translator dismisses her poet in
a most cursory fashion. Lucretius, she writes, 'With instance of a
Plague that once did wast / Renowned Athens shutts up all at last'.[26]

Notes

1 For persuasive evidence in support of dating the translation to the late 1640s
   see Samuel A. Weiss, 'Dating Mrs Hutchinson's Translation of Lucretius',
   Notes and Queries, 200 (1955), 109. Arthur Annesley, first Earl of Anglesey
   (1614–86), had professed allegiance to the Presbyterians during the 1640s
   and 1650s, whilst maintaining links with the royalists. At the Restoration
   he successfully pleaded for leniency for the opposition, Hazelrig among them,
   and it is probably in this context that the Hutchinsons had dealings with

him. See Leslie Stephen and Sidney Lee, eds, *The Dictionary of National Biography. From the Earliest Times to 1900*, 63 vols (Oxford: Oxford University Press, 1885–1900), I, 473–5. Commentators have been reserved in their praise for Hutchinson's translation, Fleischmann, for example, writing that 'a detailed comparison of lines from the translation with versions of the same Lucretius lines by Dryden and Creech leads to the conclusion that Mrs. Hutchinson's work lacks both accuracy and poetic skill'. Fleischmann, p. 158. David Norbrook writes of Hutchinson that although her version 'can ... be crabbed at times ... at her best she can rise to something of Lucretius' idiosyncratic eloquence'. See David Norbrook, 'Lucy Hutchinson's Translation of Lucretius: *De rerum natura*', *Notes and Queries*, 44 (1997), 402–3 (p. 403).

2 Lucy Hutchinson, *Memoirs of the Life of Colonel Hutchinson ... to Which is Prefixed The Life of Mrs. Hutchinson, Written by Herself, a Fragment*, ed. Julius Hutchinson (London: Longman, Hurst, Rees and Orme, 1806).

3 Hutchinson, Lucy, manuscript translation of Lucretius's *De rerum natura*, British Library, Add. MSS, 19333, p. 2.

4 Hutchinson, *Life*, p. 3.

5 *Ibid.*, p. 6.

6 *Ibid.*, p. 5.

7 Suggesting that Hutchinson exaggerates her mother's youth, B. G. Mac-Carthy writes that 'this was no mistake, but a stupid effort [on Hutchinson's part] to have her cake and eat it'. MacCarthy, p. 101.

8 Hutchinson, *Life*, p. 12.

9 *Ibid.*, p. 16.

10 *Ibid.*

11 *Ibid.*

12 *Ibid.*

13 *Ibid.*, p. 17.

14 Lucy Hutchinson, *De rerum natura*, fol. 2v.

15 *Ibid.*, fol. 4v. On Hutchinson's political and religious affiliations, and how these informed her writing see Susan Cook, '"The story I most particularly intend": The Narrative Style of Lucy Hutchinson', *Critical Survey*, 5 (1993), 271–7. Cook examines the complex generic manoeuvres Hutchinson had to perform in her biography of her husband, of the multigeneric status of which she declares: 'It is at the same time a virtual hagiography, military and political history and theological comment'. Cook, p. 272.

16 Hutchinson, *De rerum natura*, fol. 5r.

17 Cavendish, *Philosophical and Physical Opinions*, not paginated.

18 Hutchinson's own handwriting may be characterised as the 'hindsight hand', since it was added many years after the initial translation was completed.

19 Hutchinson, *De rerum natura*, fols 49v, 70v, 72v, 97r. The irony accompanying omissions such as those made in Book IV (fol. 97r), is that Lucretius's holistic philosophy, the constituents of which are atoms, must in itself be fragmented and atomised by its Puritan translator in order to be rendered

acceptable. This is less honeying the bitter pill than neglecting to administer it altogether.

20 Cavendish's socially pragmatic attitude towards religious ceremonies which bring order, and benefit the state by distracting 'Common people', is apparent in many of her texts. See, for example, Cavendish, *Olio*, p. 29.

21 Hutchinson, *De rerum natura*, fol. 5r.

22 *Ibid.*, fol. 3r.

23 Lucretius, *De rerum natura*, p. 74.

24 Hutchinson, *De rerum natura*, fol. 98r.

25 Other contemporary women were also interested in atomism, such as Anne Conway (1631–79); Christina of Sweden (1626–89) and Elizabeth of Bohemia (1618–80). These latter two were also exiles. Aphra Behn also engaged with the topic. See Marilyn Bailey Ogilvie, *Women in Science. Antiquity through the Nineteenth Century: A Biographical Dictionary with Annotated Bibliography* (Cambridge, Massachusetts: MIT Press, 1986), pp. 54, 56–7, 82.

26 Hutchinson, 'The Argument of the sixth Booke', in *De rerum natura*, fol. 128v.

Bibliography

Margaret Cavendish's publications

I have arranged the references by text, with the first edition for each followed by details of subsequent editions. Wing Catalogue numbers (Donald G. Wing, ed., *Short-Title Catalogue of Early English Books, 1641–1700* (New York: Index Committee of the Modern Language Association of America, 1972–)) are supplied in brackets after each edition.

Poems, and Fancies: Written by the Right Honourable, the Lady Margaret Countesse of Newcastle. London, Printed by T. R. for J. Martin, and J. Allestrye at the Bell in Saint Pauls Church Yard, 1653 [N869].

Poems, and Phancies, Written by the thrice Noble, Illustrious, and Excellent Princess the Lady Marchioness of Newcastle. The Second Impression, much altered and corrected. London, Printed by William Wilson, Anno Dom. M.DC.LXIV [N870].

Poems, or, Several Fancies in Verse: with the Animal Parliament, in Prose. Written by the thrice Noble, Illustrious, and Excellent Princess, the Duchess of Newcastle. The Third Edition. London, Printed by A. Maxwell, in the Year 1668 [N871].

Philosophicall Fancies. Written by the Right Honourable, the Lady Newcastle. London, Printed by Tho: Roycroft, for J. Martin, and J. Allestrye, at the Bell in St. Pauls Church-yard, 1653, 8o [N865. Douglas Grant describes this volume as 12mo in his *Margaret the First: A Biography of Margaret Cavendish, Duchess of Newcastle, 1623–1673* (London: Rupert Hart-Davis, 1957)].

The Worlds Olio. Written by the Most Excellent Lady the Lady M. of Newcastle. London Printed for J. Martin and J. Allestrye at the Bell in St. Pauls Church-Yard 1655 [N873].

The Worlds Olio. Written by the thrice Noble, Illustrious, and most Excellent Princess, the Duchess of Newcastle. The Second Edition. London, Printed by A. Maxwell, in the Year 1671 [N874].

The Philosophical and Physical Opinions, Written by her Excellency, The Lady Marchionesse of Newcastle. London Printed for J. Martin and J. Allestrye at the Bell in St. Pauls Church-Yard 1655 [N863].

197

Philosophical and Physical Opinions. Written by the thrice Noble, Illustrious, and Excellent Princess, the Lady Marchioness of Newcastle. London, Printed by William Wilson, Anno Dom. M.DC.LXIII [N864].

Grounds of Natural Philosophy: Divided into thirteen Parts: with an Appendix containing five Parts. The Second Edition, much altered from the First, which went under the name of Philosophical and Physical Opinions. Written by the thrice Noble, Illustrious, and Excellent Princess, the Duchess of Newcastle. London, Printed by A. Maxwell, in the Year 1668 [N851].

Natures Pictures drawn by Fancies Pencil to the Life. Written by the thrice Noble, Illustrious, and Excellent Princess, the Lady Marchioness of Newcastle. In this Volume there are several feigned Stories of Natural Descriptions, as Comical, Tragical, and Tragi-Comical, Poetical, Romancical, Philosophical, and Historical, both in Prose and Verse, some all Verse, some all Prose, some mixt, partly Prose, and partly Verse. Also, there are some Morals, and some Dialogues; but they are as the Advantage Loaves of Bread to a Bakers dozen; and a true Story at the latter end, wherein there is no Feignings. London, Printed for J. Martin, and J. Allestrye, at the Bell in Saint Paul's Churchyard. 1656 [N855. Includes *A True Relation*, Cavendish's autobiography].

Natures Pictures drawn by Fancies Pencil to the Life. Being several feigned Stories, Comical, Tragical, Tragi-comical, Poetical, Romancical, Philosophical, Historical, and Moral: Some in Verse, some in Prose; some mixt, and some by Dialogues. Written by the thrice Noble, Illustrious, and most Excellent Princess, the Duchess of Newcastle. The Second Edition. London, Printed by A. Maxwell, in the Year 1671 [N856].

Playes written by the thrice Noble, Illustrious and Excellent Princess, the Lady Marchioness of Newcastle. London, Printed by A. Warren, for John Martyn, James Allestry, and Tho. Dicas, at the Bell in Saint Pauls Church Yard, 1662 [N868].

Orations of Divers Sorts, Accomodated to Divers Places. Written by the thrice Noble, Illustrious and Excellent Princess, the Lady Marchioness of Newcastle. London, Printed Anno Dom. 1662 [N859. Wing lists a second edition (N860) in the same year, and one (N861) in 1663].

Orations of Divers Sorts, Accomodated to Divers Places. Written by the thrice Noble, Illustrious, and Excellent Princess, the Duchess of Newcastle. The Second Edition. London, Printed by A. Maxwell, in the Year 1668 [N862. Wing lists this as a '"Second" edition'].

CCXI. Sociable Letters, Written by the thrice Noble, Illustrious, and Excellent Princess, the Lady Marchioness of Newcastle. London, Printed by William Wilson, Anno Dom. M.DC.LXIV [N872].

Philosophical Letters: or, Modest Reflections upon some Opinions in Natural Philosophy, maintained by several famous and learned Authors of this Age, expressed by way of Letters: By the thrice Noble, Illustrious, and Excellent Princess, the Lady Marchioness of Newcastle. London, Printed in the Year, 1664 [N866].

Observations upon Experimental Philosophy. To which is added, The Description of a new Blazing World. Written by the thrice Noble, Illustrious, and Excellent Princesse, the Duchess of Newcastle. London, Printed by A. Maxwell, in the Year, 1666 [N857, appended to which is N849].

Observations upon Experimental Philosophy: To which is added, The Description of a new Blazing World. Written by the thrice Noble, Illustrious, and Excellent Princesse, the Duchess of Newcastle. The Second Edition. London, Printed by A. Maxwell, in the Year, 1668 [N858].

The Description of a New World, called the Blazing-World. Written by the thrice Noble, Illustrious, and Excellent Princesse, the Duchess of Newcastle. London, Printed by A. Maxwell, in the Year, M.DC.LX. VIII [N850].

The Life of the thrice Noble, High and Puissant Prince William Cavendishe, Duke, Marquess, and Earl of Newcastle; Earl of Ogle; Viscount Mansfield; and Baron of Bolsover, of Ogle, Bothal and Hepple; Gentleman of his Majesties Bed-chamber; one of his Majesties most honourable Privy-Councel; Knight of the most Noble Order of the Garter; his Majesties Lieutenant of the County and Town of Nottingham; and Justice in Ayre Trent-North: who had the honour to be Governour to our most Glorious King, and Gracious Soveraign, in his Youth, when he was Prince of Wales; and soon after was made Captain General of all the Provinces beyond the River of Trent, and other parts of the Kingdom of England, with power, by a special commission, to make Knights. Written by the thrice Noble, Illustrious, and Excellent Princess, Margaret, Duchess of Newcastle, his wife. London, Printed by A. Maxwell, in the Year 1667 [N853. A second edition, in quarto, was published in 1675 (N854)].

De vita et rebus gestis nobilissimi illustrissimique principis, Guilielmi ducis Novo-castrensis, commentarii. Ab excellentissima principe, Margareta ipsius uxore sanctissima conscripti. Et ex Anglico in Latinum conversi. London, Excudebat T.M.MDCLXVIII [N848. Latin translation of *Life*, by Walter Charleton].

Plays, never before Printed. Written by the thrice Noble, Illustrious, and Excellent Princesse, the Duchess of Newcastle. London, Printed by A. Maxwell, in the Year M.DC.LX.VIII [N867].

Manuscripts

Hutchinson, Lucy, manuscript translation of Lucretius's *De rerum natura*, British Library, Add. MS 19333

Secondary sources

Annas, Julia, *An Introduction to Plato's 'Republic'* (Oxford: Clarendon Press, 1981)

Anon., 'The Loyall Sacrifice', attrib. 'Philocrates' (1648)

Archibald, Elizabeth, ' "Deep clerks she dumbs": The Learned Heroine in *Apollonius of Tyre* and *Pericles'*, *Comparative Drama*, 22 (1988–89), 289–303

Auberlen, Eckhard, '*The Tempest* and the Concerns of the Restoration Court: a

Study of *The Enchanted Island* and the Operatic *Tempest*', *Restoration: Studies in English Literary Culture, 1660–1700*, 15 (1991), 71–88

Auchter, Dorothy, *Dictionary of Literary and Dramatic Censorship in Tudor and Stuart England* (Westport, Connecticut: Greenwood Press, 2001)

Babcock, Barbara A., ed., *The Reversible World: Symbolic Inversion in Art and Society* (Ithaca: Cornell University Press, 1978)

Bakhtin, M. M., 'Epic and Novel: Toward a Methodology for the Study of the Novel', in Michael Holquist, ed., *The Dialogic Imagination: Four Essays by M. M. Bakhtin* (Austin: University of Texas Press, 1981), pp. 3–40

Ballaster, Ros, 'The First Female Dramatists' in Helen Wilcox, ed., *Women and Literature in Britain, 1500–1700* (Cambridge: Cambridge University Press, 1996), pp. 267–90

Barbour, Reid, 'The Early Stuart Epicure', *English Literary Renaissance*, 23 (1993), 170–200.

Barbour, Reid, *English Epicures and Stoics* (Amherst: University of Massachusetts Press, 1998)

Barkan, Leonard, *Nature's Work of Art: The Human Body as Image of the World* (New Haven: Yale University Press, 1975)

Battigelli, Anna, *Margaret Cavendish and the Exiles of the Mind* (Lexington: The University Press of Kentucky, 1998)

Baxter, Kenneth, 'Mad, Vain and Thrice Noble', *Independent*, 12 September 1992, p. 27

Bazeley, Deborah T., 'An Early Challenge to the Precepts and Practice of Modern Science: The Fusion of Fact, Fiction and Feminism in the Works of Margaret Cavendish, Duchess of Newcastle' (unpublished doctoral dissertation, University of California at San Diego, 1990; abstract in *Dissertation Abstracts International*, 51 (October 1990), 1235-A)

Benet, Diana Treviño, and Michael Lieb, eds, *Literary Milton: Text, Pretext, Context* (Pittsburgh: Duquesne University Press, 1994)

Bentley, Gerald Eades, 'The Period 1642–60', in Philip Edwards, *et al.*, eds, *The Revels History of Drama in English*, 8 vols (London: Methuen, 1975–83 (1981)) IV, 120–4

Blaydes, Sophia B., 'Nature Is a Woman: The Duchess of Newcastle and Seventeenth-Century Philosophy', in Donald Mell, Jr, Theodore E. D. Braun and Lucia M. Palmer, eds, *Man, God, and Nature in the Enlightenment* (Studies in Literature, 1500–1800) (East Lansing: Colleagues Press, 1988), pp. 51–64

Blaydes, Sophia B., and Philip Bordinat, *Sir William Davenant: An Annotated Bibliography 1629–1985* (New York: Garland, 1986)

Bordinat, Philip, 'The Duchess of Newcastle as Literary Critic', *The Bulletin of the West Virginia Association of College English Teachers*, 5 (1979), 6–12

Bowerbank, Sylvia, 'The Spider's Delight: Margaret Cavendish and the "Female" Imagination', *English Literary Renaissance*, 14 (1984), 392–408

Bowerbank, Sylvia, and Sara Mendelson, eds, *Paper Bodies: A Margaret Cavendish Reader* (Peterborough, Ontario: Broadview, 2000)

Brodzki, Bella, and Celeste Schenck, eds, *Life/Lines: Theorizing Women's Autobiography* (Ithaca: Cornell University Press, 1988)

Brown, Sylvia, 'Margaret Cavendish: Strategies Rhetorical and Philosophical Against the Charge of Wantonness, Or Her Excuses for Writing So Much', *Critical Matrix: Princeton Working Papers in Women's Studies*, 6 (1991), 20–45

Browne, Thomas, *Religio Medici* (1643; repr. Menston: Scolar, 1970)

Bruce, Donald Williams, 'The Thwarted Epicurean: Abraham Cowley', *Contemporary Review*, 254 (1989), 139–45

Burrow, Colin, *Epic Romance: Homer to Milton* (Oxford: Clarendon Press, 1993)

Bush, Douglas, *English Literature in the Earlier Seventeenth Century, 1600–1660* (Oxford: Clarendon Press, 1962)

Campbell, Gordon, ed., *John Milton: Complete English poems* (London: Everyman, 1993)

Cavendish, Margaret, 'Bell in Campo' & 'The Sociable Companions', ed. Alexandra G. Bennett (Peterborough, Ontario: Broadview, 2002)

Cavendish, Margaret, 'The Convent of Pleasure' and Other Plays, ed. Anne Shaver (Baltimore and London: Johns Hopkins University Press, 1999)

Cavendish, Margaret, 'The Description of a New World Called The Blazing World' and Other Writings, ed. Kate Lilley (London: Pickering, 1992)

Cavendish, Margaret, *The Life of William Cavendish, Duke of Newcastle*, ed. by C. H. Firth (London: Routledge, n.d.)

Cavendish, William, *Methode et Invention Nouvelle de dresser les Chevaux par le Tres-Noble, Haut, et tres-Puissant Prince GUILLAUME Marquis et Comte De Newcastle* (Antwerp, 1658)

Cavendish, William, *Advice to Charles II*, in S. Arthur Strong, ed., *A Catalogue of Letters and Other Historical Documents Exhibited in the Library at Welbeck* (London: John Murray, 1903), pp. 173–236

Cervantes, Miguel de, *The History of Don Quixote of the Mancha. Translated from the Spanish of Miguel de Cervantes by Thomas Shelton, Annis 1612, 1620*, ed. James Fitzmaurice-Kelly, 4 vols (London: David Nutt, 1896), I

Charleton, Walter, *Physiologia Epicuro-Gassendo-Charltoniana: Or a Fabrick of Science Natural, Upon the Hypothesis of Atoms* (London, 1654; facsimile repr. New York: Johnson Reprint Corporation, 1966)

Charleton, Walter, *Oeconomia Animalis: Novis in Medicina Hypothesibus Superstructa & Mechinice Explicata* (London, 1669, Wing C3687)

Cixous, Hélène, 'The Laugh of the Medusa', in Elaine Marks and Isabelle de Courtivron, eds, *New French Feminisms: An Anthology* (Amherst: University of Massachusetts Press, 1980), pp. 245–64

Clucas, Stephen, 'Poetic Atomism in Seventeenth-century England: Henry More, Thomas Traherne and "Scientific Imagination"', *Renaissance Studies*, 5 (1991), 327–40

Clucas, Stephen, 'The Atomism of the Cavendish Circle: A Reappraisal', *The Seventeenth Century*, 9 (1994), 247–73

Cocking, Helen Muriel, 'Originality and Influence in the Work of Margaret Cavendish, First Duchess of Newcastle' (unpublished MPhil. dissertation, University of Reading, 1972)

Colie, Rosalie L., *The Resources of Kind: Genre-theory in the Renaissance*, ed. Barbara K. Lewalski (Berkeley, California: University of California Press, 1973)

Collins, Howard S., *The Comedy of Sir William Davenant* (Paris: Mouton, 1967)

Cook, Albert, 'The Angling of Poetry to Philosophy: The Nature of Lucretius', *Arethusa*, 27 (1994), 193–222

Cook, Susan, ' "The story I most particularly intend": The Narrative Style of Lucy Hutchinson', *Critical Survey*, 5 (1993), 271–7

Cotton, Charles, 'Melancholy. Pindaric Ode', in *Poems of Charles Cotton 1630–1687*, ed. John Beresford (London: Cobden-Sanderson, 1923)

Cotton, Nancy, *Women Playwrights in England c. 1363–1750* (Toronto: Associated University Presses, 1980)

Cowley, Abraham, *The Civil War*, ed. Allan Pritchard (Toronto: University of Toronto Press, 1973)

Davenant, *The Platonick Lovers* (London, 1636)

Davies, Stevie, *Unbridled Spirits: Women of the English Revolution: 1640–1660* (London: The Women's Press, 1998)

Davis, Lennard, *Factual Fictions: Origins of the English Novel* (New York: Columbia University Press, 1983)

Dennison Jr, James T., *The Market Day of the Soul: The Puritan Doctrine of the Sabbath in England, 1532–1700* (Lanham: University Press of America, 1983)

De Quehen, Hugh, ed., *Lucy Hutchinson's Translation of Lucretius: 'De rerum natura'* (London: Duckworth and Co., 1996)

De Santis, Maria, 'Projecting a New Science: Restoration and Eighteenth-Century Scientific Method' (unpublished doctoral dissertation, Columbia University, 1992; abstract in *Dissertation Abstracts*, 54 (1993), p. 186)

Dobson, Austin, ed., *The Diary of John Evelyn*, 3 vols (London: Macmillan, 1906; repr. London: Routledge/Thoemmes, 1996)

Doody, Margaret Anne, *The True Story of the Novel* (London: Harper Collins, 1997)

Dreistadt, Roy, 'An Analysis of the Use of Analogies and Metaphors in Science', *The Journal of Psychology*, 68 (1968), 97–116

Duff, David, ed. and intro., *Modern Genre Theory* (Longman Critical Readers) (Harlow: Pearson Education, 2000)

Edwards, Philip, 'The Closing of the Theatres', in Philip Edwards, *et al.*, *The Revels History of Drama in English*, 8 vols, vol. IV (London: Methuen, 1975–83 (1981)), pp. 61–7

Ezell, Margaret J. M., *Writing Women's Literary History* (Baltimore: Johns Hopkins University Press, 1993)

Ferguson, Moira, 'A "Wise, Wittie, and Learned Lady": Margaret Lucas Cavendish', in Katharina M. Wilson and Frank J. Warnke, eds, *Women Writers of the Seventeenth Century* (Athens: University of Georgia Press, 1989), pp. 305–40

Findley, Sandra, and Elaine Hobby, 'Seventeenth-century Women's Autobiography', in Francis Barker, *et al.*, eds, *1642: Literature and Power in the Seventeenth Century* (Proceedings of the Essex Conference on the Sociology of Literature) (Colchester: University of Essex, 1981), pp. 11–36

Fitzmaurice, James, 'Fancy and the Family: Self-characterizations of Margaret Cavendish', *Huntington Library Quarterly*, 53 (1990), 198–209

Fitzmaurice, James, 'Margaret Cavendish on Her Own Writing: Evidence from Revision and Handmade Correction', *Papers of the Bibliographical Society of America*, 85 (1991), 297–307

Fitzmaurice, James, 'Frontispieces, Prefaces, and Commendatory Verses in Books by Margaret Cavendish' (unpublished paper presented to the Margaret Cavendish Reading Group, Gonville and Caius College, Cambridge University, Spring 1996)

Fitzmaurice, James, 'Front Matter and the Physical Makeup of *Natures Pictures*', *Women's Writing*, 4 (1997), 353–67

Fitzmaurice, James, ed., *Margaret Cavendish: Sociable Letters* (New York: Garland, 1997)

Fleischmann, Wolfgang Bernard, *Lucretius and English Literature 1680–1740* (Paris: A. G. Nizet, 1964)

Foucault, Michel, *The Order of Things* (London: Tavistock, 1970; London: Routledge, 1991)

Fowler, Alastair, *Kinds of Literature: An Introduction to the Theory of Genres and Modes* (Oxford: Clarendon Press, 1982)

Fowler, Ellayne, 'Margaret Cavendish and the Ideal Commonwealth', *Utopian Studies*, 7 (1996), 38–45

Frank Jr, Robert G., 'The Image of Harvey in Commonwealth and Restoration England', in Jerome J. Bylebyl, ed., *William Harvey and his Age: The Professional and Social Context of the Discovery of the Circulation* (Baltimore: Johns Hopkins University Press, 1979) pp. 103–43

Gale, Monica, 'Lucretius 4.1–25 and the Proems of the *De Rerum Natura*', *Proceedings of the Cambridge Philological Society*, 40 (1994), 1–17

Gale, Monica, *Myth and Poetry in Lucretius* (Cambridge: Cambridge University Press, 1994)

Gallagher, Catherine, 'Embracing the Absolute: The Politics of the Female Subject in Seventeenth-century England', *Genders*, 1 (1988), 24–39

Gardiner, Judith Kegan, '"Singularity of Self": Cavendish's *True Relation*, Narcissism, and the Gendering of Individualism', *Restoration: Studies in English Literary Culture, 1660–1700*, 21 (1997), 52–65

Genette, Gérard, *Seuils* (Paris: Éditions du Seuil, 1987)

Genette, Gérard, *Paratexts: Thresholds of Interpretation*, trans. Jane E. Lewin (Cambridge: Cambridge University Press, 1997)

Gilbert, Allan H., *Literary Criticism: Plato to Dryden* (Detroit: Wayne State University Press, 1962)

Gilbert, Sandra, and Susan Gubar, *The Madwoman in the Attic: The Woman Writer and the Nineteenth-century Literary Imagination* (New Haven: Yale University Press, 1980)

Gim, Lisa, 'Representing Regina: Literary Representations of Queen Elizabeth I by Women Writers of the Sixteenth and Seventeenth Centuries' (unpublished doctoral dissertation, Brown University, 1992; abstract in *Dissertation Abstracts International*, 53 (May 1993), p. 3918)

Goddard, Charlotte, 'Pontano's Use of the Didactic Genre: Rhetoric, Irony and the Manipulation of Lucretius in *Urania*', *Renaissance Studies*, 5 (1991), 250–62

Gouge, William, *Of Domesticall Duties: Eight Treatises* (London: for William Bladen, 1622)

Graham, Elspeth, *et al.*, eds., *Her Own Life: Autobiographical Writings by Seventeenth-century Englishwomen* (London: Routledge, 1989)

Grant, Douglas, ed., *The Phanseys of William Cavendish* (London: Nonesuch Press, 1956)

Grant, Douglas, *Margaret the First: A Biography of Margaret Cavendish, Duchess of Newcastle, 1623–1673* (London: Rupert Hart-Davis, 1957)

Gregory, Elizabeth, 'Unravelling Penelope: The Construction of the Faithful Wife in Homer's Heroines', *Helios*, 23 (1996), 3–20

Grundy, Isobel, and Susan Wiseman, eds, *Women, Writing, History, 1640–1740* (London: Batsford, 1992)

Guffey, George R., 'Politics, Weather, and the Contemporary Reception of the Dryden–Davenant *Tempest*', *Restoration*, 8 (1984), 1–9

Hageman, Elizabeth, 'Women's Poetry in Early Modern Britain', in Helen Wilcox, ed., *Women and Literature in Britain, 1500–1700* (Cambridge: Cambridge University Press, 1996), pp. 190–208

Hart, Kingsley, ed., *The Letters of Dorothy Osborne to Sir William Temple, 1652–54* (London: The Folio Society, 1968)

Harvey, William, *Lectures on the Whole of Anatomy: An Annotated Translation of Prelectiones Anatomiae Universalis*', ed. C. D. O'Malley, F. N. L. Poynter and K. F. Russell (Berkeley: University of California Press, 1961)

Harvey, William, *The Circulation of the Blood, and Other Writings*, trans. Kenneth J. Franklin, and intro. by Andrew Wear (London: Everyman, 1990)

Hernadi, Paul, *Beyond Genre: New Directions in Literary Classification* (Ithaca: Cornell University Press, 1972)

Herrera, C. Andrea O'Reilly, 'Nuns and Lovers: Tracing the Development of Idyllic Conventual Writing' (unpublished doctoral dissertation, University of Delaware, 1993; abstract in *Dissertation Abstracts*, 54 (1994), p. 2588)

Bibliography

Hesiod, 'Theogony' and 'Works and Days', ed. M. L. West (Oxford: Oxford University Press, 1988)

Hill, Christopher, *Puritanism and Revolution: Studies in Interpretation of the English Revolution of the Seventeenth Century* (London: Mercury Books, 1962)

Hill, Christopher, 'William Harvey and the Idea of Monarchy', in Charles Webster, ed., *The Intellectual Revolution of the Seventeenth Century* (London: Routledge, 1974) pp. 160–81

Hill, Christopher, 'William Harvey (No Parliamentarian, No Heretic) and the Idea of Monarchy', in Charles Webster, ed., *The Intellectual Revolution of the Seventeenth Century* (London: Routledge, 1974), pp. 189–96

Hillman, David, and Carla Mazzio, eds, *The Body in Parts: Fantasies of Corporeality in Early Modern Europe* (London: Routledge, 1997)

Hintz, Carrie, '"But One Opinion": Fear of Dissent in Cavendish's *New Blazing World*', *Utopian Studies*, 7 (1996), 25–37

Hobbes, Thomas, 'Answer' to Davenant's preface to *Gondibert*, in David F. Gladish, ed., *Sir William Davenant's 'Gondibert'* (Oxford: Clarendon Press, 1971)

Hobbes, Thomas, *Leviathan*, ed. C. B. Macpherson (Harmondsworth: Penguin, 1985)

Hobby, Elaine, '"Discourse so unsavoury": Women's Published Writings of the 1650s', in Isobel Grundy and Susan Wiseman, eds, *Women, Writing, History, 1640–1740* (London: Batsford, 1992)

Hobby, Elaine, *Virtue of Necessity: English Women's Writing, 1649–88* (Ann Arbor: University of Michigan Press, 1989)

Honderich, Ted, ed., *The Oxford Companion to Philosophy* (Oxford: Oxford University Press, 1996)

Hudson, Roger, ed., *The Grand Quarrel: From the Civil War Memoirs of Mrs Lucy Hutchinson; Mrs Alice Thornton; Ann, Lady Fanshawe; Margaret, Duchess of Newcastle; Anne, Lady Halkett, & the Letters of Brilliana, Lady Harley* (London: The Folio Society, 1993)

Hume, Robert, 'Texts Within Contexts: Notes Toward a Historical Method', *Philological Quarterly* 71 (1992), 69–100

Hutchinson, Lucy, *Memoirs of the Life of Colonel Hutchinson ... to Which is Prefixed The Life of Mrs. Hutchinson, Written by Herself, a Fragment*, ed. Julius Hutchinson (London: Longman, Hurst, Rees and Orme, 1806)

Ingram, Angela, 'Introduction: On the Contrary, Outside of It', in Mary Lynn Broe and Angela Ingram, eds, *Women's Writing in Exile* (Chapel Hill: University of North Carolina Press, 1987) pp. 1–15

Italiano, Gloria, 'Two Parallel Biographers of the Seventeenth Century: Margaret Newcastle and Lucy Hutchinson', in Mario Curreli and Alberto Martino, eds, *Critical Dimensions: English, German and Comparative Literature Essays in Honour of Aurelio Zanco* (Cuneo: Saste, 1978), pp. 241–51

Jackson, W. T. H., *The Hero and the King: An Epic Theme* (New York: Columbia University Press, 1982)

Jacob, James R., and Timothy Raylor, 'Opera and Obedience: Thomas Hobbes and *A Proposition for Advancement of Moralitie* by Sir William Davenant', *The Seventeenth Century*, 6 (1991), 205–50

Jelinek, Estelle C., *The Tradition of Women's Autobiography: From Antiquity to the Present* (Boston: Twayne, 1986)

Jenkins, Edward, ed., *The Cavalier and his Lady: Selections from the Works of the First Duke and Duchess of Newcastle* (London: Macmillan, 1872)

Jones, Kathleen, *A Glorious Fame: The Life of Margaret Cavendish, Duchess of Newcastle, 1623–1673* (London: Bloomsbury, 1988)

Josten, C. H., ed., *Elias Ashmole (1617–1692): His Autobiographical and Historical Notes, His Correspondence, and Other Contemporary Sources Relating to His Life and Work*, 5 vols (Oxford: Clarendon Press, 1966)

Kahn, Victoria, 'Margaret Cavendish and the Romance of Contract', in Lorna Hutson, ed., *Feminism and Renaissance Studies* (Oxford: Oxford University Press, 1999), pp. 286–316

Kargon, Robert, *Atomism in England from Hariot to Newton* (Oxford: Clarendon Press, 1966)

Kargon, Robert, 'Introduction', in Walter Charleton, *Physiologia Epicuro-Gassendo-Charltoniana: Or a Fabrick of Science Natural, Upon the Hypothesis of Atoms* (New York: Johnson Reprint Corporation, 1966)

Keeble, N. H., ed., *The Cultural Identity of Seventeenth-century Woman: A Reader* (London: Routledge, 1994)

Kenshur, Oscar, *Open Form and the Shape of Ideas: Literary Structures as Representations of Philosophical Concepts in the Seventeenth and Eighteenth Centuries* (London: Associated University Presses, 1986)

Killigrew, Thomas, *Thomaso: or, The Wanderer* (London, 1664)

Kroll, Richard W. F., *The Material Word: Literate Culture in the Restoration and Early Eighteenth Century* (Baltimore: Johns Hopkins University Press, 1991)

Kunzle, David, 'World Upside Down: The Iconography of a European Broadsheet Type', in Barbara A. Babcock, ed., *The Reversible World: Symbolic Inversion in Art and Society* (Ithaca: Cornell University Press, 1978), pp. 39–94

Latham, Robert, and William Matthews, eds, *The Diary of Samuel Pepys*, 11 vols (London: Bell & Hyman, 1983)

Leslie, Marina, 'Gender, Genre and the Utopian Body in Margaret Cavendish's *Blazing World*', *Utopian Studies*, 7 (1996), 6–24

Lieb, Laurie Yager, '"The Works of Women are Symbolical": Needlework in the Eighteenth Century', *Eighteenth-century Life*, 10 (1986), 28–44

Lilley, Kate, 'Blazing Worlds: Seventeenth-century Women's Utopian Writing', in Clare Brant and Diane Purkiss, eds, *Women, Texts and Histories, 1575–1760* (London: Routledge, 1992), pp. 102–33

Livy, *The Romane Historie Written By T. Livius of Padua ... Tran[slat]ed out of Latin into English* [*Ab Urbe Condita*], *by PHILEMON HOLLAND, Doctor in Physick* (London, 1659, Wing No. L2613)

Livy, *Works*, trans. B. O. Foster, 14 vols (London: Heinemann, 1919–67)

Lucretius, *De rerum natura*, ed. Ronald Latham (Harmondsworth: Penguin, 1968)

MacCarthy, B. G., *The Female Pen: Women Writers and Novelists, 1621–1744* (Oxford: Blackwell, 1945)

Macheski, Cecilia, 'Penelope's Daughters: Images of Needlework in Eighteenth-Century Literature', in Mary Anne Schofield and Cecilia Macheski, eds, *Fetter'd or Free? British Women Novelists, 1670–1815* (Athens: Ohio University Press, 1986), pp. 85–100

Machiavelli, *The Prince*, ed. Robert M. Adams (London: Norton, 1992)

Maidment, James, and W. H. Logan, eds, *The Dramatic Works of Sir William D'Avenant*, 5 vols (New York: Russell & Russell, 1872–74; repr. 1964)

Marcus, Jane, 'Alibis and Legends: the Ethics of Elsewhereness, Gender and Estrangement', in Mary Lynn Broe and Angela Ingram, eds, *Women's Writing in Exile* (Chapel Hill: University of North Carolina Press, 1987), pp. 269–94

Markley, Robert, ' "Shakespeare *to thee was dull*": The Phenomenon of Fletcher's Influence', in Robert Markley and Laurie Finke, eds, *From Renaissance to Restoration: Metamorphoses of the Drama* (Chagrin Falls: Bellflower Press, 1984), pp. 88–125

Marks, Elaine, and Isabelle de Courtivron, eds, *New French Feminisms: An Anthology* (Amherst: University of Massachusetts Press, 1980)

Martz, Louis L., ed., *Poet of Exile: A Study of Milton's Poetry* (New Haven: Yale University Press, 1980)

Maskell, David, *The Historical Epic in France, 1500–1700* (Oxford: Oxford University Press, 1973)

Mason, Mary G., 'The Other Voice: Autobiographies of Women Writers', in Bella Brodzki and Celeste Schenck, eds, *Life/Lines: Theorizing Women's Autobiography* (Ithaca: Cornell University Press, 1988), pp. 19–44

Masten, Jeffrey, *Textual Intercourse: Collaboration, Authorship and Sexualities in Renaissance Drama* (Cambridge: Cambridge University Press, 1997)

Mendelson, Sara Heller, *The Mental World of Stuart Women: Three Case Studies* (Brighton: Harvester, 1987)

Mendelson, Sara, and Patricia Crawford, *Women in Early Modern England, 1550–1720* (Oxford: Clarendon, 1998)

Merchant, Carolyn, *The Death of Nature: Women, Ecology and the Scientific Revolution* (New York: Harper and Row, 1980; repr. London: Wildwood House, 1982)

Merrens, Rebecca, 'A Nature of "Infinite Sense and Reason": Margaret Cavendish's Natural Philosophy and the "Noise" of a Feminized Nature', *Women's Studies: An Interdisciplinary Journal*, 25 (1996), 421–38

Meyer, Gerald Dennis, *The Scientific Lady in England, 1650–1760: An Account of*

Her Rise, With Emphasis on the Major Roles of the Telescope and Microscope (Berkeley: University of California Press, 1955)

Miller, J. Hillis, Ariadne's Thread: Story Lines (New Haven: Yale University Press, 1992)

Milton, John, John Milton: Complete English Poems, ed. Gordon Campbell (London: Everyman, 1993)

Nagler, A. M., A Source Book in Theatrical History (Sources of Theatrical History) (New York: Dover, 1952)

Newman, John Kevin, The Classical Epic Tradition (Madison: The University of Wisconsin Press, 1986)

Newton, Judith, 'History as Usual? Feminism and the "New Historicism"', Cultural Critique, 40 (1998), 87–121

Nichols Jr, James H., Epicurean Political Philosophy: The De rerum natura of Lucretius (Ithaca: Cornell University Press, 1976)

Nicholson, Marjorie Hope, Voyages to the Moon (New York: Macmillan, 1960)

Nicoll, Allardyce, ed., Chapman's Homer: The Iliad, The Odyssey and the Lesser Homerica, 2 vols (London: Routledge and Kegan Paul, 1957)

Nicoll, Allardyce, 'The Origin and Types of the Heroic Tragedy', Anglia, 44 (1920), 325–36

Norbrook, David, 'Lucy Hutchinson's Translation of Lucretius: De rerum natura', Notes and Queries, 44 (1997), 402–3

Nugent, S. Georgia, 'Mater Matters: the Female in Lucretius's De Rerum Natura', Colby Quarterly, 30 (1994), 179–205

Nuttall, A. D., Openings: Narrative Beginnings from the Epic to the Novel (Oxford: Clarendon Press, 1992)

Ogilvie, Marilyn Bailey, Women in Science: Antiquity Through the Nineteenth Century: A Biographical Dictionary with Annotated Bibliography (Cambridge, Massachusetts: MIT Press, 1986)

Ollard, Richard, The Escape of Charles II After the Battle of Worcester (London: Hodder and Stoughton, 1966)

O'Malley, C. D., F. N. L. Poynter and K. F. Russell, eds., William Harvey, Lectures on the Whole of Anatomy: An Annotated Translation of 'Prelectiones Anatomiae Universalis' (Berkeley: University of California Press, 1961)

Otis, Brooks, Virgil: A Study in Civilised Poetry (Oxford: Clarendon Press, 1964)

Ovid, Heroides and Amores, in Works, trans. Grant Showerman, 6 vols (Loeb Classical Library) (London: Heinemann, 1977–89 (1986))

Ovid, Metamorphoses, ed. and trans. Mary M. Innes (Harmondsworth: Penguin, 1955)

Paloma, Dolores, 'Margaret Cavendish: Defining the Female Self', Women's Studies, 7 (1980), 55–66

Parker, Rozsika, The Subversive Stitch: Embroidery and the Making of the Feminine (London: The Women's Press, 1984)

Patterson, Annabel, *Censorship and Interpretation: The Conditions of Writing and Reading in Early Modern England* (Madison: University of Wisconsin Press, 1984)

Payne, Lynda, 'Dramatic Dreamscapes: Women's Dreams and Utopian Vision in the Works of Margaret Cavendish, Duchess of Newcastle', in Mary Anne Schofield and Cecilia Macheski, eds, *Curtain Calls: British and American Women and the Theater, 1660–1820* (Athens: Ohio University Press, 1991), pp. 18–33

Pearson, Jacqueline, '"Women may discourse [...] as well as men": Speaking and Silent Women in the Plays of Margaret Cavendish, Duchess of Newcastle', *Tulsa Studies in Women's Literature*, 4 (1985), 33–45

Penwill, J. L., 'Image, Ideology and Action in Cicero and Lucretius', *Ramus: Critical Studies in Greek and Roman Literature*, 23 (1994), 68–91

Perry, Maria, *Elizabeth I: The Word of a Prince. A Life from Contemporary Documents* (London: Folio Society, 1990)

Peters, Richard, *Hobbes* (Harmondsworth: Penguin, 1967)

Plato, *The Republic*, ed. Desmond Lee (Harmondsworth: Penguin, 1987)

Plato, *The Symposium*, ed. Walter Hamilton (Harmondsworth: Penguin, 1951)

Plato, *Timaeus*, ed. and trans. John Warrington (London: Dent Everyman, 1965)

Potter, Lois, 'Closet Drama and Royalist Politics', in Philip Edwards, *et al.*, eds, *The Revels History of Drama in English*, 8 vols (London: Methuen, 1975–83 (1981)) IV, 263–79

Potter, Lois, *Secret Rites and Secret Writing: Royalist Literature, 1641–1660* (Cambridge: Cambridge University Press, 1989)

Prasad, Kashi, 'Margaret Cavendish's *Blazing World*: A Seventeenth-Century Utopia', in R. K. Paul, ed., *Essays Presented to Amy G. Stock, Professor of English, Rajasthan University 1961–65*, (Jaipur: Rajasthan University Press, 1965), pp. 58–67

Price, Bronwen, 'Feminine Modes of Knowing and Scientific Enquiry: Margaret Cavendish's Poetry as Case Study', in Helen Wilcox, ed., *Women and Literature in Britain, 1500 1700* (Cambridge: Cambridge University Press, 1996), pp. 117–39

Prynne, William, *Histriomastix: The Players Scourge* (London, 1633; facsimile repr. New York: Garland, 1974; preface by Arthur Freeman)

Quintilian, *Institutio oratoria*, trans. H. E. Butler, 4 vols (Loeb Classical Library) (London: Heinemann, 1969)

Radzinowicz, Mary Ann, 'Forced Allusions: Avatars of King David in the Seventeenth Century', in Diana Treviño Benet and Michael Lieb, eds, *Literary Milton: Text, Pretext, Context* (Pittsburgh: Duquesne University Press, 1994), pp. 45–66

Raylor, Timothy, 'Samuel Hartlib and the Commonwealth of Bees', in Michael Leslie and Timothy Raylor, eds, *Culture and Cultivation in Early Modern England: Writing and the Land* (Leicester: Leicester University Press, 1992), pp. 91–129

Riley, Denise, *'Am I that name?' Feminism and the Category of 'Women' in History* (Basingstoke: Macmillan, 1988)

Rogers, John, 'Margaret Cavendish and the Gendering of the Vitalist Utopia', in *The Matter of Revolution: Science, Poetry and Politics in the Age of Milton* (Ithaca: Cornell University Press, 1996), pp. 177–211

Roots, Ivan, ed., *'Into another mould': Aspects of the Interregnum* (Exeter: University of Exeter Press, 1998)

Rosse, Alexander, *Mel Heliconium: Or, Poeticall Honey, Gathered Out of the Weeds of Parnassus* (London: L. N. and J. F. for William Leak, 1642. Wing No. R1962)

Rostenberg, Leona, *Literary, Political, Scientific, Religious and Legal Publishing, Printing and Bookselling in England, 1551–1700: Twelve Studies*, 2 vols (New York: Burt Franklin, 1965)

Samuel, Irene, *Plato and Milton* (Ithaca: Cornell University Press, 1965)

Sarasohn, Lisa T., 'A Science Turned Upside Down: Feminism and the Natural Philosophy of Margaret Cavendish', *Huntington Library Quarterly*, 47 (1984), 289–307

Sawday, Jonathan, 'The Fate of Marsyas: Dissecting the Renaissance Body', in Lucy Gent and Nigel Llewellyn, eds, *Renaissance Bodies: The Human Figure in English Culture c. 1540–1660* (London: Reaktion, 1990), pp. 111–35

Sawday, Jonathan, *The Body Emblazoned: Dissection and the Human Body in Renaissance Culture* (London: Routledge, 1995)

Schiesaro, Alessandro, 'The Palingenesis of *De Rerum Natura*', *Proceedings of the Cambridge Philological Society*, 40 (1994), 81–107

Schoenfeldt, Michael, 'Fables of the Belly in Early Modern England', in David Hillman and Carla Mazzio, eds, *The Body in Parts: Fantasies of Corporeality in Early Modern Europe* (New York and London: Routledge, 1997), pp. 243–61

Scott, Wilson L., *The Conflict Between Atomism and Conservation Theory 1644–1860* (London: Macdonald, 1970)

Scott-Douglass, Amy, 'Self-crowned Laureatess: Towards a Critical Revaluation of Margaret Cavendish's Prefaces', *Pretexts: Literary and Cultural Studies*, 9:1 (2000), 27–49

Seelig, Sharon Cadman, *Generating Texts: The Progeny of Seventeenth-century Prose* (Charlottesville: University Press of Virginia, 1996)

Shakespeare, William, *Hamlet*, ed. Harold Jenkins (London and New York: Routledge, 1982)

Shakespeare, William, *The Tragedy of Coriolanus*, ed. R. B. Parker (Oxford: Clarendon Press, 1994)

Sharpe, Kevin, *Remapping Early Modern England: The Culture of Seventeenth-century Politics* (Cambridge: Cambridge University Press, 2000)

Shepherd, Alan, ' "O seditious Citizen of the Physicall Common-Wealth!": Harvey's Royalism and His Autopsy of Old Parr', *University of Toronto Quarterly*, 65 (1996), 482–505

Sherman, Sandra, 'Trembling Texts: Margaret Cavendish and the Dialectic of Authorship', *English Literary Renaissance*, 24 (1994), 184–210

Sidney, Philip, *An Apology for Poetry or The Defence of Poesy*, ed. Geoffrey Shepherd (Manchester: Manchester University Press, 1984)

Slaughter, Thomas P., ed., *Ideology and Politics on the Eve of the Restoration: Newcastle's Advice to Charles II* (Philadelphia: American Philosophical Society, 1984)

Smith, Hilda, *Reason's Disciples: Seventeenth-century English Feminists* (Urbana: University of Illinois Press, 1982)

Smith, Nigel, *Literature and Revolution in England, 1640–1660* (New Haven and London: Yale University Press, 1994)

Smith, Sidonie, '"The Ragged Rout of Self": Margaret Cavendish's *True Relation* and the Heroics of Self-disclosure', in Anita Pacheco, ed., *Early Women Writers: 1600–1720* (London: Longman, 1998), pp. 111–32

Steiner, George, ed., *Homer in English* (Harmondsworth: Penguin, 1996)

Stephen, Leslie, and Sidney Lee, eds, *Dictionary of National Biography*, 63 vols (Oxford: Oxford University Press, 1885–1900)

Stevenson, Jay, 'The Mechanist-vitalist Soul of Margaret Cavendish', *Studies In English Literature*, 36 (1996), 527–43

Summers, Claude J., and Ted-Larry Pebworth, eds, *Renaissance Discourses of Desire* (Columbia: University of Missouri Press, 1993)

Suzuki, Mihoko, 'The Essay Form as Critique: Reading Cavendish's *The World's Olio* through Montaigne and Bacon (and Adorno)', *Prose Studies*, 22:3 (1999), 1–16

Taneja, Gulshan, ed., *In Between: Essays and Studies in Literary Criticism* (Special Cavendish edition), 9:1 & 2 (2000)

Thirsk, Joan, and J. P. Cooper, *Seventeenth-century Economic Documents* (Oxford: Clarendon Press, 1972)

Todd, Janet, *The Sign of Angellica: Women Writing and Fiction, 1660–1800* (London: Virago, 1989)

Tomlinson, Sophie, '"My Brain the Stage": Margaret Cavendish and the Fantasy of Female Performance', in Clare Brant and Diane Purkiss, eds, *Women, Texts and Histories, 1575–1760* (London: Routledge, 1992), pp. 134–63

Toohey, Peter, *Reading Epic: An Introduction to the Ancient Narratives* (London: Routledge, 1992)

Trease, Geoffrey, *Portrait of a Cavalier: William Cavendish, First Duke of Newcastle* (London: Macmillan, 1979)

Trubowitz, Rachel, 'The Reenchantment of Utopia and the Female Monarchical Self: Margaret Cavendish's *Blazing World*', *Tulsa Studies in Women's Literature*, 11 (1992), 229–45

Trussler, Simon, *The Cambridge Illustrated History of British Theatre* (Cambridge: Cambridge University Press, 1994)

Tuck, Richard, *Hobbes* (Oxford: Oxford University Press, 1992)

Underdown, David, *Pride's Purge: Politics in the Puritan Revolution* (London: Allen & Unwin, 1985)

Underdown, David, *A Freeborn People? Politics and the Nation in Seventeenth-century England* (Oxford: Clarendon Press, 1996)

Van Nortwick, Thomas, *Somewhere I Have Never Travelled: The Second Self and the Hero's Journey in Ancient Epic* (Oxford: Oxford University Press, 1992)

Veevers, Erica, *Images of Love and Religion: Queen Henrietta Maria and Court Entertainments* (Cambridge: Cambridge University Press, 1989)

Wagner, Hans-Peter, *Puritan Attitudes Towards Recreation in Early Seventeenth-century New England: With Particular Consideration of Physical Recreation* (Frankfurt: Verlag Peter Lang, 1982)

Wallwork, Jo, and Paul Salzman, eds, *Women Writing 1550–1750* (Bundoora, Victoria: *Meridian*, 18:1, 2001(special book issue))

Warrington, John, ed., *The Diary of Samuel Pepys*, 3 vols (London: Everyman, 1964)

Webster, Charles, 'William Harvey and the Crisis of Medicine in Jacobean England', in Jerome J. Bylebyl, ed., *William Harvey and his Age: The Professional and Social Context of the Discovery of the Circulation* (Baltimore: Johns Hopkins University Press, 1979), pp. 1–27

Weiss, Samuel A., 'Dating Mrs Hutchinson's Translation of Lucretius', *Notes and Queries*, 200 (1955), 109

Wheeler, Stephen M., 'Ovid's Use of Lucretius in *Metamorphoses* 1.67–8', *Classical Quarterly*, 45 (1995), 200–3

Whitaker, Katie, *Mad Madge: The Extraordinary Life of Margaret Cavendish, Duchess of Newcastle, the First Woman to Live by Her Pen* (New York: Basic Books, 2002)

White, Hayden, *Tropics of Discourse: Essays in Cultural Criticism* (Baltimore: Johns Hopkins University Press, 1978; repr. 1992)

Whitteridge, Gweneth, 'William Harvey: a Royalist and No Parliamentarian', in Charles Webster, ed., *The Intellectual Revolution of the Seventeenth Century* (London: Routledge, 1974), pp. 182–8

Williams, Tamsyn, 'Polemical Prints of the English Revolution' in Lucy Gent and Nigel Llewellyn, eds, *Renaissance Bodies: The Human Figure in English Culture c. 1540–1660* (London: Reaktion, 1990), pp. 86–110

Williamson, Marilyn L., *Raising Their Voices: British Women Writers, 1650–1750* (Detroit: Wayne State University Press, 1990)

Wilputte, Earla A., 'Margaret Cavendish's Imaginary Voyage to *The Blazing World*: Mapping a Feminine Discourse', in Donald W. Nichol, ed., *Transatlantic Crossings: Eighteenth-Century Explorations* (St Johns, Nfld: St John's Memorial University of Newfoundland, 1995), pp. 109–17

Wing, Donald G., *Short-title Catalogue of Early English Books, 1641–1700* (New York: Index Committee of the Modern Language Association of America, 1972–)

Wiseman, Susan, 'Gender and Status in Dramatic Discourse: Margaret Cavendish, Duchess of Newcastle', in Isobel Grundy and Susan Wiseman, eds, *Women, Writing, History, 1640–1740* (London: Batsford, 1992), pp. 159–77

Wither, George (attrib.), *The Great Assises Holden in Parnassus by Apollo and his Assessors* (1645; repr. Oxford: Luttrell Society/Blackwell, 1948. Wing W3160)

Woodbridge, Linda, 'Patchwork: Piecing the Early Modern Mind in England's First Century of Print Culture', *ELR*, 23 (1993), 5–45

Woolf, Virginia, *A Room of One's Own* (London: Hogarth Press, 1929; repr. London: Grafton Books, 1990)

Woolf, Virginia, 'The Duchess of Newcastle', in *The Common Reader* (London: The Hogarth Press, 1925; repr. *A Woman's Essays* (Harmondsworth: Penguin, 1992)), pp. 107–14

Worden, Blair, *The Rump Parliament 1648–1653* (Cambridge: Cambridge University Press, 1974)

Zwicker, Steven N., *Lines of Authority: Politics and English Literary Culture, 1649–1689* (Ithaca: Cornell University Press, 1993)

Index

Note: literary works can be found under authors' names; 'n.' after a page reference indicates the number of a note on that page; page numbers in **bold** refer to main entries.